THE BUSINESS OF WAR

The Business of Modern Life Series

Series Editors: Justin Bronson Barringer and James McCarty

The Business of Modern Life Series explores the ways that neoliberal global capitalism has infiltrated and come to dominate virtually all spheres of modern life including incarceration, healthcare, agriculture, technology, education, non-profit organizations, immigration, and church along with, of course, war. Various industrial complexes have popped up all around us, and this series will grapple with the effects that they have on our daily lives. It will be the first series of its kind—that is, one addressing a variety of theological and ethical issues of the modern world through the lens of capitalism's pervasive domination. Many books have been published on the areas we hope this series will explore, but for the most part they have neglected how finance capitalism, global markets, and economic philosophy and policy drive, or often eschew, theological and ethical concerns. Each book in this series will take on one of the industrial complexes (e.g., the military-industrial complex, the prison-industrial complex, the agricultural-industrial complex, etc.), all following the same basic format, which first addresses the biblical and theological foundations relevant to the topic, then reflects on the theological and moral state of affairs in history and in the world today, before finally closing with some uniquely Christian proposals for responding to the issues raised.

The Business of War

Theological and Ethical Reflections on the Military-Industrial Complex

Edited by
**James McCarty,
Matthew Tapie,**
and
Justin Bronson Barringer

Foreword by
Jonathan Tran

CASCADE *Books* · Eugene, Oregon

THE BUSINESS OF WAR
Theological and Ethical Reflections on the Military-Industrial Complex

The Business of Modern Life Series 1

Copyright © 2020 Wipf and Stock Publishers. All rights reserved. Except for brief quotations in critical publications or reviews, no part of this book may be reproduced in any manner without prior written permission from the publisher. Write: Permissions, Wipf and Stock Publishers, 199 W. 8th Ave., Suite 3, Eugene, OR 97401.

Cascade Books
An Imprint of Wipf and Stock Publishers
199 W. 8th Ave., Suite 3
Eugene, OR 97401

www.wipfandstock.com

PAPERBACK ISBN: 978-1-5326-4104-6
HARDCOVER ISBN: 978-1-5326-4105-3
EBOOK ISBN: 978-1-5326-4106-0

Cataloguing-in-Publication data:

Names: Barringer, McCarty, James, editor. | Tapie, Matthew A., editor. | Justin Bronson, editor. | Tran, Jonathan, foreword.

Title: The business of war : theological and ethical reflections on the military-industrial complex / edited by James McCarty, Matthew Tapie, and Justin Bronson Barringer ; foreword by Jonathan Tran.

Description: Eugene, OR : Cascade Books, 2020 | The Business of Modern Life Series 1 | Includes bibliographical references.

Identifiers: ISBN 978-1-5326-4104-6 (paperback) | ISBN 978-1-5326-4105-3 (hardcover) | ISBN 978-1-5326-4106-0 (ebook)

Subjects: LCSH: War—Religious aspects—Christianity. | War—Economic aspects—United States.

Classification: BT736.15 .B87 2020 (paperback) | BT736.15 .B87 (ebook)

Manufactured in the U.S.A.   07/08/20

Scripture quotations are from New Revised Standard Version Bible, copyright © 1989 National Council of the Churches of Christ in the United States of America. Used by permission. All rights reserved worldwide.

The Holy Bible, English Standard Version (ESV) is adapted from the Revised Standard Version of the Bible, copyright Division of Christian Education of the National Council of the Churches of Christ in the U.S.A. All rights reserved.

Contents

Series Foreword | vii
Foreword by Jonathan Tran | ix
Acknowledgments | xiii
Introduction | xv
  —Justin Bronson Barringer, James McCarty, and Matthew Tapie

Part One: Theological Foundations

1 The Business of War in the Bible | 3
    —Myles Werntz

2 Christian Ethics and the Problems of War and Business | 23
    —Christina G. McRorie

Part Two: The Business of War in History

3 Globalization and Warmaking: People, Planet, and Peace in Peril | 47
    —Pamela K. Brubaker

4 Free Souls, Free People, Free Enterprise: Business, the Cold War, and American Evangelicalism | 68
    —David R. Swartz

5 The Business of War in Latin America | 86
    —Matthew Philipp Whelan

6 The Business of War on the Korean Peninsula | 109
    —Wonchul Shin

Part Three: Practicing the Business of War Today

7 Contracting Justice? Private Military and Security Contractors and the Commodification of War | 125
    —Bradley B. Burroughs

8 The Military-Educational Complex | 141
    —Kara N. Slade

Part Four: Resisting the Business of War

9 Communal Responses to the Business of War | 161
    —Justin Bronson Barringer

10 Building Peace in a Violent Nation: A Kingian Response to the Interconnected Violence of Racism, Materialism, and Militarism | 179
    —James McCarty

11 The Costs of *Jus Ante Bellum* and *Jus Post Bellum* | 193
    —Tobias Winright and Nathaniel Hibner

12 Masquerade: Public Policy and the Military-Industrial Complex | 207
    —Stan Goff

Bibliography | 231
Contributors | 255

Series Foreword

Over the centuries the Church has been a source of guidance to many about the provision of goods and services that contribute to the common good. St. Basil started what might be considered one of the first hotels and hospitals in his Basiliad in the fourth century. Monastic communities served as a model for modern educational institutions, and sometimes served as places of sanctuary for those whose lives were in danger. And countless Christians through the centuries have sought guidance from the church about their participation in warfare or how they were going to run their businesses. To many in the modern world such a role for the Church seems absurd because we have come to believe that state actors and business leaders should dictate the what and why and how of our lives, often even letting business trends or patriotic commitments order the life of the Church.

However, there has also been resistance to the rise of nation-state and business logics ordering our moral lives. In 1961 Dwight Eisenhower warned us that the ever-deepening relationship of private companies' profits to the United States's participation in war was creating a "military-industrial complex" that threatened the very practice of democracy. In 1983 political philosopher Michael Walzer warned us that the moral logic of the market is imperialistic and threatens to become the dominant way we relate to each other by turning nearly every human interaction into a market transaction. And Christian theologian-activists—from Martin Luther King Jr. to Dorothy Day to Desmond Tutu—have shown us ways to resist these trends through social movements and lives of radical hospitality.

These phenomena—the rise of various industrial complexes, the colonialist expansion of market logics into every aspect of our lives, and the seeming completion of market expansion around the world—have become so commonplace that we rarely question them anymore. We now speak not only of a military-industrial complex, but of the prison-industrial complex, the medical-industrial complex, and even the nonprofit-industrial complex (to name only a few). These industrial complexes are economic subsystems within the larger global market that are dependent on private actors influencing, and even shaping, public policies and practices to promote their continual expansion. Increasingly and with growing speed, sectors of our common life once considered public and shared are increasingly becoming privatized and dominated by market forces: our schools, our medical institutions, and even our churches.

The books in *The Business of Modern Life* take these developments seriously as theological and ethical problems to be examined, critiqued, and resisted. The Christian tradition has long taught us that humans are more than consumers or commodities, but bearers of God's image. The Church has long reminded us that we belong not only to ourselves or our appetites but to each other and to God. And the words of Jesus have long challenged us to believe that it is the poor rather than the rich, the oppressed rather than the powerful, who are blessed by God. In *The Business of Modern Life* you will find a series of books examining the social ethics of our contemporary economic life in ways that seek to resist turning everything we do into "business" and reclaiming a vision of shared life that orients us toward the business of loving God and our neighbors.

The books in this series will address these topics through four primary lenses: theological foundations for understanding and addressing the industrial complex in question, the history of that particular industrial complex, the global impact of that industrial complex today, and finally, possible Christian responses to the industrial complex being addressed. Collectively, then, these volumes should be a compendium of neo-liberal, global, capitalism's effects on nearly the entirety of human lives. They will also suggest ways that followers of Jesus might think about and act faithfully in response to these realities, seeking out the good, the true, and the beautiful as a declaration that it is not the market and Mammon that ultimately reign, but Jesus Christ.

Foreword

JONATHAN TRAN

One way to think about the relationship between an industry and the political economy within which it unfolds is to envision the two as contingently, and externally, related. In this case the industry is seen as being non-indicative of the political economy and could rather exist without it. One will be especially drawn to this line of thought if one views the industry in question as morally dubious but feels okay about the political economy. So, with industries like human trafficking and arms trading, we capitalists (few of us are exempted) will ward off suggestions that the industries are proper to capitalism. We would rather think of them as operating outside the proper channels of the capitalist economy, accidental to an otherwise innocuous, and sometimes even morally praiseworthy, set of arrangements.

This was for some time the line taken by historians regarding American chattel slavery. The thought was that the whole untoward affair was at worst an unfortunate precursor to capitalism, perhaps some strange outlier arising out of the messy transition from feudalism to mercantilism. The case for this triumphant periodization hung on the premise that the difference between wage labor and slave labor issued as a difference in kind. This premise carried through no matter how much the respective labor relations resembled one another. The premise ultimately proved untrue, and so the line of thought was shown to be mistaken. Researchers comprising the "History of Capitalism"—taking their cues from Marxist structural analysis, labor historians, business school economists, and most significantly, the Black radical tradition—have helped us see that both factory-based wage labor and plantation-based slave labor constituted the extractive operations of modern capitalism. Indeed, it was through these two specific enterprises that capitalism realized itself.

When the Black Marxist Cedric Robinson referred to the Atlantic's political economy as "racial capitalism," he was saying that the relationship between capitalism and its racist regimes is necessary and internal, and not at all contingent and external.[1] History of Capitalism researchers have followed suit, primarily by sifting through the material histories of chattel slavery's many technological innovations. They have demonstrated how inventions like the whips used to drive cotton-picking lines coupled with advances in agricultural sciences allowed cotton production to reach unprecedented heights, eventually becoming the nineteenth century's biggest industry, in turn propelling US capitalism to tops in the world. Yet, it wasn't just those innovations already negatively associated with slavery that bore out the necessary and internal relationship between slavery and capitalism. Slavery also birthed capitalist techniques in accountancy (e.g., the slaver's ledger book), finance (e.g., mortgage credit lines utilizing enslaved bodies as leveraged capital), and international trade (e.g., American-based slave labor produced the raw materials for English millworkers, who, while technically "waged," subsisted under slavelike conditions). As researchers turn up more and more evidence (and take the Black Marxist tradition with greater and greater seriousness) the rest of us are coming to recognize slavery's necessary and internal relationship to capitalism. We are also coming to recognize why we wanted to hold those two apart for so long. Namely, the distinction allowed us to conveniently distance the capitalism that very much defines our contemporary lives from those things we consider immoral. We could have our slave-made cake and eat it too.[2]

We capitalist Americans find consolation in a second distinction. Given the too-close-for-comfort relationship between capitalism and moral dubiousness, at least America is not *officially* involved. Our government insulates us by maintaining a laissez-fare relationship to filthy lucre. The premise here is the aspiration that the government has, by distancing itself from capitalism, made us better than we would be left to our own devices. Neoliberal capitalism has disabused us of this pretension. The post-Keynesian realization that nation-states would need to, going forward, tightly manage and

---

1. Robinson, *Black Marxism: The Making of the Black Radical Tradition*. See also Eric Williams, *Capitalism and Slavery*.

2. On the History of Capitalism, see the following: Beckert and Rockman, *Slavery's Capitalism: A New History of American Economic Development*; Zakim and Kornblith, *Capitalism Takes Command: The Social Transformation of Nineteenth-Century America*; Rockman, "Review: What Makes the History of Capitalism Newsworthy?," 439–66; Beckert and Desan, *American Capitalism: New Histories*; Johnson, "The Pedestal and the Veil: Rethinking the Capitalism/Slavery Question," 299–308; and Baptist, *The Half Has Never Been Told: Slavery and the Making of American Capitalism*. For a philosophical analysis, see Fraser, "Is Capitalism Necessarily Racist?"

thereby enable and empower global capitalism—that globalization's market could not be permitted a free hand after all—removed even the pretense of the nation-state's relative independence. Of course, all of this was already the case when it came to racial capitalism, where federal and state action continuously enabled and empowered its many operations, from slavery to "second slavery" and from Jim Crow to "the New Jim Crow."[3] The global transition to neoliberal capitalism now means that there is no consolable distance between our governments and our markets. This is equally the case with what this present volume calls "the business of war."

We Americans are now, and have been for some time, inextricably in bed with some of the most immoral industries the world has ever seen. We are talking about a single political economy that produces Apple iPhones, Amazon Prime same-day deliveries, human slaves, and, as the authors here show, trading in arms, mercenaries, militarization, despotic regimes, dark wars, torture, so on and so forth—the same raw materials and basic concepts cycling through crisscrossing circuits of imagination. No light gets between the constituent parts of this industrial complex. Like the research comprising the New Histories of Capitalism, the chapters in this volume trace out the necessary and internal lines of development between capitalism and the business of war and reveal how all of this is not only stewarded by the US government but also largely determines it. As is the case with slavery's capitalism, the business of war is not simply an enterprise where specific industries make up the constituent parts of the military-industrial complex such that the government as its steward is, in order to serve its interests, required to protect those industries. It is also that the cozy relationship innovates new capitalist technologies, availing ever new applications to industries beyond the business of war.

The volume also points to possibilities for resistance. But not, wisely, in ways that will conveniently console us. Just the opposite, in fact. The Christianity comes in by rendering such consolations morally dubious.

---

3. Regarding "second slavery," see Tomich, *Through the Prism of Slavery*, 56–71; Tomich and Zeuske, "Introduction, the Second Slavery: Mass Slavery, World-Economy, and Comparative Microhistories," 91–100; and Kaye, "The Second Slavery: Modernity in the Nineteenth-Century South and the Atlantic World," 627–50. Regarding "the New Jim Crow" see Michelle Alexander's so-titled book.

Acknowledgments

This book has been years in the making. It has only come to completion due to the hard work and patience of our contributors, and the communities that have supported us along the way. The book began as a panel discussion at the Christian Scholars Conference, at Lipscomb University, in 2013. To all those involved in organizing that excellent conference, especially David Fleer, we give our thanks.

We would like to give special thanks to those initial panelists, most of whom have contributed to this volume: Justin Barringer and Matt Tapie, who organized the panel; Kara Slade; Jimmy McCarty; and Logan Isaac. The conversation was lively, and the audience engaged us with helpful questions. A number of attendees, some of whom were pastors, convinced us that expanding that conversation into a book would be a worthwhile endeavor. We would like to thank everyone who attended that session and encouraged the completion of this project.

This volume would never have existed without the keen insights and hard work of our contributors. We are deeply grateful for their scholarship and partnership. We would also like to acknowledge Charlie Collier, and the rest of the Cascade Books/Wipf and Stock team, for their interest in the project, and for working with us with grace and encouragement. We are grateful to Danae Casteel for her editorial work. Finally, we thank our families, friends, and communities for their support.

Feast of St. Ignatius, 2019
Seattle, Washington

Introduction

JUSTIN BRONSON BARRINGER, JAMES MCCARTY, AND MATTHEW TAPIE

H. Richard Niebuhr once said that the first question to ask when doing ethics is, "What is going on?" Since at least World War II, war has become big business, and addressing this problem is what inspires and charts the course for this book. War as business is a moral problem that has largely gone underexplored in Christian theology and ethics. We call this the problem of "the business of war." There have been important works on the theology and ethics of modern economic systems, and the ethics of war and peace have expanded into many subdisciplines in the last century. However, very few people have explored the theological and ethical aspects of the intersections of contemporary global capitalism and modern warfare, and we are unaware of an extended examination of this important area in Christian theology and ethics.

The essays in this book attempt to remedy this problem by exploring the history of Christian teaching on the topics of economics and war alongside the unique historical and contemporary manifestations of the business of war in the twentieth and twenty-first centuries. The focus of the book then shifts to suggest ways for Christians to respond to and resist the ever-encroaching moral logics and practices of the business of war in our lives. We hope that readers will gain a familiarity with the relevant resources in the Christian tradition on war and economy and that this will prepare them to address the injustices caused by the rise of the business of war. Moreover, we hope Christians who read these chapters will be better equipped to resist the business of war in their local contexts.

Many of the essays in the volume, especially in part four, focus on the United States. Indeed, even those chapters with an explicit focus outside of the United States often refer back to the US and its economic and political policies. This is because the US has been the most dominant driving force of the business of war as a global phenomenon. The US would not have become the global superpower it is if it had not become the best in the world at harnessing war's business potential. However, the impacts of the business of war are not limited to the borders of the US. The economic, environmental, and human costs of the business of war are felt in every country in the world. The business of war has been central to the growth of international stock markets and the global arms trade. It has produced multi-nation wars and weapons of mass destruction. And it has created the conditions that facilitate some of the largest global migration flows in human history—including the contemporary global refugee crisis—and the exploitation of fossil fuels that spurred and are accelerating climate change.

There is, then, no political, economic, or moral problem more pressing than the problem of the business of war. This makes the dearth of resources available to help people, including Christians, think critically about this phenomenon even more troubling. This dearth, however, illuminates the difficulty of speaking accurately and with clarity about this complex problem that permeates nearly every aspect of our lives. In light of this difficulty, the present volume is not a comprehensive accounting of the business of war and all its components or every way it might be understood or resisted. It is, however, a first step toward naming the problem clearly, examining it rigorously, and taking steps to resist it, and even transform it.

The volume is organized in four parts: "Theological Foundations," "The Business of War in History," "Practicing the Business of War Today," and "Resisting the Business of War." The essays build on one another, but each of them can be read as a stand-alone essay as well. The book progresses from biblical and theological foundations to the rise of the business of war in the twentieth century, then from contemporary implications of the business of war to suggestions of practices that resist and might defeat the business of war in the future.

Theological Foundations

The first part of the book explores biblical and theological foundations for thinking about the business of war. These chapters address the biblical narrative and the Christian tradition as a way of setting the stage for understanding what resources are available to Christians when considering our contemporary conundrum with the business of war. In particular, this opening section includes overviews of biblical texts relevant to the business of war and an in-depth analysis of the ethics of business and the ethics of war in Christian thought.

Myles Werntz provides a survey of Old Testament and New Testament scriptures that highlight the ambiguous account of the intersection of economics and war in the Christian Scriptures and points us toward understanding. Werntz argues that the interrelationship between the military and economics has an ambiguous scriptural lineage. Exploring the contours of the canon, he finds that these two elements of political life are envisioned as running together faithfully, with the people of God called to exercise faithfulness in both their political and economic affairs, as these elements are intertwined. But what it means for the people of God to live faithfully at the intersection of these elements of political life changes over time. Werntz not only attends to the typology present within both Testaments but looks toward present possibilities of faithful practice in these intersecting elements of political life.

Christina McRorie walks the reader through the history of Christian thinking on economic life and the ethics of war to highlight the historical resources available to Christians and the historical uniqueness of our contemporary situation. McRorie's chapter provides a brief overview of the range of perspectives on business and war found within Christian thought and practice, highlighting points of congruence and contrast in the modes of moral reasoning used to respond to the concrete issues these distinct fields raise. McRorie proposes that theological reflection on each subject can be loosely plotted along a spectrum ranging from "rejection" to "embrace," and that the recurrent disagreement over the ethics of wealth and warfare reflects a deeper ambivalence on these issues within the tradition that can be found even within Scripture itself. McRorie concludes by suggesting that this ambivalence has been productive of modes of analysis and habits of critical and prudential judgment that may be useful in facing the new questions that the business of war itself raises for Christians today.

The Business of War in History

The next part of the book provides several case studies that trace the historical impacts of the business of war around the globe. In this section, we learn of the rise of the business of war, its unique impacts in Latin America and the Korean Peninsula, and its global impacts on peace, justice, and sustainability.

The business of war is integral to economic globalization, but it is costly. Pamela Brubaker argues that military spending produces fewer jobs than other areas of the economy and reduces funds for job creation in other sectors, such as education, healthcare, infrastructure, and clean energy. It is a major contributor to the international arms trade and climate change, which harm people, the planet, and peace.

David Swartz offers a historical survey of evangelical debates related to business and war. In the 1970s, several discourses emerged to challenge the mid-century evangelical consensus around free enterprise, anticommunism, patriotism, and missionary work. An evangelical left, marshaling New Left critiques of the neoliberal consensus, argued against the military-industrial-corporate-university complex. International evangelicals argued against American cultural, economic, and political imperialism. While this pacific stream of the evangelical movement did not win the day in the context of 1980s America, the debate suggests a striking "ambivalence of the sacred" at work even within American evangelicalism.

Matthew Whelan looks for clues regarding the functional and ideological interdependence of economics and warfare by examining Latin America's Cold War and how it became what Greg Grandin calls "a workshop for empire." The chapter concludes by reflecting upon the fact that there are now martyrs of the Church among the countless victims of this period, which presses the question, how should we approach the business of war in Latin America given that one of its products is martyrdom?

Wonchul Shin critically examines the key factors in the competitive militarization between North and South Korea—highlighting the US-Republic of Korea (South Korea) military alliance rather than the so-called threat of North Korea—and points out the ways that the US military-industrial complex is one of the greatest beneficiaries of the arms race between the two countries. This chapter then contextualizes this critical analysis of the militarization through the recent case of the controversial deployment of a Terminal High Altitude Area Defense (THAAD) system on the Korean Peninsula. Finally, this chapter calls for moral imagination, liberating people from fear and envisioning the peace of Christ, reflected in the peace movement led by the National Council of Churches in Korea.

Practicing the Business of War Today

This section brings us more explicitly into the present by examining the impacts of the business of war on the education of engineers in the United States, and in the evolving practice of state-sponsored violence through the use of private military contractors. These essays expose the increasing privatization and corporatization of war in our world. They also reveal to us the ways that the logics of business and war have permeated each other, and our educational practices, to such an extent that their marriage has ceased to raise eyebrows.

Bradley Burroughs' chapter begins by tracing the rise of private military and security contractors (PMSCs), who have come to play a critical role in staffing recent wars, particularly the United States' wars in Afghanistan and Iraq. Despite its growing prominence, Burroughs argues that Christians should regard this trend toward increasing use of PMSCs as problematic, because it reduces the possibility of justice in war. Christian communities should respond to such challenges by seeking to cultivate individuals who recognize that, even if it might in some cases be justified, war is full of tragedy and anguish and thus must be placed under clear limits—and not simply reduced to a business.

Articles in the popular press regularly proclaim "our" need for graduates trained in the STEM disciplines (science, technology, engineering, and mathematics). Kara Slade asks who is the "we/our" in these accounts, and what needs are engineers and other practitioners in technological professions being expected to fulfill? This chapter addresses the extent to which engineering education in the United States is tied to the anxieties of the nation-state. It also explores the implications of this relationship for those who teach, and those who learn, in the contemporary university.

Resisting the Business of War

In the final section several authors examine ways of resisting the business of war in a variety of contexts. These essays propose individual, ecclesial, and policy recommendations for resisting the business of war.

Justin Barringer explores possible Christian responses to modern warfare. Christians have employed a number of tactics to demonstrate opposition to war, including public protest, destruction of military property, prayer services outside weapons manufacturing sites, draft dodging, and signing petitions. With the changing face of modern warfare, it is pertinent to ask how Christians might adapt our peace witness in response. By combining insights from the work of scholars such as James William McClendon and Andrew Bacevich, and the example of activists such as the Berrigan brothers and Bayard Rustin, the essay attempts to map possible Christian responses to the increasingly complex business of war. These possible Christian responses include the Christian virtues and practices of simplicity, community, charity, and spirituality.

James McCarty draws on the example of Martin Luther King Jr.'s resistance to the Vietnam War to propose ways of resisting the cultural and moral logics of war in conjunction with resisting racism, poverty, and classism. These injustices are interrelated and dependent upon one another, King taught us, and McCarty provides us concrete examples for resisting them in exactly those places where they overlap and reinforce each other.

Tobias Winright and Nathaniel Hibner show how the just-war tradition recognizes the costs of war. In preparing for war and in conducting war, there are costs. But just war holds that these costs should be limited and minimized. In recent decades, as just-war theorists have expanded their attention to postwar justice, there are even more costs to be weighed for war to be considered morally justified, justly conducted, and justly concluded.

Finally, Stan Goff explores how the military-industrial complex is not a fixed establishment but a meshwork of power relations, which has expanded over the last fifty years into something more akin to a military-industrial-financial-digital media complex. His essay discusses how the military-industrial complex is embedded in economic, political, sociological, psychological, and ecological contexts. He then addresses the challenges facing the church, especially the need to unlearn what he refers to as popular discourses on the relation between war, church, and policy.

We hope this book provokes what we believe are vital conversations among religious leaders and scholars on how government and various institutions in civil society benefit financially from the business of war. We also hope the book contributes to a larger discussion in seminaries, and in our universities, about the relationship between modern neoliberal global capitalism and attitudes to war in local, national, and global contexts. We pray these discussions lead to greater clarity about the problem of the business of war in our communities and empower Christians to act faithfully to resist this business wherever they find it.

Part One

THEOLOGICAL FOUNDATIONS

1

The Business of War in the Bible

MYLES WERNTZ

Introduction

In the pages of Scripture there is little that could be called straightforward or univocal about the relation between military endeavors and economic processes. Ample critical analysis exists on the modern forms of the military-industrial complex, but one is hard-pressed to find a one-size-fits-all approach within Scripture.[1] At times the relationship between military endeavors and economic life is commended, and at other times the relationship is condemned. The separate issues of Scripture's vision of military life and Scripture's vision of economic life have been amply described and dissected, but seldom have they been explored in relation to one another. But in this chapter, I will explore what I take to be the three categories of this relation in Scripture: (1) warfare without economy, (2) just military engagements accompanied by economic expansion, and (3) unjust economies supporting military engagements. After laying out these three

---

1. Selected recent analyses on the relationship between militaries and economy in contemporary life include Aizenman and Glick, "Military Expenditure," 129–55; Brzoska, "World Military Expenditures," 45–67; Kang and Meernik, "Civil War Destruction," 88–109; Murdoch and Sandler, "Economic Growth," 91–110.

arrangements, I will suggest what I take to be a workable hermeneutic for adjudicating among these options for the modern world.

Insofar as Scripture treats moral topics together, Scripture likewise judges these topics synthetically. The synthetic nature of Scripture's moral reasoning has to do with the manner in which moral topics arise within Israel's life and are discussed in Scripture. As John Barton explains, Scripture's laws and rules manifest themselves narratively, drawing together not only laws that have been transgressed, but motive, effect, and derivative actions that stem from the initial transgression.[2] In narrative accounts of ethics, then, there is never simply one issue in play. In light of this, treating any topic individually requires being attentive to the multiple aspects of the moral question in play. As Waldemar Janzen explains, moral topics emerge within social matrices of various kinds and often involve multiple matrices. Scripture offers multiple paradigms of the good life, ranging from the priestly life to the wise life, with all of the descriptions of these lives touching on another paradigm or on the most fundamental of these paradigms, family life.[3]

The synthetic nature of ethics in the Hebrew Bible/Old Testament carries forth in the New Testament as well. As Richard Hays has argued, the New Testament presupposes that the moral life is known not by the interpretative vision of the individual but by the community, as the Scriptures themselves are a canonical community.[4] Hays' focus is on the communal context of interpretation, but he makes a similar point to Barton and Janzen: moral questions emerge narratively and are dealt with narratively, meaning that moral issues never appear in isolation. The synthetic manner in which moral issues appear in Scripture means, in part, that Scripture's judgments upon moral actions—particularly confluences of moral actions, as with the relation between the military and economic systems—are never simply of one piece.

Narratively, in both military and economic ventures, the focus of the Scriptures is on the ways in which these human endeavors serve as occasions for the worship of God. This is not to say, however, that simply because these two ventures are enacted for maximal efficiency they are commended; faithful joint performances of military and economic life are envisioned within Scripture as well as idolatrous ones. Thus it will be the goal of this chapter not only to describe the pluriform relations present within Scripture but also to assess what the contemporary manifestation of

2. Barton, *Understanding Old Testament Ethics*, 7–8.
3. Janzen, *Old Testament Ethics*, 1–44.
4. Hays, *Moral Vision of the New Testament*, 4–5.

the military-economic relation might consist of. In what follows, I will not offer an exhaustive exploration of these forms but a typology that will help us see the overarching logic of these associations within Scripture.

Category One: YHWH's Warfare, Israel's Economy

The first confluence of warfare and economy that appears in Scripture is a peculiar one, for it is one of warfare independent of an economic matrix. Throughout the Hebrew Bible there are multiple descriptions of God going to war for the people of Israel,[5] ventures that require no corresponding economic resources from the people. While there are any number of accounts of this across the Hebrew Bible, our focus here will center on three accounts that specifically implicate the people's economic life: Exodus 14–15, 2 Kings 6:8—7:20, and the imagery of Psalms 33 and 44.

Broadly, the evaluation of these events by Scripture is positive, as these events are the work of God independent of any contribution by the people, initiated by God and not by the people.[6] In these instances, the economy of Israel benefits as a byproduct of God's actions but is not a direct contributor to the military victories. The spoils of the Egyptians (Exod 12:35–36) that accrue to Israel as a result of the plagues of YHWH, for example, are put to use in the treasury of Israel and used for constructing various aspects of the tabernacle.[7] From the vantage point of this essay, what is interesting is the *divorce* between economy and military in these instances and what this might tell us regarding the synthesis of economic and military concerns.

Exodus 14–15: YHWH against Pharaoh's Economy

The first occurrence of this type is in Exodus 14–15. In these chapters, the people of Israel experience their deliverance from slavery not by armed rebellion but by the plagues sent by YHWH against the Egyptians. In this culminating act, then, we see YHWH acting in a manner consistent with Exodus 7–11, delivering Israel independent of any armed action by the people. The people of Israel, according to the narrative, are deprived on both economic and military accounts: though having plundered the Egyptians of

---

5. I am using "Israel" and "people of Israel" here as shorthand to designate the people descending from Jacob/Israel, rather than an organized nation-state.

6. Longman and Reid, *God Is a Warrior*, 33–47.

7. Ostensibly, the gold used in fashioning the ark of the covenant in Exodus 25:10–22, as well as the gold that formed the golden calf in Exodus 32:1–4, were taken from Egypt.

their precious stones and livestock (Exod 12:35-38), they are ill-equipped against Egyptian armies.

Pharaoh's armies are characterized by their technological dominance, equipped with chariots and horses, in contrast to an absence of weaponry by the people of Israel. This is no matter, however, as YHWH destroys the Egyptian armies without any corresponding military action from the fleeing Hebrews. The arc of Exodus is one of deliverance: YHWH is a god who saves the people from slavery and tyranny. This familiar reading, however, ignores that the deliverance of the people of Israel is not only a political deliverance but an economic deliverance as well. As J. G. McConville has argued, the salvation of Israel is one that allows for a new economic possibility to emerge. If Genesis 1–3 provides a picture of human labor as a proper response to God's benevolence, then Israel's slavery in Egypt is a perversion of this picture, for the labor of the people is conscripted toward the worship of the Pharaoh.[8] Put differently, the wars of YHWH against Egypt were, by one reading, for the sake of restoring to Israel their economic agency, an integral part of their worship of God.

But the larger lens of the Hebrew Bible casts this story as one concerned with the worship of God: in Exodus 15 this event is remembered as an instance of God's power over the nations, in Exodus 20 as the basis for the commandments, and in Judges 6:9 as an anti-idolatry polemic. This is not to negate the economic import of God's work in Exodus 14 but to contextualize these economic concerns within a liturgical framework. This liturgical framework reminds us that a properly ordered economy is one of the aspects of right worship of YHWH.[9] YHWH's unaided military victory serves to provide the basis for the establishment of a just economy, which is an aspect of right worship.

Second Kings 6:24—7:20: YHWH, Restorer of Israel's Economy

By the time of the divided kingdom, the framework of YHWH fighting on behalf of the people was well established. Not excluding more routine military ventures, the Hebrew Bible is not shy of describing the ways in which YHWH unilaterally defends the people of Israel from attack. In 2 Kings 6:24—7:20 we find another one of these narratives during a time of siege by Ben-hadad of Aram. In this narrative, centering on the prophet Elisha, Samaria is under assault and starving. As a consequence of the siege, food

---

8. McConville, *God and Earthly Power*, 53.
9. For more examples, see Fox, *Reverberations of the Exodus*.

scarcity has become such that typically inedible or taboo foods are the measure of the market (the head of a donkey and the bitter Star of Bethlehem flower [6:25], for example).[10] Beyond this, even accounts of cannibalism are surfacing, indicating the depth of the famine.[11]

What is significant in describing the famine in these terms is twofold. First, the narrator emphasizes not simply that people are resorting to extreme food sources but that the metrics associated with these foods are exorbitant, charging eighty shekels for a horse head and a quarter of a cab for five shekels.[12] Unjust valuation of necessities is criticized by the prophets when done for unscrupulous reasons, but here the whole of Samaria suffers economic imbalance because of Aram's siege. Secondly, however, the Israelite economy, which is one of the measures of the people's fidelity to YHWH, has become linked to the valuation of foods that are expressly forbidden by the law.[13] In sum, the Aramean siege has created a cultural situation in which the people—in order to survive—are engaging in activities prohibited by the law and which are unjust under normal circumstances.

The departure of the Aramean army due to a great confusion caused by YHWH (7:6–7) creates a restoration of the Samarian economy. Not only are the foodstuffs of the Aramean army plundered by the Samarians after it is reported that their camp has been abandoned, but the narrator notes the way in which once again the food economy has returned to a proper scale (7:18). This detail is significant not only because the food economy is no longer characterized by prohibited foods or unjust prices but because this was the specific reason given by the prophet Elisha for YHWH's action (7:1–2).

---

10. For a guide to the botanical references, see Duke, Duke, and duCellier, *Medicinal Plants*.

11. Other instances of this surface in the accounts of Deuteronomy 28:53–57, Jeremiah 19:9, and Lamentations 4:10.

12. For a sense of the disproportion, the threshing floor of Aravna the Jebusite is bought by King David (2 Sam 24:24) for fifty shekels, and the mountain of Samaria is purchased for six hundred shekels (1 Kgs 16:24). To pay eighty shekels for a horse head, even given the generational gap between the time of David and the time of the divided kingdom, indicates profound inflation due to scarce resources. For an overview of biblical economics of scale, see Levine, *Oxford Handbook of Judaism and Economics*, particularly 564–84.

13. Donkeys fall under the prohibition against eating hooved creatures who do not chew cud (Lev 11:3).

Imagery of the Psalms: Economy and YHWH's Wars in Liturgical Celebration

The Psalms, unlike the histories or the Pentateuch, offer little direct narrative exploration of these themes. Rather, they recount how YHWH has unilaterally delivered the people in ways that provide the basis for economic flourishing. As with the previous examples, what is important about this connection for the Psalms is how the economic life of Israel has flourished in a way consistent with the law due to the unilateral action of YHWH. Any number of Psalms could be explored for this relation, including Psalms 60, 107, and 144, but our discussion will encompass only two examples.

In Psalm 33, for example, the psalmist contrasts the plans of the nations with the plans of the Lord (vv. 10–11), a contrast that is carried out with respect to the size of the nations' armies (v. 16) and Israel's deliverance from famine (v. 19). The psalm's historical narrative is bookended by exhortations to praise God, casting this restoration of Israel both politically and economically in a liturgical framework. The effect is that the filling of the earth with unfailing love (v. 5) is made manifest through a plentiful economy. If Lynn Jost is correct that Psalm 33 is authored in the wake of David's conquest of Bathsheba, the psalm's affirmation that "no king is saved by the size of his armies" (v. 16) is all the more poignant: the deliverance that YHWH brings is unmatched by any military force, along with the economic fruit that comes from YHWH's work.[14]

The converse is also true for the Psalms: the failure of YHWH to act militarily leads to economic injustice. In Psalm 44, the psalmist laments that God "no longer goes out with our armies" (v. 9), which has resulted in the people's enslavement (v. 12). And yet the people have kept the covenantal obligations, despite their destitution (vv. 17–18). The psalmist calls for God to act, for in acting, not only will the people be able to keep the covenant, but their economic situation will be restored to a just state that reflects the faithfulness of the people to God (vv. 23–26).[15]

Summing Up: YHWH's Wars, Israel's Economy

As we survey the first category, the link between YHWH's intervention and the subsequent economic life of Israel is not one that guarantees Israel's faithfulness. YHWH's acts on behalf of Israel are designed to provide Israel

---

14. Jost, "Psalm 33," 71.

15. Rom-Shiloni, "Psalm 44," reads the psalm as a protest against the unjust action of God. See also Crow, "The Rhetoric of Psalm 44."

with the physical means by which it can be justly sustained. As seen in Exodus 32, however, this is no guarantee that Israel will utilize these material goods toward just ends. What is important to note is that there is a positive link between YHWH's defense of a people and their social flourishing: YHWH acts on behalf of a people's political and social flourishing.

No consideration is given here to the justice of YHWH's actions, as the acts of YHWH are not subject to these kinds of judgments in the same way that the acts of humans are; what is of concern, however, is whether Israel responds rightly to the work of God. This theme broadly resonates with the whole of the Old Testament: when God acts unilaterally (whether with creation, liberation from Egypt, or return from exile), the people are expected to respond to YHWH by being the people whom YHWH has called them to be, in this case by justly ordering their economic goods.

Category Two: Israel's Just Wars, Israel's Just Economy

Explicating the unilateral work of YHWH against Israel's adversaries is fairly straightforward, but now we move into the more contested field of how to describe the wars of Israel itself. In these sections, I will not engage questions of divine command or questions of the ethics of warfare directly but will instead explicate the relation between wars that are commanded by God and the economic benefits that accrue to Israel through these wars. The valuation of these Old Testament conflicts, in particular, stem from their divine sanction, though not exclusively; as we will see, both those conflicts that are undertaken by Israel's initiative while sanctioned by YHWH and those that are by YHWH's direct command are designed to be accompanied by just economic growth.

In these occasions, warfare leads to Israel's economic growth, through the acquisition of land and goods. As with the previous category, valuations of economic life are interrelated, both positively and negatively. For example, when the goods of warfare are used for private gain, and not devoted to the worship of God or the common good, judgment from God is rendered. These events, as with the first section, are primarily drawn from the Hebrew Bible but have resonances in the New Testament's imagination as well.

Genesis 14: The Spoils of Conflict and Abram's Distribution

The first instance we see of the wars of the people of YHWH occurs in Genesis 14, as a prototype of future events. A battle between a coalition of five kings (Sodom, Gomorrah, Admah, Zeboyim, and Bela) and four kings

(Elam, Goyim, Shinar, and Ellasar) takes place. Overwhelmed by the five kings, the four-king coalition flees, carrying away Abram's nephew Lot with them (vv. 10–12). In the wake of the fight, Abram follows after the kings until Lot and his possessions have been returned. This event ostensibly leads to Abram being treated as an equal among the kings, as the king of Sodom visits Abram, who had single-handedly defeated the four kings. In the wake of this recognition by the winning coalition of the kings, Melchizedek comes to Abram, recognizing that God has been with Abram in the fight (v. 20), at which point Abram divests himself of the spoils of the battle. The king of Sodom offers the spoils of the battle to Abram, who refuses to keep anything belonging to Sodom (vv. 22–24).

Economically, there are two aspects of this event that are significant. First, in the wake of his battle with the four kings, Abram offers a self-imposed tithe to the mysterious priest Melchizedek, who speaks a blessing over Abram. Secondly, when offered the spoils of battle, Abram refuses any payment except "what my men have eaten and the share that belongs to the men who went with me" (v. 24). Rather than opting to use war as an occasion for self-glorification, Abram views the economic boon of war as an occasion for a tribute to the priest Melchizedek and for the just treatment of his companions.

Joshua 6–7: Just War, Just and Unjust Accumulation

If the story of Abram is the prototype for how the people of YHWH are to view the spoils of conflict, Joshua 6–7 serves as an important antitype. Joshua 6 tells the familiar story of the people of Israel's victory over the walled city of Jericho. In a manner mirroring both the battle of Abram and the earlier unilateral battles of YHWH, the battle of Israel is preceded by liturgical activity, namely, the blowing of the ceremonial trumpets and the procession of the ark of the covenant (6:1–6). And in a manner akin to Exodus 14–15, the precious metals of Jericho are taken for the people's treasury, even as their enemies are devoted to the Lord as a *herem* offering. Beyond the collection of Jericho's goods into the people's treasury, the boundaries of Israel's generosity are expanded to include Rahab and her family; initially kept outside the camp (6:23), Rahab and her Canaanite family are included within Israel and made the beneficiaries of the battle against Jericho (6:25).

Joshua 7 begins in a parallel manner to Joshua 6, including spies sent out to canvass the territory, with the people afraid of the citizens of Ai as they were of Jericho. But in this instance, military defeat followed as a consequence of economic hoarding.[16] In the aftermath of the battle of Jericho, Achan and his family had taken those things that were meant to be devoted to the treasury, resulting in Israel's military defeat. In one respect, Israel fails in its military venture because of its covenantal infidelity to YHWH, but this covenantal infidelity is expressed particularly in Achan's upending of the covenantal economy that is intrinsic to Israel's corporate life. To take the goods of battle and hide them under his tent (7:21) was akin to building the economic goods into the family line, as opposed to the economic life of the people.

In view of our exploration, what occurs here is consistent with what we have seen thus far: the goods that YHWH provides through military conflict are to be ordered toward the good of the people and toward right worship. When this economic order is upended—whether by hoarding the goods of battle (Josh 7) or by ordering the goods of battle toward idolatry (Exod 32)—the relation between war and economics becomes perverse and destructive for Israel.

Luke 14:31–32:
Military and Economic Alliance in the New Testament

Following the exile and return of Israel, the theocratic arrangement, which makes the military-economic nexus of this section possible, comes into question. Following the Maccabean period, Israel as a political entity is no longer the dynastic rule that had comprised a previous age; this is not to say that this memory was entirely gone, however. As many have noted, the expectations of the Messiah involved a restoration of Israel as a military force. Whatever else we make of military actions in Scripture broadly, it is important to note the ways in which Jesus' own actions move away from this ideal. This is important as we examine one of the only links between economic life and military life in Jesus' teachings, the parable of the king who plans for war. As with other parables, Jesus uses these images not to bless or condemn certain vocations, but because they are easily accessible.

As such, the parable of Luke 14 concerns the nature of discipleship and is not designed to confirm the military-economic link one way or another. In the pericope, the illustration of 14:31–32 carries other meanings. The illustrations before and after it both concern endurance—of completing a

---

16. "Israel has sinned; they have violated my covenant, which I commanded them to keep. They have taken some of the devoted things; they have stolen, they have lied, they have put them with their possessions.... I will not be with you anymore unless you destroy whatever among you is devoted to destruction" (Josh 7:11–12).

large-scale task and of the ongoing value of salt's preservative powers—and point the reader toward that meaning in the case of the king as well. That these three illustrations (building a tower, planning a conflict, preserving food) speak to diverse social contexts (business, politics, domestic life) confirms this reading. We will return to this point shortly with respect to modern application, but the silence on the military-economic valuation, an arrangement that was so prevalent in the Old Testament, raises important questions for what to make of this link in the contemporary world.

Summing Up: Just Wars and Just Economies

In this type, Israel enacts wars under the guidance and/or command of YHWH, though no less is expected of Israel in terms of the just relation between the military and economy. In the first type, the acts of YHWH both make possible and restore just economic life to Israel. What we see here in the second type follows from this: justified conflict should be accompanied by just economic relations that benefit the community and do not lead to private acquisition or unequal social conditions. As I have suggested already, however, this relation is largely one that is restricted to the Old Testament. What explicit mention there is in the New Testament of this union by Jesus appears to be illustrative and not meant to affirm or disconfirm this relation.

What these sections leave relatively undiscussed, however, is the human cost of divine violence latent within the Old Testament passages, most evidently with *herem*. What should we make of Israel's economic flourishing at the expense of human life? One could argue that it is simply normalized, that the parables of Jesus simply assume an unjust arrangement. But this ignores, I think, the expectation of economic fidelity, which is placed upon Israel, in keeping both with the vocation of Israel and with the blood-cost associated with Israel's financial state. The copious commands of Israel to treat the foreigner well, to care for their poor, and to be characterized by economic justice point us toward acknowledgment of the attention paid toward what has been lost. When Israel engages in economic injustice—either by ignoring their own poor or by using forced labor to build Solomon's temples—it is problematic not only because of the divine covenant but because of what has been involved in Israel's economic success.

Consider, for example, Achan, who hoarded the wealth plundered from Ai rather than donate it rightly to God (Josh 7). On one level, this is a story about fidelity to God and using the wealth rightly toward God. But considered from another angle, this is a way of acknowledging the high cost of war: that the wealth gained cannot be for one's private benefit but must be put to use in dispossessed service to God—for the sake of the poor, for worship, and for the stranger. To incorporate the wealth gained through war seamlessly into the foundations of Israel's aggrandizement is to make the blood of the Canaanites into an analogy of Abel's blood, crying out from beneath the floor of the temple for vindication.

Category Three: Economy and Military Arrangements Gone Wrong

The third relation between military and economy in Scripture is that of unjust economies supporting warfare. Unlike the first two categories, this third relation appears in both the pagans and among the people of God. The Egyptians and Assyrians—in their enslavement and conquest of the people of Israel—exhibit this relation. Both of these groups are named by the prophets as oppressing the people of God, both in the economic arrangement that they conscript Israel into and in their conquest of the people. As with the first two categories, the worship of the people is indicative of how it unfolds in practice. Put differently, because the Egyptians and Assyrians do not turn to YHWH, their economic-military relation proceeds in an unjust fashion, which is condemned. But this military-economic arrangement present within Assyria and Egypt is mirrored at times within Israel as well. The prophets likewise link together the abuses of Israel's kings in this way: trusting in horses and in wealth accompanies idolatry. As with the first two types, reliance upon military strength and economic injustices are not linked together, but the malformation of both economy and military is linked to infidelity to God.

Nahum 2–3: The Injustice of the Military-Economic Relation among the Nations

There are any number of instances in which the nations beyond Israel are judged for the combined disorder of violently supported economics, including Amos 1, Habakkuk 1, and Micah 1, but we will briefly focus on Nahum 2–3. Putting to one side what it means that the nations beyond Israel are judged according to Israel's law, we find YHWH rendering judgment on the nations for the very disorders we see emerging from Israel even prior to the giving of the law (Exod 32).[17] This is most often the case with respect to the

---

17. If the covenant given to Abraham is, among other things, that he is to be a light

idolatry of the nations, but in Nahum 2–3, the military-economic relation of Assyria is brought under judgment as well.

Chapter 2 opens with judgment being rendered upon Nineveh by a foreign invader, stripping away its economic resources (2:7, 9–10). Nineveh's manifold military technologies (2:5–6, 13) cannot defend it from being plundered, in a dual judgment encompassing both their economic and military prowess. In 3:1–4, in contrast to other nations who are judged explicitly for their devotion to idols, we find Assyria coming under judgment for its military prowess (vv. 1–2) but also for how its economic goods have been ordered toward the prowess of Assyria and not the worship of God. In the wake of their defeat, their manifold merchants—built up as a consequence of Assyria's wars—will turn on Assyria, stripping the land bare (3:16).

Though in Assyria's case the relation runs from military corruption to economic injustice, this is not the only arrangement for which condemnation occurs. In Nahum, for example, the violence of Assyria has led to the economic flourishing of the nation, and it is thus the brutality of Assyria that first comes under judgment. Other nations, however, are condemned in their reversal of this relation. In Exodus 2, we first encounter Egypt as the one who is exploiting Israel economically, an exploitation that funds their military.

The Judgment of Israel: Varieties of Pathologies between Economy and Military

As we turn our attention to Israel, it is not the wars of Israel that are condemned by Scripture but the economic mechanisms that fund those wars. As I suggested in the opening of this essay, Scripture treats the issues of warfare and economy synthetically, such that for Israel, the corruption of one implicates the other. This is true because of the integrated nature of Israel: as a people called together under God, there is no area of life that does not contribute to the peoplehood of Israel. Accordingly, a failure in one area of Israel's life cannot be cordoned off from its effect on other areas of life. For the Old Testament, there is no discussion of whether or not the wars of YHWH or of Israel are *just*, but, rather, whether the wars and that which follows from them (such as economic gains) contribute to the faithfulness of Israel. This being said, the fates of these two facets of Israelite life are intertwined: if the economy that supports the wars of Israel is deficient, the

---

to the nations, then it is not surprising that the standard by which Abraham's people are judged is the standard by which all nations are judged.

military life of Israel also comes to ruin, and vice versa. How we evaluate Israel's practices of war is an important question but not one that the Old Testament performs independent of other considerations.

Three instances will help illustrate the manifold ways in which these two aspects of Israelite life rise and fall together. In Isaiah 3:5–8, the prophet foretells the manner in which, following their military defeat, economic injustice will be normalized. According to Isaiah, the economic despair to follow comes, in part, because of the people's reliance upon military might instead of YHWH (2:7). By looking to other sources of power (pagan idols and military might), the people were able to build their national economy (2:7) independent of YHWH. The focus of Isaiah's prophecy is not against military resources as such but against a military-economic nexus that is ordered independent of trust in YHWH.

A narrative similar to Isaiah 2–3 appears in 1 Kings 9–10, where Solomon conscripts the Jebusite people into forced labor to build not only the temple but his own palaces (9:15–19). Solomon is commended for not enslaving his own people, but the cheap source of labor artificially enables Israel's economy to blossom, drawing the attention of foreign leaders. Not accidentally, 1 Kings 10–11 displays the downward spiral that this leads to, as Solomon continues to accumulate wealth and foreign wives, which gives rise to external rebellions against Solomon and the dissolution of Israel. The text does not solely attribute the decline of Israel to the enslavement of the Jebusites, but from an economic perspective, the decline of Israel would not have been possible *without* their unjust enslavement.

In the previous two examples, we have instances in which (1) excessive concern for military strength results in economic injustice, and (2) unjust economies create military difficulties. In 1 Kings 21, we find a final configuration: military force used for purely economic ends, resulting in divine judgment. King Ahab follows the pattern set by David before him—using government force for private ends (2 Sam 11)—but rather than terminating in repentance, Ahab's story results in political disaster. Ahab sees the vineyard of Naboth and uses the force of the government to murder Naboth and take the vineyard (21:11–16). This single act sets in motion a prophecy against Ahab's house that ends in Ahab's death on the field of battle (22:39–40).

The first two instances show particularly traditional arrangements: the failures of military and economic life to mutually support one another. In the third instance, however, governmental force is used over against proper economic life, creating a competitive relation between the two. To take Naboth's ancestral land is not only to transgress the role of governmental force within Israel, but it is to transgress and reconfigure a divinely instituted economic arrangement. One's ancestral land preserved one's place within Israelite society; Ahab's taking of the land is the ultimate destruction of the military-economic relation that had preserved Israelite society since Egypt.

Summing Up: Unjust Military and Economic Arrangements

In this third category, we find a whole host of deformed relations between military and economy, all of which lead to the destruction of Israel. Analytically, the differences between these instances provide interesting vantage points to understand the manifold ways that economic and military aspects of society become intertwined and corrupt one another. But, theologically, however these aspects become malformed, the scriptural narratives are more interested in the ways in which these intertwined aspects of life draw the people either toward God or away from God.

Excurses: What of the New Testament?

As observed thus far, much of the explicit treatment of the relationship between economy and military occurs within the Old Testament. Throughout the New Testament—particularly in the letters of Paul—there are military metaphors that are used to indicate the rigor with which Christians are to approach their discipleship. But there is a transposition of the terminology that takes place which, in turn, affects what I take to be the plurality of the Old Testament witness. Thus, we must briefly take stock of these texts to see if there is any similar relation as seen in the Old Testament and, if so, what it might indicate.

In 1 Corinthians 9:7, Paul uses the analogy of a soldier receiving their pay to argue for the validity of paying him as an apostle. As seen in the preceding sections, a defender arising from the ranks of Israel—provided that the cause was one authorized by God—should not be economically burdened by their service.[18] In this passage, however, there is an inversion that occurs between economic gain and the service which an apostle, that is, the Christian "soldier," renders. Arguing that while he has the right to economic compensation (as soldiers do), Paul, as an apostle, would rather offer his service free of charge (9:18), for this more deeply corresponds to the free work of Christ than paid service. A similar distancing between

---

18. Compare to Deuteronomy 24:5. Other exemptions are observed within the Old Testament for not serving in the military, such as being faint of heart (Judg 7:3) or age (Num 1:45), but the exemption from service for the reason of economically establishing one's household after marriage is most pertinent here.

compensation and service is seen in Philippians 2:25, in which his "fellow soldier" Epaphroditus serves without thought of reward but rather focuses on excellent service, a pattern seen in Paul's advice to Timothy as well (2 Tim 2:3).

This broken link in Paul between service and compensation, using the metaphor of the soldier, bears closest resemblance to the first type of Old Testament material, in which the people of God are provided for by the act of God, independent of their engagement in a military venture. In these instances, it is God who works and the people who are provided for economically. These usages by Paul of the soldier are not for the sake of validating military service one way or another,[19] but to indicate the manner in which Christians are to serve. In terms of our survey thus far, there is in Paul a distance between the provision of God and the mode by which that provision will come. Whereas in national Israel there may have been a faithful mode of correspondence between the two, that mode no longer seems applicable in Paul's day.

Given that Christians are not encouraged to be soldiers and that when soldiering is used as an analogy it is being used as a *disanalogy* for the military-economic relation, there is, I suggest, a returning of Christians to the first type of material: God provides and the people receive, independent of their taking those resources by justified means. This broken link between soldiering and economics is akin to what we find with Jesus' Sermon on the Mount, in which the use of interpersonal force is also ruled out, whether in legally legitimate forms of force or court actions (Matt 5:21-26, 38-48). In this sermon, likewise, the people are instructed to trust in God's provision and not in whatever forms of legalized force they might avail themselves of: the link between force and material provision is ruled out for disciples of Jesus.

Moving Forward: What to Make of the Military-Economic Arrangements in Scripture?

The interpersonal teachings of the Sermon on the Mount are not the same as the wars described in the Hebrew Bible, to be sure. But the use of soldiering as a metaphor and not as an actual practice in the New Testament,

---

19. The use of a profession illustratively as Paul does in these passages is akin to what Jesus does, in using tax collectors, unjust managers, and kings as professional examples in parables. To say that Paul is commending the specific profession of a soldier by his use of it as an example here makes no more sense than to say that Jesus is doing the same in his parables: appeal to a commonly understood profession and example is not a commendation of the profession itself or an encouragement to take up that profession.

combined with the use of soldiering in ways that distinctly breaks the link between violence and economic provision, points us in a direction indicated by the words of Jesus. But this does not yet resolve the question of the contemporary use of the economic-military link, for asserting that Christians live as *disanalogous* soldiers, awaiting God's provision apart from violence, still requires us to say what this all has to do with contemporary military-economic arrangements.

As we have seen, the bulk of the scriptural witness does not univocally condemn the link between economic development and military life as such. In the life of Israel, both a just economy and certain military engagements are described as components of a manifold social arrangement by which the people of Israel live in faithfulness before God. That being said, there are any number of ways in which this arrangement can be corrupted, ranging from unjustly manipulating an economy, to unjustly intervening in society with military force, to using that which is gained by military ventures for private gain and not for the good of the people. However—despite the affirmation of this arrangement in the Old Testament—justifying this arrangement in contemporary nation-states is fraught with difficulties. First, as I have argued, the image for Christian practice, rooted in the New Testament, is one that not only disavows even the just application of this arrangement but also repurposes the imagery of the justly paid soldier for practices contrary to the Old Testament.

Even if we were to set this hermeneutical argument aside, making contemporary application of this relation as seen in Israel is fraught with several difficulties. First, as William Cavanaugh has suggested, there seems to be no contemporary analogue here, as there is no theonomous political entity.[20] In the absence of such a theonomous political entity, the question of what to make of the military-economic relation is without a direct analogy and thus without a sure basis for advocacy: the just war/economy relation rests upon the polity's liturgical relation to God. Since Israel, as a theocentric political entity, no longer exists, making any simple analogy between the benevolent nature of the military-economic arrangement of the Old Testament and today's world simply cannot be done. Second, the majority

---

20. As an aside, the way in which Scripture portrays warfare does not comport to either traditional just war or pacifist categories. By just war reasoning, the Old Testament mirrors certain modern concerns, such as proper authority and just cause, but because of its commitment to war only because of God, falls much closer to holy war than anything resembling modern just war thinking. The disanalogy between modern thinking and the Old Testament favors Christian pacifist arguments, who would cite the implausibility of enacting an Old Testament vision in the present, except that the Old Testament generally only speaks in opposition to the *excesses* of certain wars and not against war as such.

of the material that speaks to the theological nature of this arrangement rests in the Old Testament and not in the New. As this chapter indicated, allusions to a proper military-economic arrangement are made, but with the demise of Israel as a political entity by the time of Jesus, the relationship between military and economy has to be rethought in a non-nationalized fashion. It is here that contemporary thinkers point to the ways in which the New Testament church embodies a particular vision of the relation between economic life and conflict that is distinctly different from that of Israel. As I argued earlier, in the wake of Jesus, the assumption of the New Testament is broadly that God provides for the people apart from their taking those provisions by force or engaging in war against their enemies.

What I have proposed thus far—that there can be no legitimate applicability of the justified military-economy arrangement of the Old Testament—does not have the immediate benefit of these proposals, namely, a basis for judgments upon national arrangements of military-economy. In other words, because we do not live in ancient, theonomous Israel, the bulk of the material described above does not have direct application. In addition, Christians must consider not simply the good of their own nation but also the good of other nations in the global community, of which their own nation is a part. To understand what import the scriptural witness has, and how it can be seen in our world, we have to relocate these critiques of the Old Testament to the locus of the church, and, more properly, a church that is scattered across nations, peoples, and places.

In a globalized economy—where events in the Chinese market have dramatic ramifications for the American market, or where subprime mortgages in America trigger global banking meltdowns—these questions of how to conceive of the relation between military and economy become even more complicated. Just as our economies are now globally shared and affect global interests, so the same is true with respect to our militaries. We now live in an age in which American arms are shipped and used across the world and American military interests are bound up in global security interests. In an earlier era, including the ages depicted in Scripture, the intertwined relation of economic and military concerns could be thought of in circumscribed ways: faithfulness toward God in areas both economic and military were linked together and could be thought of within national boundaries.

In an age in which economic and military interests are shared globally, I would suggest, it is becoming increasingly impossible to think of how to judge the military-economic arrangements of a *nation*, insofar as (at least in an American context) these are intimately intertwined with international interests. For us to judge the scope of America's military-economic arrangements, we must consider that America remains the largest weapons exporter in the world and maintains the largest military force globally. The ways this nexus is interwoven into economies and conflicts throughout the world makes it nearly impossible to account for all its permutations. By limiting our judgments upon this arrangement to how America benefits economically from its military, or how the military funds the economy, obscures the ways in which our military expenditures hamper or harm other polities worldwide. Thus, making judgments upon these arrangements must be done in a way that can account for the multitude of national arrangements, but from within the larger scope of their global impacts; just as Israel could not live on Canaanite gold in a way that rehearsed Canaanite idolatry, so the contemporary people of God cannot engage in these arrangements as if global others were not immediately affected by their actions.

As I argued earlier, America does not solely bear the costs of its military-economic arrangements. As such, judgments by Christians upon *American* arrangements cannot belong exclusively to American Christians. Put differently, if the military-economic relation is now no longer national but international, Christians must join their witness across national boundaries to address these arrangements. Churches, embedded within polities that not only originate these arrangements but are affected by these arrangements, are able to join together in their transnational critiques of an arrangement with international scope and effect.

This, of course, was always the way that Paul envisioned the churches: as transnational realities that shared not only their peaceable witness but their economic goods across cultural lines (2 Cor 8). For readers of Scripture to wrestle with how to call the nexus of economy and our military to account, to limit them (or perhaps to annul them) for the sake of God, they must recognize the Christian churches as a global body that is in principle able to meet the challenge of a global military-economic complex. This will require, among other things, Christians recognizing one another as sharing a common worshipping life and having an interconnected moral life, moving beyond the frame of nationalism, and recognizing the scope of our challenges as global. It will require Christians materially supporting one another's judgments, across national lines, and listening to the critiques of Christians elsewhere as the voice of the Spirit builds from multiple spaces, pushing back on the deformations of the military-economic arrangement in the manifold places in which it takes root.

Being able to hear the full force of Scripture's vision of the military-economic arrangement will require that Christians recover their fundamental identity as Christians, who inhabit certain spaces in an almost ironic fashion, as those who belong to a place but are yet not at home there.

As creatures *sub aeterni*, churches are both of their particular cultures and yet allied in connatural ways with those who are not of their home culture, determined in practice and orientation by commitments that are both germane to their culture and alien to them. It is only in this way that we can hear Scripture's message on this topic, remembering that to take up arms internationally means to take up arms at times against other sisters and brothers in Christ around the globe, gaining from their loss both politically and economically. As we find in the *Epistle to Diognetus*,

> The Christians are distinguished from other men neither by country, nor language, nor the customs which they observe. For they neither inhabit cities of their own, nor employ a peculiar form of speech, nor lead a life which is marked out by any singularity. . . . But, [they inhabit] Greek as well as barbarian cities, according as the lot of each of them has determined. . . .
>
> . . . What the soul is in the body, that are Christians in the world. The soul is dispersed through all the members of the body, and Christians are scattered through all the cities of the world.[21]

The inhabitation of cities described here can be read as a quasi-gnostic one, but it is better read as an inhabitation by those who, in an Augustinian sense, "make use of" what is at hand in a transformative sense, drawing their affiliations and their citizenships toward the kingdom of God. This is achieved by claiming their common worship with other Christians, a common worship that propels them to identify the malformations which another country's military-economic nexus is perpetuating on their own country. This orientation toward critique may seem insufficiently Augustinian, identifying only the dark possibilities, but as we see in our scriptural typology, absent a liturgical center for this nexus, idolatry lies close on the horizon when war and moneymaking are intertwined.

The scriptural witness on this arrangement, as it moves through Pentecost to the proliferation of the people of God to the far corners of the world, points us to a much different context of its use: any theological justification of the military-economic arrangement must be lived out in a transnational context, in which Christians and their neighbors are among many nations, and speak many languages. Gone are the days when the people of God could think in a circumscribed, theocratic way about the good of military-economic arrangements. Christians are opened up into a world where the arms taken up in one place will radically impact the people

---

21. *Epistle to Diognetus* 5, 6, in Roberts and Donaldson, *Ante-Nicene Fathers*, 1:26–27.

of God elsewhere. In short, readers of Scripture are given a legacy that does not invite easy usage but, if anything, endless circumspection about how we have used this legacy badly, and an endless invitation to rethink whether this relation is usable today.

2

Christian Ethics and the Problems of War and Business

CHRISTINA G. MCRORIE

Introduction

Over the years, Christianity has had rather a lot to say about both business and war. And although business and war present quite different "problems" for moral reflection, much of what has been said about the two issues has been similar. In fact, at times Christian thought treats the two as interchangeable problems; we can see places where war is treated as business and where business is treated as war.

An analogy or comparison between business and war is not perfect, for many reasons. For one thing, however dangerous the conditions of labor, the purpose of business is not itself killing. For another, although war can be avoided, business, at least in some form, cannot; as the word itself implies, business is simply what humans do in order to collectively provision themselves with the resources required for everyday life. If we are to live more than a mere subsistence life, we cannot avoid busying ourselves with some form of exchange and commerce. This might seem to imply that business and war should be dealt with rather differently—by, say, embracing the one practice but rejecting the other. And in fact, it is not hard to call to mind stark scriptural injunctions against violence (e.g., Jesus' teaching regarding not resisting evil in Matthew 5:39 and Luke 6:29), whereas business qua business is nowhere so clearly prohibited.

But of course, in truth the moral status of these issues is nowhere near this straightforward, either in Scripture or in the tradition more generally. Although Jesus' teachings in the New Testament do seem to condemn violence, narratives in the Hebrew Bible—the Christian Old Testament—seem to endorse it. Christians hold the Old Testament to be Scripture as well, and so these narratives must be reckoned with when thinking about a Christian ethic of war. Likewise, although Scripture nowhere plainly says "Thou shalt not be a capitalist, or a businessman," Jesus' teachings often do appear to enjoin a radical divestment of wealth and property that can be read to imply a condemnation of business, capitalist or otherwise. These too must be reckoned with alongside other Scriptures that appear to endorse honorably gained wealth, the ownership of property, and virtue in commerce. In short, the Christian scriptural witness on questions of business and war is decidedly ambivalent—and perhaps even conflicted. We should not be surprised then that the development of Christian thought on these two questions in the last two millennia is likewise a story of ambivalence and disagreement.[1]

This chapter introduces a variety of responses within the Christian tradition to the moral challenges of business and war and does so in particular by foregrounding similarities in the treatments of the two issues. It does not provide a linear historical narrative but rather sketches key forms of moral reasoning used to think about these issues at different points in Christian history. It roughly groups these according to the general posture of the approach: *rejection, embrace, and cautious restraint and reflection*. But of course, such broad categories cannot tell the whole story; we must also ask, rejection or embrace of what? A denunciation of war might mean a condemnation of all forms of killing whatsoever or of particular forms of warfare—say, imperialist expansion or torture. Likewise, it is necessary to distinguish between the rejection of business that denounces all forms of commercial activity (or even the use of money itself) and that which condemns only certain ways of making profit, such as lending at interest. This chapter will attempt to clarify what key moments and figures in the tradition have meant by "business" and "war" by asking how ethical reflection on each issue might illuminate treatment of the other. Were there any forms of warfare that Christians understood as a kind of business,

---

1. For a more detailed analysis of this ambivalence, see Myles Werntz's chapter in this volume.

for example? How did (and do) Christians conceive of market activity as warlike and apply ethical concepts applicable to war to questions of profit and wealth? Searching for the points of contact and contrast in the analysis of each of these issues promises to enrich our understanding of the modes of moral reasoning used to respond to both.

Following this, the chapter concludes with a reflection on some of the problems that business and war present to Christian moral reflection today. These include concerns raised by the way that the increasingly complex and interconnected nature of the global economy now causes the two issues to frequently overlap and merge, a new problem we might call "the business of war." Coping with this new issue, this chapter suggests, will require an adaptation of the moral reasoning used to address these issues at prior moments. What is needed now is moral reflection on business and war that is creatively innovative while still remaining faithful to the central commitments animating Christian moral reflection.

Critical Approaches to Business and War

Rejection and Withdrawal

The earliest Christian response to both business and war—however they are construed—was undoubtedly one of rejection and withdrawal. This moral orientation was underwritten by the general conviction among the first-century Christians that following Jesus Christ meant living in opposition to "the world" which was passing away,[2] and therefore meant rejecting the logic of prudential self-preservation which animates worldly pursuits such as commerce and military service. However, this rejection was not solely one of indifference to the affairs of the world. It also sprung from the moral judgment that the requirements of Christian *askesis* (moral training in discipleship and in the *imitatio Christi*) precluded all forms of violence. This was to a lesser extent true with regard to participation in the hierarchical and often exploitative economy of the Roman Empire. The earliest Christians seemed to endorse what now can be seen as an "interim ethic" of nonparticipation in wider cultural practices.[3]

This ethic of nonparticipation was both more obvious and feasible with regard to questions of war: the earliest church was pacifist. As best as historians can tell, Christians generally avoided military and civil service in

---

2. For a concise introduction to the role of the concept of "the world" in Christian thought, see Pyper, "World," 761–762.

3. Mohrmann, unpublished manuscript on the history of Christian ethics.

the first two hundred years (although some disagreement exists over whether this was most fundamentally driven by an absolute refusal of violence or by a desire to avoid participation in public religious rites). As Tertullian memorably reminded his flock, Christ, "in disarming Peter, unbelted every soldier."[4]

The record of the earliest Christian attitudes toward business is less clear. The book of Acts records that the Jerusalem churches engaged in a kind of radical economic sharing in which "no one claimed that any of their possessions was their own, but they shared everything they had" (4:32–35). This approach to economic life is also encouraged by the teachings of the *Didache*, the oldest surviving catechism, which exhorts, "You shall not turn away from someone in need, but shall share everything with your brother or sister, and do not claim that anything is your own."[5] The earliest Christians were probably still involved in business and trade outside the Christian community, but the ethical goal was clear that inside the community the external relations of business and socioeconomic stratification and inequality were to be overcome. This sort of radical ethic was more possible to sustain in the centuries before Christianity became the official religion of the state, when Christian communities were small, voluntary communities, and a minority within the larger culture of the Greco-Roman world.

This ethic began to change even before Christianity became the official religion of the Roman Empire, and eventually both military service and wealth (if not business; more on Christian views of business below) were widely accepted as legitimate within Christianity.[6] However, the radical witness of the early churches has continued to influence Christian thought on these two issues.

Counsels of Perfection and Room for Conscience

At times this influence has been direct, and Christian communities have pointed to the example of the early churches, as well as to the life and teachings of Jesus Christ, to explain a refusal to participate in either violence or worldly commercial activity. More frequently, however, Christians have endorsed the ideals of nonviolence and/or poverty not as binding moral requirements but as acts of supererogation or "counsels of perfection," which

---

4. Tertullian, *On Idolatry*, in Roberts and Donaldson, *Ante-Nicene Fathers*, 3:73.

5. *Didache* 4.8, in Holmes, *Apostolic Fathers*, 351.

6. For a magisterial introduction to the development of early Christian conceptions of wealth, and to the way that the admittance of wealthy Romans into the faith in late antiquity ultimately changed the religion, see Brown, *Through the Eye of a Needle*.

take their name from Jesus' advice to the rich young man in Matthew 19:21: "If you wish to be perfect, go, sell your possessions, and give the money to the poor."[7] The voluntary poverty and pacifism of mendicant and monastic orders such as the Franciscans is based on such a two-tiered ethic. Although Francis of Assisi certainly interpreted Jesus' advice to the rich young man literally, he did not think it binding upon all Christians. Rather, Francis described poverty as a "special way to salvation."[8] Christian communities have used such two-tiered systems of ethics (sometimes also referred to as "dual morality") in order to retain respect for Jesus' rigorous teachings, while also developing an ethic suitable for a church much larger than the earliest Christian communities.[9]

Within this supererogatory ethic of perfection, the desire to conform to Christ's radical example has led to some stark moralizing about the temptations of the world. Francis, for example, regularly spoke as if money were intrinsically morally dangerous—akin to "a venomous serpent."[10] Despite such dramatic imagery, however, those following such counsels of perfection rarely elaborate fully developed moral condemnations of business, as such. The Franciscans' withdrawal from commercial life and the ownership of property, for example, necessitated their dependency on alms, which meant their ethic existed within (and relied upon) a larger moral cosmology in which business was acceptable. Given this, the radical ethic of the Franciscans simultaneously challenged and reaffirmed the prevailing Christian economic ethic of the day.[11] This is often the case more generally

---

7. To be clear, the classic list of counsels of perfection includes poverty, chastity, and obedience, and not nonviolence. However, in a two-tiered Christian ethic, the regard for nonviolence as a morally superior ideal is roughly in keeping with the elevated moral status of these counsels.

8. Bonaventure, *Life of St. Francis of Assisi*, 64.

9. The room within this sort of two-tiered ethic for gradations of purity and holiness was especially instrumental in enabling the medieval church to embody what theologian Ernst Troeltsch has called the "Church-type" expression of Christianity. In this, the perennial Christian impulses toward asceticism, perfectionism, and social withdrawal are balanced by and subsumed within a larger moral synthesis, such that Christianity could eventually encompass and morally organize an entire social order. See Troeltsch, *Social Teaching*.

10. Bonaventure, *Life of St. Francis*, 68.

11. For more on the complicated ways that the voluntary renunciation of wealth by mendicants both challenged *and* reaffirmed the medieval social orders in which they occurred, see Wolf, *The Poverty of Riches*, and Little, *Religious Poverty*. See also Johnson, *The Fear of Beggars*, which examines the ironic way that "Christian mendicants played a role in fostering a renewed sense of the moral importance of property, the centrality of rights in public discourse, and the market as a pervasive organizational component of society" (51).

as well; those who practice radical economic ethics that reject most contemporary business practices at best cannot avoid existing alongside widespread acceptance of some form of commerce by others, and in some cases, are still deeply reliant upon the pursuit of commercial livelihoods in the wider society (if not in their own churches).

Another nonbinding approach to the issues urging rejection can be seen in the Roman Catholic Church's teaching on conscientious objection to war in the twentieth and twenty-first centuries. While the Catholic Church has always had a presumption against violence and war (more on this in the following section), only in recent years has it placed an increasing emphasis upon the right of conscientious objection. This is in part in light of the new shape of war in a post-atomic age, in which terrorism and counterterrorism occupy much of the discussion. Noting that the Pastoral Constitution of Vatican II urged "a completely fresh reappraisal of war" in light of the "development of armaments by modern science," for example, the United States Conference of Catholic Bishops declared in 1983 that the "new moment in which we find ourselves sees the just-war teaching and nonviolence as distinct but interdependent methods of evaluating warfare."[12] They accordingly encourage Catholics to "assess their attitudes toward war and military service in the light of Christian pacifism."[13] The vagueness of this advice means it can be read as encouraging support for pacifism construed broadly, as anywhere on a spectrum between an absolutist position to a more contextual "technological" pacifism that uses the logic of just war theory to determine that specifically modern forms of warfare cannot be justified.[14]

Counter-polis Politics and the Economics of Liberation Theology

Not all Christians have viewed repudiating business and war as optional or as an elective higher calling; some groups have argued that one or the other of these is in fact incumbent upon Christians. The problem with this, of course, is that the larger world appears simply not to be able to go a day without either business or war, and so it is generally only possible to successfully meet this moral expectation within small Christian communities. The most visible of such dissenting minority communities are the inheritors of the Anabaptist movement that arose from the Radical Reformation.

12. USCCB, *Challenge of Peace*, 120.
13. USCCB, *Challenge of Peace*, 118.
14. For more on this bridge position between a pacifist and just war theoretical approach to contemporary warfare, see Childress, "Contemporary Pacifism," 109–31.

The claim of the *Schleitheim Confession* (a 1527 statement of Anabaptist principles) that "the sword is an ordering of God outside of the perfection of Christ" neatly encapsulates the perspective most frequently taken by Anabaptists toward war.[15] While Anabaptists recognized that the offices and activities of soldiers and governors were not illegitimate and may be divinely ordained for the preservation of order in the world, they believed Christ "forbids the violence of the sword" for Christians.[16] As such, Christians cannot even serve as magistrates if elected or asked to do so, given that these supervise, and therefore can be said to engage in, violence.

Contemporary inheritors of this Anabaptist legacy of radical discipleship have focused less on withdrawal from the world and increasingly emphasized that the church ought to live in the world differently, so as to witness to the reality and possibilities of grace (although various groups differ on the degree to which they are called to be separate from or involved with the unredeemed, fallen world). Anabaptist theologians in particular have argued that creative communities of faith may offer resources and alternatives to a larger society trapped in agonistic patterns,[17] and in fact Mennonite and Amish scholars and communities are known for pioneering peacebuilding and restorative justice theory and practices[18] and creative alternative economic practices,[19] and for providing exemplary witnesses to the transformative role that radically nonviolent responses to violence (including forgiveness) play in communal healing after trauma.[20]

In recent decades, similar arguments have been made from Protestant and evangelical corners by scholars and pastors advocating a "kingdom

15. *Schleitheim Articles/Brotherly Union (1527)*, in Koop, *Confessions of Faith*, 30.

16. *Schleitheim Articles/Brotherly Union (1527)*, in Koop, *Confessions of Faith*, 30.

17. Mennonite theologian John Howard Yoder was particularly interested in the ways that putatively sectarian groups can provide creative resources for social change to the larger societies in which they exist. See Yoder, *Christian Witness*, especially 18–22; Yoder, "Evangelical Social Action," 184–89; and Yoder, *Body Politics*.

18. See the work of Howard Zehr and the Center for Justice and Peacebuilding at Eastern Mennonite University.

19. See the work of Mennonite theologian and activist Ched Myers and the Bartimaeus Cooperative Ministries (https://www.bcm-net.org) and Sabbath Economics Collaborative (http://www.sabbatheconomics.org/Sabbath_Economics_Collaborative/Home.html).

20. See the media coverage around notable cases such as that of the 2006 shooting of ten Amish girls at the West Nickel Mines School, in which the Amish community offered support—both emotional and financial—to the family of the shooter; and the coverage of the death of NHL player Dan Snyder due to a friend's reckless driving, in which his Mennonite family forgave and supported the driver and opposed his imprisonment when he plead guilty to second-degree vehicular homicide. Ruth, *Forgiveness: A Legacy*.

theology" approach to Christian ethics that emphasizes embodying God's already here and yet not fully present kingdom on earth. Like much Anabaptist theology, this focuses on how living proleptically into the grace of God's kingdom transforms the agonistic relations of the world into relations of peace and mutual giving.[21] Among other ethical concerns, these voices also urge nonviolence, and enjoin Christians to refrain from competitive and predatory economic behavior (and, in more radical versions, call for a kind of communal sharing and caretaking that draws upon the example of the Jerusalem church). This approach to social reflection and individual ethics shares with Anabaptist ethics the sense that the church should embody a robust *polis* that is visibly distinct from the larger society in which it resides.

Although in many ways similar to Anabaptist and evangelical kingdom ethics, another and distinct strand of recent theological reflection has voiced condemnation of both modern business and war, in this case as part of a larger rejection of the terms of modern life presented in liberal, pluralistic societies. Sometimes labeled as "radical Orthodoxy," theologians writing in this vein see capitalism today as foreign to the Christian faith, whether because political economy has "obliterat[ed]" Christian charity and is now Machiavellian,[22] or because a perverse and idolatrous crypto-theology is at work in markets today in which money "posits itself as the supreme being."[23] The rejection they encourage is more conceptual than practical; although such figures may advocate a (variant of) Christian socialism, their critiques are more academic thought experiments than they are practical, ecclesially grounded proposals.[24] Such theologians encourage a general suspicion of theological engagements with business ethics, and social sciences such as economics, based on the claim that secular social theory is irremediably compromised by the theological and heretical assumptions woven into modernity itself.

A final strand of theological reflection deserves mentioning in the rough category of "rejection," and that is liberation theology. Liberation theology began as a movement in Latin America in the mid-twentieth century as a reaction to the systemic poverty and extreme inequality experienced by Central and South American nations.[25] As a method of theological

21. See Gushee and Stassen, *Kingdom Ethics*.

22. Milbank, *Theology and Social Theory*, 31.

23. Goodchild, *Theology of Money*, 106.

24. Consider Goodchild's ambitious proposal to resubmit contemporary finance to theological evaluations; while Goodchild nowhere says this proposal is *anti*-business, per se, it would require entirely refashioning the market as we know it today.

25. The term was originally coined by Peruvian priest Gustavo Gutiérrez in his *Theology of Liberation*.

reflection, it emphasizes the integral role of praxis (radical practice) and centers on interpreting the Christian faith from the perspective of the poor and socially vulnerable and dispossessed. Liberation theologians interpret the salvation promised by the gospel as a full-orbed liberation of the whole human person, from economic, social, and political oppression as well as from the bondage of personal sin. At times, this emphasis on liberation has led advocates of liberation theology to endorse social revolution; although individual theologians or advocates of liberation theology may be pacifist, as a whole it is not generally a pacifist school of theology. It is generally characterized by a rejection of capitalist modes of social organization, however, given that these have so far only led to continued oppression and exploitation in Latin America (and in other contexts in which liberation theology has emerged, including parts of Asia and Africa). A central and distinctive contribution of liberation theology has been the experience of ecclesial base communities in Latin America.[26] Not all liberation theologians advocate Marxian social theory or socialism; however, if and where "business" is taken to mean free markets and capitalist modes of social organization, liberation theology certainly must count as a strand of Christian ethical reflection that firmly rejects the injustices of "business as usual."

Embracing Business and War

The polar opposite ethical response to a rejection of our themes would be that of embrace, based on the normative judgment that it is morally appropriate for Christians to conduct both business and war according to norms internal to these activities themselves. While Christian arguments for wholly embracing war and business can be found at different times and places within the tradition, this is an ideal-typical ethical stance that is not, in fact, very typical of most of the history of Christian ethics. As this section will explain, this fully welcoming orientation toward trade, finance, and profit has emerged only in recent centuries. Regarding warfare, instead of direct defenses or celebrations, it is more common to encounter arguments that seem to "embrace" war indirectly, as a result of the assumption that war is a tragic necessity and cannot be avoided.

---

26. This term has been used to refer to local Catholic communities committed to studying Scripture and worshiping together and engaging in radical action for social justice. Because they often fall outside the formal organizational structure of the Catholic Church and because of their radical political commitments, such communities have sometimes been seen as subversive to church authorities as well as political authorities.

The Unfortunate Necessity of War

Reformation theologian Martin Luther's "two kingdoms" theology provides the classic Christian formulation of this approach to violence. (Although it is interesting to note that when it came to business, Luther actually urged Christians to adhere to a rather rigorous ethic; his economic ethics had a bit more "bite" than his approach to war, as it were. The following section will mention this.) This "two kingdom" theology is founded on two key commitments: to the separation of sanctification and justification in the Christian life (which was, at the time, an innovation in the tradition) and to the idea that the Christian lives at once in two kingdoms: the inner (sanctified) Christian in the kingdom of Christ and the outer (still sinning) Christian in the kingdom of the world. These led Luther to proclaim that the Christian who receives salvation by grace through faith is *simul iustus et peccator*: at once both justified and still a sinner. Accordingly, the noticeable change salvation brings is largely an epistemological one; while Christians do and ought to gratefully respond to God's grace by acting in a more righteous manner, their good works are not tied in any way to—either by causing, or being required for—the gift of justification.

Once saved, according to Luther, the Christian is at once "a perfectly free lord of all, subject to none" and "a perfectly dutiful servant of all, subject to all."[27] This apparent contradiction refers to the fact that while the inner Christian is a free and justified citizen of the spiritual kingdom of Christ, the outer Christian is still a *peccator*, living in the temporal world among other sinners. The spiritual kingdom is run according to the rule-less love ethic given by Christ in the Sermon on the Mount (and instituted by God the Creator); the temporal kingdom is led by earthly rulers who have been given authority by God the Redeemer to keep order.[28] Christians owe obedience to these rulers for the sake of preserving this order; if Christians did not fulfill their duties by serving as hangmen and soldiers and governors, Luther feared, the world would be overrun with unruly lawbreakers. State-sponsored violence—whether putting down rebellions, defending against invasions, or punishing individual wrongdoers—is therefore a divinely ordained concession to sin and part of what later theologians termed the "orders of preservation," or a version of the order of creation that has been warped as a result of and remedy for sin. On this theological reading of the

---

27. Luther, *Freedom of a Christian*, 53.

28. With this teaching, Luther collapsed the earlier two-tiered systems of double morality, such as that seen earlier in the case of the medieval mendicant orders and evangelical poverty, into the internal life of the Christian.

issue, then, war may be unfortunate but is nonetheless often morally justified by its necessity.

Luther's approach to the problem of war, in particular, and to Christian ethics more generally, has its origins in the writing of Augustine of Hippo (and, before him, the Apostle Paul). Like Luther, Augustine's moral reasoning around issues of war and money focused on the importance of dispositions, rather than upon concrete moral rules or literal obedience to the teachings of Christ. His influential teachings on wealth, for example, center on his argument that Christians ought to relate to their wealth in an appropriate and ordinate manner and accordingly use, rather than enjoy, their possessions (because only God can truly be enjoyed). With regard to violence, Augustine wrote of Christ's injunction not to resist evil and to turn the other cheek: "What is here required is not a bodily action, but an inward disposition. The sacred seat of virtue is the heart."[29] Indeed, Augustine's deep awareness of evil in the world and the priority he placed upon assuring the stability of the social order led him to conclude that there were many cases in which war may be just and therefore morally permissible.[30] Moreover, he taught that Christians ought to obey their rulers and, when in a position to do so (as are judges, hangmen, and members of the military), participate in restraining evil within society as well—even up to and including, for example, the use of torture, something Augustine lamented but endorsed.[31] This was consistent with his reading of the gospel given his interpretation of Christian ethics as a matter of interior intentions, motives, and dispositions, rather than the details of the acts themselves. In short, for Augustine, like Luther, violence itself was not a good—but neither was it out of the question for the good Christian life.

Unqualified Embrace: The Crusades

The only argument in the Christian tradition that might be said to construe war as an actual *good* is found in the strange and terrifying history of the Crusades. These were a series of military campaigns fought by western Europeans in the Middle Ages to subject Jerusalem, Palestine, and other

---

29. Augustine, *Against Faustus* 22.76, in O'Donovan and O'Donovan, *From Irenaeus to Grotius*, 118.

30. Because Augustine was the first influential Christian thinker to use the term "just war" in his book *The City of God* he is often seen as the father of Christian just war theory which now identifies a central line of Christian reflection on war discussed in the following section.

31. Augustine, *City of God*, Bk. 19.

parts of the Middle East to Christian rule and were regularly conceived of as having divine sanction, even in their excesses—including the slaughter of innocent noncombatants and captured prisoners.[32] Moral arguments for the Crusades drew upon God's apparently frequent approval of war in the Hebrew Bible, as have other (although usually less enthusiastic) defenses of Christian involvement in war.[33]

This moral orientation has generally been absent in the tradition since the Enlightenment. To be sure, political leaders still do regularly employ religious rhetoric when justifying military action. However, they tend to frame this action primarily in terms of tragically necessary humanitarian intervention and only secondarily as enacting divine wrath or punishment. While it is up for debate whether this development represents an actual change in Christian moral attitudes toward war or simply a shift in publicly acceptable rhetoric, it is nonetheless true that Christian moral discourse on war has evolved; an orientation of "embrace" used to be a more visible minority moral logic than it is now.

Embracing Business

Usury

While the unrestrained embrace of business is as anomalous in the early history of Christian ethics as is the embrace of war, developments leading up to and during the early modern era enabled the emergence of a gradually more accepting attitude toward commerce and finance as means of accumulating wealth. Integral in paving the way for this was the gradual transformation of the classical prohibition of usury inherited from Christianity's roots in Judaism. Originally, this norm was understood as forbidding the receipt of any sum in excess of the principal when lending, regardless of the loan's purpose. However, as lending practices developed to meet new demands—to insure mercantile goods shipped over long distances, for example—so did the understanding of money and loans—from a "sterile" consumption good to a vendible good capable of reproducing itself and from primarily

---

32. On the Crusades as a central category of Christian thinking about war, see Bainton, *Christian Attitudes to War*; in Bainton's classic typology, Christian responses to war fall into three categories: pacifist, crusading, and just war.

33. Pope Gregory VII, who was instrumental in mobilizing support for the first crusade, for example, was apparently "especially fond" of Jeremiah 48:10: "Accursed is the one who keeps back the sword from bloodshed." Seibert, *Violence of Scripture*, 17.

an act of charity to those in distress to an ordinary business contract, respectively. The scope of usury was itself gradually refined in light of these practical and conceptual developments, and by the late sixteenth century, the usury prohibition only forbade interest rates deemed to be excessive and exploitative.[34]

The Protestant Work Ethic

In his *Protestant Ethic and the Spirit of Capitalism*, sociologist Max Weber noticed what he called an "elective affinity" between capitalism and the work ethic that emerged in Protestant, and particularly Calvinist, parts of Europe after the Reformation. As Weber identified it, this ethic centered on the Protestant affirmation that all believers (and not merely the priestly class) have a calling and the growing belief that the diligence with which one attends to one's vocation in the world may be a sign of election. As proof of one's diligence (or "worldly asceticism"), profit was thus viewed within the Protestant work ethic as a potential sign of grace, and God's favor. This more appreciative moral appraisal of profit and trade was a marked transition from the earlier Christian suspicion of these worldly pursuits.[35]

Prosperity Theology

In the late nineteenth and then twentieth centuries, a new Protestant theological perspective emerged that even more directly links financial gain with divine favor: prosperity theology, sometimes also called the prosperity gospel. This centers on the belief that God wills physical and financial well-being for Christians and will reward faithfulness with prosperity. However, whereas profit was to be acquired through industry and frugality in Weber's Protestant work ethic (and not to be spent on luxury or idleness, for that matter), prosperity theology does not focus on trade or business and emphasizes instead God's miraculous provision. Although this perspective has received much criticism from other denominations and within academic Christian ethics, a 2006 poll reported that 17 percent of American Christians identified with the movement, and prosperity congregations are growing rapidly in Africa, Asia, and Latin America.[36] While prosperity

---

34. For a concise overview of this transformation, see Jonsen and Toulmin, *Abuse of Casuistry*, 181–94.

35. Max Weber, *The Protestant Ethic and the Spirit of Capitalism*.

36. Van Biema and Chu, "Does God Want You to Be Rich?"; Jenkins, *Next Christendom*, 99. For more on the history and beliefs of this movement, see Bowler, *Blessed*.

theology does not directly address business per se, it arguably represents an emerging strand of Christian ethics that "embraces" many aspects of contemporary capitalism.

The Invisible Hand and the Hand of God

One further perspective within Christian thought deserves mention for its clear embrace of capitalism, and that is scholarship claiming that free markets operate according to providential design—or, more modestly, that markets are compatible with, if not the actual result of, a society based on Christian ideals.[37] This particular claim, it is worth noting, does not have an analogue in the ethics of war. In fact, it is premised upon the view that market activity is the exact *opposite* of war: it asserts that markets turn agonistic relations (of zero-sum competition) toward public peace and prosperity. The *doux commerce* thesis that market relations civilize and the "invisible hand" thesis that self-interest in business promotes communal prosperity has existed for some time but was not originally cast in a Christian register.[38] It entered Christian ethics through the work of thinkers like Michael Novak in the 1980s, in part as a defense of capitalism against emerging liberationist critiques that market society is inherently sinful and unjust.

Even these enthusiastic endorsements of markets, however, admitted two caveats: first, that markets are most moral when supported by a moral culture; and second, that individual Christians must always engage in honest behavior within those markets—by telling the truth, being faithful to contracts, and so forth.[39] That is, while this view suggests that the demands of Christian life are fully consonant with following profit-maximizing economic rationality in business, even this most appreciative of Christian embraces of business has never suggested that "anything goes."

---

37. For example, Max Stackhouse sees capitalism as grounded in Protestant covenant theology, and Michael Novak argues it is compatible with Catholic social teaching. See Novak, *The Spirit of Democratic Capitalism*; and, for Novak's extension of this to the corporation, see Novak and Cooper, *The Corporation*.

38. For a history of the *doux commerce* thesis, see Hirschman, *The Passions and the Interests*.

39. See Stackhouse, "Business, Economics and Christian Ethics," and Stackhouse et al., *On Moral Business*.

Judicious Restraint and Social Reflection

In the centuries since the earliest Christian communities, the vast majority of Christian thought has fallen somewhere in between the two ideal-typical approaches just introduced. Most Christian reflection characterizes both business and war as morally ambivalent means through which it is appropriate to pursue good ends (albeit proximate and not ultimate ones) but which may also present grave temptations to sin. The one is always more perilous than the other, to be sure—Christian thought generally presumes that violence is necessarily a concession to sin, whereas business is a natural response to the need to provision human life using the scarce resources of creation.

In both arenas, however, Christian moral reflection has urged placing limits on selfish and wasteful excesses and aligning all action with appropriate ends, such as the common good, peace, and the protection of the vulnerable. Often this reflection focuses on exhorting the individual or community to moral care in identifying and pursuing appropriate ends. At other times, however, Christian moral discourse assumes that the pursuit of good ends requires a certain amount of tragedy, in either markets or political life. This grammar of "tragedy" is applied most often to warfare, based on a fundamental presumption against killing.

Just War Ethics

The previous section mentioned Augustine's introduction of the just war doctrine into Christian ethics. With regard to the rough categories of this chapter, it is arguably a matter of perspective whether to place this doctrine here or in the "embrace" category. This chapter addresses just war here in light of the fact that the doctrine has been interpreted more restrictively in recent years (particularly as it has been used in Catholic social thought), and many argue that it now rests on a fundamental presumption against the use of force.

This was not necessarily the case at earlier points in this tradition. On Augustine's view, for example, the "real evils in war" are all dispositional in nature, such as the "love of violence" and "revengeful cruelty."[40] Wars may thus be justified when "conducted with the intention of peace, even when they are conducted by those who are concerned to exercise their martial

---

40. Augustine, *Against Faustus* 22.74, in O'Donovan and O'Donovan, *From Irenaeus to Grotius*, 117.

prowess in command and battle."⁴¹ Augustine's emphasis was on the justice of the warrior or political leader's intentions—and, moreover, on the overriding moral importance of maintaining social order—rather than upon the evil of violence itself, and he demonstrates what can be called a "pragmatic" or "realist" conception of peace.⁴² Thomas Aquinas' treatment of just war was likewise framed by a concern for the sovereign's duty to defend the common good. His classic and influential articulation of the doctrine was also fairly minimal and contained only three criteria, all pertaining to *jus ad bellum*: that a war be fought for a just cause, undertaken by a legitimate authority, and with a right intent.⁴³

In the last decades of the twentieth century, however, Catholic teaching on war has been reframed within a commitment to peace, understood theologically as integral to the church's mission to follow Christ.⁴⁴ Papal encyclicals have identified war as an aspect of the "culture of death" into which the gospel must be spoken,⁴⁵ and along with the US bishops show greater appreciation for conscientious objection and pacifism as a "witness of evangelical charity" that offers a necessary complement to just war thinking.⁴⁶

This shift in tone and emphasis has been accompanied by the development of additional and more restrictive criteria for judging the permissibility of conflicts. In their pastoral letter *The Challenge of Peace*, the US Conference of Catholic Bishops, for example, list seven standards for adjudicating *jus ad bellum* (justice before war) and three for *jus in bello* (justice in war), including proportionality and discrimination between combatants and noncombatants. As they explain, the point of elaborating these limits is not so much to *justify* certain wars as to determine which wars and forms of conduct in war are *un*justified. Their use of the concept of "comparative evil" illustrates this clearly:

> In essence: which side is sufficiently "right" in a dispute, and are the values at stake critical enough to override the presumption against war? The question in its most basic form is this: do the rights and values involved justify killing? For whatever the means used, war, by definition, involves violence, destruction, suffering, and death. The category of comparative justice is

---

41. Augustine, *City of God* 19.12.
42. Norris, "'Never Again War,'" 112.
43. Aquinas, *Summa Theologica*, II.II 40.1.
44. For more on this development, see Norris "'Never Again War.'"
45. See Paul VI, *Humanae Vitae*, and John Paul II, *Evangelium Vitae*.
46. USCCB, *Challenge of Peace*, 121.

> designed to emphasize the presumption against war which stands at the beginning of just war teaching. In a world of sovereign states recognizing neither a common moral authority nor a central political authority, comparative justice stresses that no state should act on the basis that it has "absolute justice" on its side. Every party to a conflict should acknowledge the limits of its "just cause" and the consequent requirement to use only limited means in pursuit of its objectives. Far from legitimizing a crusade mentality, comparative justice is designed to relativize absolute claims and to restrain the use of force even in a "justified" conflict.[47]

In their pastoral letter, the bishops thus effectively introduced into Catholic moral discourse on war what ethicist James Childress had called a *prima facie* principle against killing. This represents a marked departure from the "presumption for justice" foundational to earlier just war theory, which viewed war itself as more morally neutral.[48]

This shift in theological framework has been prompted in no small part by changes in the nature of warfare itself, including the advent of nuclear weapons, the emergence of terrorism, and debate over "humanitarian intervention." Many contemporary situations do not neatly fit within the criteria for the justified use of force. Further, technological advancements have rendered the possibility of limited wars simply less likely—as the *Compendium of Social Doctrine* observes, "It is hardly possible to imagine that in an atomic era, war could be used as an instrument of justice. . . . The terrifying power of the means of destruction . . . make it very difficult or practically impossible to limit the consequences of a conflict."[49] The contemporary Catholic movement toward a more pacifist kind of just war thinking is, as a result, at once both theological and pragmatic, and analogous to the development of Catholic opposition to the use of the death penalty in light of the "increased effectiveness of modern penal systems."[50]

Business Ethics

Whereas much just war thinking now presumes that violence, which is the essence of war, is a *prima facie* evil, the mainlines of modern Christian

---

47. USCCB, *Challenge of Peace*, 92–93.
48. Griffiths and Weigel, "Just War," 33–36.
49. Pontifical Council for Justice and Peace, *Social Doctrine of the Church*, paras. 497–98.
50. Griffiths and Weigel, "Just War," 32.

reflection on business harbor no equivalent concern about business, whether its essence is described as buying, selling, lending, or even profiting. This was not always the case; in premodern times Christianity was characterized by a general distaste for the social role played by merchants and a deep and particular suspicion of the idea of finance, profit, and effortless gain. This moral orientation made especial sense in the context of a subsistence and agrarian world characterized by a "limited good" worldview in which the amount of wealth in the world was fixed and zero-sum.[51] However, as a generally feudal social order developed into an increasingly capitalist one—and as it became clear that it was possible to gain wealth without having taken it from one's neighbor—so too did the church's stance evolve so as to become more appreciative of markets.

As noted above, a few voices within the tradition today retain this suspicion of markets and profit and reject modern business in favor of, for example, Christian socialism. For the most part, however, Christian ethics today affirms business as "a calling to serve the common good through transformational service."[52] In this view, virtuous commercial activity achieves real social goods and is not merely an unfortunate necessity. This fact indicates the limits of any attempt to draw a line between ethics of "embrace" and those of "cautious restraint" with regard to business. It also points toward significant differences between contemporary Christian treatments of business and war.

As long as any analogy is held lightly, however, it may be possible to view the genre of Christian business ethics as roughly parallel to just war thinking, given that both aim to provide practical guidance on how to pursue legitimate goods while avoiding illicit behavior. And as with just war thought, business ethics has its roots in Scripture and early Christian practice and teaching but was not developed into anything resembling its current case-oriented genre until the medieval period when scholastics began to evaluate specific practices of lending, insuring, pricing, and so forth.[53]

In both its premodern and modern forms, Christian analysis of business practices has had to find a way to hold the aim of business—to provide for oneself through profit—in constructive tension with Christ's

---

51. For more on the "limited good" view of wealth, see Malina, *The New Testament World*.

52. See Wong and Rae, *Business for the Common Good*, and the Pontifical Council for Justice and Peace, *Vocation of the Business Leader*.

53. In this regard, it could be argued that Christian business ethics is a genre of surprising antiquity, especially when considered alongside secular philosophical business ethics, which dates to only the middle of the twentieth century.

commands to self-sacrifice. The difficulty of this is visible, for example, in Martin Luther's memorable advice to Christian merchants, in which he was uncharacteristically specific with his moral guidance (although, it could be argued, his direction of this ethic solely to the inner Christian somewhat blunts its rigor). According to Luther, only four modes of exchange are available to the Christian merchant: allowing others to steal one's property, freely giving one's property to those who need it, lending one's property to those who ask but forgoing assurance of repayment, and buying and selling but without recourse to credit or insurance, on the grounds that these indicated a failure to rely upon God.[54] Moreover, Luther harshly condemned merchants of his day who held that "I may sell my goods as dear as I can," claiming that "this maxim flies squarely in the face of not only Christian love but natural law."[55]

Since Luther's time, this genre of reflection has come to accept the moral legitimacy of both insurance and credit and has expanded to address new issues and situations arising in global capitalism. Modern business ethics does retain, however, one aspect of Luther's cautious restraint: the conviction that the Christian must discern the appropriate level of gain in each market interaction and that this may require refraining from some practices that are legal within wider society, such as payday lending.[56] Developing this insight to speak to the complexities of financial markets, recently theologians and ecclesial leaders have also urged Christians to abstain from investing and holding stock in companies that rely upon child labor, slavery, and prostitution, and other practices that harm the common good, such as the arms trade and fossil fuel production.

Reflection on the Whole: Social Ethics

Thus far, this section has primarily discussed practical ethics; both just war and business ethics aim at providing individual agents guidelines for right action. A slightly different type of Christian ethical reflection takes society as a whole as its subject and considers the morality of its institutions and culture and how these encourage certain kinds of attitudes and behaviors. This strand of Christian ethics emerged in the late nineteenth century in response to the new issues presented by industrial society, many of which centered precisely on questions about economics and war.

54. Luther, *Trade and Usury*, 255–60.
55. Luther, *Trade and Usury*, 247.
56. See Presbyterian Church (USA), *A Reformed Understanding of Usury*.

In 1891, Pope Leo XIII issued *Rerum Novarum* and initiated what is now referred to as Catholic social teaching, the body of Catholic moral theology that addresses social justice. Following the teachings of Thomas Aquinas, *Rerum Novarum* affirmed social institutions that protect private property but harshly condemned the way that unregulated capitalism subordinates the common good and the dignity of the worker to those rights (while also condemning Marxism). Subsequent encyclicals and pastoral letters built upon this foundation to develop a robust body of teaching that uses the themes of solidarity, subsidiarity, human dignity, and a preferential option for the poor to analyze contemporary political and economic concerns, ranging from healthcare legislation to care of the natural environment. Although liberationist thought was mentioned earlier under the rubric of "rejection," it is in many ways deeply consistent and in sustained conversation with this tradition.

A parallel body of thought, Protestant social ethics, likewise had its origin in the late nineteenth century with the discovery of "society" itself and the need to address new problems generated by urbanization, industrialization, and globalization. Social gospelers such as Walter Rauschenbusch identified correspondences between the patterns of modern life and the social vision of gospel and reflected theologically on how churches ought to address gaps between the two.[57] Contemporary inheritors of this tradition have especially focused on the importance of grounding social reflection within a particular context and increasingly push Christian ethical discourse to consider questions of race, gender, class, and power.

Finally, a third strand of social reflection is described by the term "public theology," which was originally associated with the "Christian realism" of the twentieth-century Protestant theologian Reinhold Niebuhr but has since been used to describe a range of thinkers from Catholic theologians[58] to Augustinian liberals who seek a via media between the "neo-sectarian" social ethic of Stanley Hauerwas and the realism of Niebuhr.[59] Such thinkers propose a moral and theological imagination that combines both appreciation of and criticism for the economic and political (including and especially martial) practices of modern nation-states. Although public theologians generally do not primarily focus on issues of war and business, their attempts to creatively refashion theological conversations in light of

---

57. For more on this history, see Dorrien, *Social Ethics*, particularly 60–125.

58. See Tracy, *The Analogical Imagination*.

59. See Bretherton, *Christianity and Contemporary Politics*; Gregory, *Politics and the Order of Love*; and Mathewes, *A Theology of Public Life*.

pressing issues in contemporary public life offer resources for the task of Christian ethics to continually discern the nature of the good life, right moral action, and the shape of God's call to the churches in each new historical era.

Conclusion: New Problems in the Business of War and the Need for Creative Adaption in Christian Social and Practical Ethics

Political, technological, and economic developments in the past half-century have changed the nature of the problems that business and war present to Christian ethics. On the "war" side of this equation, we now face the possibility of nuclear warfare and must reckon with an ongoing and widespread arms trade, the regular recurrence of ethnically motivated and genocidal actions, and the emergence and increasing incidence of terrorist activity. On the "business" side, recent decades have seen the rapid financialization and globalization of capitalism and, at times and in places, "the economic" surpassing "the political" as a site and mode of global governance for a host of reasons ranging from the terms of bilateral and regional trade treaties to the sheer size of the finance industry and of multinational corporations. We also face a world of increasing income and wealth inequality.

The new scope and character of issues arising in these conditions threaten to overwhelm and confound existing frameworks of moral description and analysis in Christian thought. As noted, the classical criteria of just war, for example, are less politically illuminating in an age of nuclear weapons, terrorism by nonstate parties, and the constant surveillance enabled by Big Data. Likewise, received concepts of moral responsibility and agency seem inadequate to make sense of our relations to distant harmful economic outcomes, given the complex, decentered, interdependent, and highly dynamic nature of global markets today. This is especially true with regard to the increasing interconnection of these issues.

These are new problems raised in what this collection is calling "the business of war"—of conflict and violence as a profitable business, of war undertaken in a businesslike manner, and, to a certain extent, of business itself undertaken in a mercenary manner. What is Christian ethics to make of this new business of war? This is the question asked in this essay collection, and it is a timely one. What ought we to make of the fact that the success of our economy today (which determines so many aspects of our lives, including our living standards) is in no small part due to the large portion of the economy devoted to violence, both domestic and international? What should the Christian response to this be—in churches, in schools, and in our roles as market agents, investors, consumers, citizens, and neighbors to our fellow humans, both near and far?

Both business and war today call for new and creative thinking in Christian ethics around classical concepts of responsibility, complicity, and agency. Christian ethics must adapt (again) to our historically new context—both to provide practical guidance on these problems and more generally to retain the vibrancy and comprehensibility of its moral tradition. With this urgent need in mind, it strikes this author that although there is much to learn from all three general approaches sketched in this chapter, our moral imaginations are best served by sitting in the creative tension between the first (alternative polis) and third (cautious restraint and reflective social analysis) approaches. Christians in America simply do not have the option to totally withdraw from the business of global capitalist markets or from involvement in a global political order engaged in extensive surveillance and perpetual war. What is especially crucial now is to find a way to let classical Christian commitments fund a creative social imagination that resists being ideologically captured by the implicit terms of our current political, social, and economic moment.

Part Two

THE BUSINESS OF WAR IN HISTORY

3

Globalization and Warmaking

People, Planet, and Peace in Peril

PAMELA K. BRUBAKER

Introduction

Although globalization and warmaking may seem to be distinct and unrelated processes, the business of war is integral to economic globalization. "Globalization is not just a trend, not just a phenomenon, not just an economic fad," *New York Times* foreign affairs columnist Thomas Friedman proclaimed in the spring of 1999. "It is the international system that has replaced the cold-war system."[1] Although free-market capitalism is the driving idea behind globalization, "the hidden hand of the market will never work without a hidden fist." And the United States military is "the hidden fist that keeps the world safe" for "*the spread of free-market capitalism to virtually every country in the world*."[2] Friedman contends that the US is a "benign superpower" and that this system will bring peace and prosperity.

---

1. Friedman, "Manifesto for the Fast World."

2. Friedman, "Manifesto for the Fast Word"; emphasis added. Friedman cites foreign policy historian Robert Kagan, who said that "good ideas and technologies need a strong power that promotes those ideas by example and protects those ideas by winning on the battlefield."

In this essay, I contend that this system is militarized globalization—and militarized globalization (with neither the hand nor the fist so hidden) has put people, the planet, and peace in peril.³

One of the most recent developments in the process of militarized globalization is the spread of both US military and economic tentacles across Asia. In "Sustaining US Global Leadership: Priorities for 21st Century Defense (2012)," the US Department of Defense laid out the rationale for what has been called its pivot to Asia. It clearly illustrates the connection between globalization and militarism.

> US economic and security interests are inextricably linked to developments in the arc extending from the Western Pacific and East Asia into the Indian Ocean region and South Asia, creating a mix of evolving challenges and opportunities. Accordingly, while the US military will continue to contribute to security globally, *we will of necessity rebalance toward the Asia-Pacific region*. . . . The maintenance of peace, stability, the free flow of commerce, and of US influence in this dynamic region will depend in part on an underlying balance of military capability and presence.⁴

In his introduction to this document, President Obama declared that meeting the challenges we face "cannot be the work of the military alone." But his conclusion stressed its importance: "There should be no doubt . . . we will keep our Armed Forces the best-trained, best-led, best-equipped fighting force in history. And in a changing world that demands our leadership, the United States of America will remain the greatest force

---

3. *The New Oxford Dictionary of English* defines militarism as "the belief or desire of a government or people that a country should maintain a strong military capability and be prepared to use it aggressively to defend or promote national interests." Globalization is "the process by which businesses or other organizations develop international influence or start operating on an international scale." I first heard the term "militarized globalization" from Peace for Life: A Peoples' Forum for Global Justice and Peace. I have participated in various People for Life meetings and forums since 2005 (https://peaceforlife.wordpress.com/). Although I do not cite it in this chapter, the work of Cynthia Enloe has also been helpful in thinking about this reality.

4. United States Department of Defense, "Sustaining Global Leadership," 2; emphasis in the original. This document reflects the move to "full-spectrum dominance"—land, sea, air, space, and information—introduced in the Joint Chiefs of Staff publications *Joint Vision 2010* (1996) and *Joint Vision 2020* (2000). Alfred McCoy points out that freedom of the seas for trans-Pacific commerce became a "critical strategic priority" because of "the economic significance of East and Southeast Asia's booming manufactures for the country's [US] new economy of information and consumer goods." McCoy, *Shadows of the American Century*, 216.

for freedom and security that the world has ever known."[5] Both President Obama's introduction and the document itself convey militarism.

The approximately eight hundred US bases in foreign countries, where hundreds of thousands of US troops are stationed, are crucial to this "fighting force." In *Base Nation*, David Vine notes that "this massive global deployment of military force was unknown in U.S. history before World War II." These overseas bases, he claims, are "in even more complicated ways than major weapons systems . . . the true incarnation of the military-industrial complex."[6]

Part One: The Military-Industrial Complex and Militarized Globalization

The term *military-industrial complex* was first used by President Dwight Eisenhower in his 1961 Farewell Address. He noted that although our military establishment is a crucial element in keeping peace, its combination with "a large arms industry" is new. Furthermore, its overall influence is "economic, political, even spiritual." It led to annual spending on military security "that was more than the net income of all US corporations." He warned that "we must guard against the acquisition of unwarranted influence" in the councils of government by what he called "the military-industrial complex."[7]

Its origins were in World War II (1939–45). In *The American Way of War*, filmmaker Eugene Jarecki discusses a series of WWII films entitled *Why We Fight*. These brought "popular support not only for the war effort but for a new and expanded way of seeing America on the world stage." The war "also represented a shift in America's political economy," Jarecki contends, "producing unprecedented closeness between the federal government and corporate America."[8]

---

5. President Barack Obama, in United States Department of Defense, "Sustaining Global Leadership," n.p.

6. Vine, *Base Nation*, 4–5, 331. Nami Kim and Wonhee Anne Joh draw on the work of sociologist Seungsook Moon to point out that "US military bases that have been built in over 150 countries do 'territorialize US empire.'" Kim and Joh, introduction to *Critical Theology*, xi. I contend that US militarism is a form of imperialism.

7. Eisenhower, "Farewell Address (1961)."

8. Jarecki, *American Way of War*, 57–58. Jarecki also made a film called *Why We Fight*, which won the Grand Jury Prize for Documentary at the 2005 Sundance Film Festival and a 2006 Peabody Award. It is a powerful, engaging, and moving examination of the US way of war, drawing on Eisenhower's warning about the military-industrial complex and interviews with a wide range of people with different perspectives.

World War II

World War II started when Germany invaded Poland on September 1, 1939. In response, France and Great Britain declared war on Germany. On September 2, 1940, President Roosevelt authorized an agreement with Britain which provided fifty World War I-era destroyers to Britain in exchange for US control over a group of air and naval bases in Britain's Caribbean colonies.[9] On December 29, 1940, Roosevelt charged in a speech broadcast throughout the nation that "*we must be the great arsenal of democracy*." This great arsenal would be built in America "by workers and managers and engineers with the aid of machines which in turn have to be built by hundreds of thousands of workers."[10]

The US entered the war only after the Japanese attack on Pearl Harbor, December 7, 1941. By the end of the war, the US had produced almost two-thirds of all the military equipment for the Allied military. This came to 297,000 aircraft, 193,000 artillery pieces, 86,000 tanks, and two million army trucks. US industrial production, already the global leader at the start of the war, doubled in size during the war.[11]

---

9. Vine, *Base Nation*, 17–18. The US acquired 99-year leases and near sovereign powers over these bases. Vine calls this the birth of the base nation as we know it. He reports that "after the war started, [Roosevelt] pushed his military leaders to develop plans for a postwar network of military bases around the globe that could ensure U.S. dominance." He also wanted to secure US economic dominance in the airline industry and in accessing natural resources, international markets, and investment opportunities around the world. "Commercial and military planning often went hand in hand" (*Base Nation*, 26–27). In 1939, Roosevelt began warning that "no attack is so unlikely or impossible that it may be ignored." In a world of "permanent danger," the military needed to be a "permanently mobilized force" ready to confront threats wherever they might appear. "If the US is to have any defense," he declared, "it must have total defense" (*Base Nation*, 31).

10. Roosevelt, "The Great Arsenal of Democracy." Roosevelt began by saying, "My friends: This is not a fireside chat on war. It is a talk on national security; because the nub of the whole purpose of your President is to keep you now, and your children later, and your grandchildren much later, out of a last-ditch war for the preservation of American independence, and all of the things that American independence means to you and to me and to ours."

11. From the website associated with the 2007 PBS series *The War*, produced by Ken Burns and Lynn Novick (http://www.pbs.org/thewar/at_home_war_production.htm). Economist Ismael Hossein-zadeh contends that there are two important differences between the market-driven behavior of military and nonmilitary industries in the US. First, in contrast to most civilian industries, the profits of military contractors are usually guaranteed. "These profits also tend (on average) to be higher than those of their civilian counterparts—especially during times of war and international conflicts." The second difference is that "the quality of arms manufacturers' products is measured in terms of death and destruction." This serves as an incentive for contractors to develop

On May 12, 1942, President Roosevelt signed an order creating a secret project to develop a nuclear weapon. Research had already begun in 1939 at Columbia University in Manhattan. The Manhattan Project grew to employ more than 130,000 people at over thirty sites in the US, Canada, and the United Kingdom. It cost nearly two billion US dollars. Less than 10 percent of the cost was for development and production of the nuclear weapons. The rest went to build factories and to produce the fissile material.[12] Although the impact of this project was immense, the monetary cost of the Manhattan Project was a pittance of the total cost of US military operations during 1941–45: 296 billion dollars, which was 37 percent of GDP.[13]

"Without the development of nuclear weapons," asserts William Hartung, "the military-industrial complex would never exist in the form it exists today." The Manhattan Project "was one of the largest government-funded research and manufacturing projects in history." It was the first building block of a "permanent arms establishment": "Today's nuclear warhead complex is built largely around facilities and locations that date back to that time."[14]

Postwar Period

During World War II, the United States developed immense economic, financial, and military power. It was the only one of the Allies whose country and economy were not ravaged by the war, although there was a significant loss of life by US armed forces.[15] Its major military buildup had stimulated

---

more efficient instruments of death and destruction. Hossein-zadeh, *Political Economy of U.S. Militarism*, 201–2. During World War I, military contractors were guaranteed cost plus 13.4 percent; this amount was cut some during World War II to 9 to 10 percent. Hartung, *Prophets of War*, 49.

12. Fissile material is material capable of sustaining a nuclear fission chain reaction (CTBTO, "Manhattan Project"). Late in 1939, President Roosevelt had received a letter signed by Albert Einstein suggesting that uranium could undergo nuclear fission, resulting in a great burst of energy. It was probable that this kind of reaction could be developed to construct extremely powerful bombs. The letter also said that it was likely that Germany would pursue this research.

13. All estimates are of the costs of military operations only and do not reflect costs of veterans' benefits, interest on war-related debt, or assistance to allies (Daggett, "Costs of Major US Wars"). This section focused on the relation between military and economic interests. A later section looks at human and environmental cost of these policies, especially nuclear weapons.

14. Hartung, "Nuclear Politics," 110. For example, Lockheed Martin had a contract with the Department of Energy worth "2 billion per year to run the Sandia National Laboratories, one of three US nuclear labs." Hartung, *Prophets of War*, 199.

15. World War II was the deadliest military conflict in history in absolute terms of

the economy, ending the Great Depression. Its nuclear weapons, used to project US force against the Soviet Union, added to its military strength. The US aimed to maintain its global military dominance, power and wealth during the postwar era.

Global Governance

The project of global governance began before the end of the war. US Secretary of the Treasury Henry Morgenthau Jr., president of the 1944 United Nations Monetary and Financial Conference, declared that its aim was "the creation of a dynamic world economy in which the peoples of every nation will be able to realize their potentialities in peace and enjoy increasingly the fruits of material progress."[16] The US led in the creation of the World Bank and the International Monetary Fund, enhancing its role by backing a fixed exchange rate of the dollar against gold, rather than a global currency outside of the control of any one nation.[17] It wanted "institutions designed to ensure an open, capitalist international economy."[18]

The US also played a crucial role in establishing the United Nations. The Preamble to the United Nations Charter, its founding document, proclaimed that "the peoples of the United Nations determined to save succeeding generations from the scourge of war . . . to reaffirm faith in fundamental human rights, in the dignity and worth of the human person, in the equal rights of men and women and of nations large and small . . . and to promote social progress and better standards of life in larger freedom." It came into force on October 24, 1945, after ratification by the five permanent

---

total casualties. More than 60 million people were killed, which was about 3 percent of the 1940 world population (est. 2.3 billion). More than 400,000 US soldiers were killed and nearly 700,000 wounded. The Soviet Union had the most casualties. See "World War II Casualties," available at https://everipedia.org/wiki/World_War_II_casualties.

16. Cited in Korten, "Sustainability and Global Economy," 40.

17. For the Bretton Woods negotiations, see Harvey, *Enigma of Capital*, 32. The US Congress scuttled the International Trade Organization proposed at Bretton Woods. It was opposed by US businesses as too friendly to labor and developing countries. Instead, the General Agreement on Tariffs and Trade (GATT) was negotiated during the United Nations Conference on Trade and Employment, signed in 1947 and took effect in 1948. The original GATT text (GATT 1947) is still in effect under the WTO framework, subject to the modifications of GATT 1994. I present an in-depth discussion and analysis of the Bretton Woods institutions in my chapter in *Globalization and Economic Justice* (Brubaker, "Neoliberalism and Economic Development").

18. US Department of State, "Post-War Economy."

members of the Security Council (China, France, Great Britain, the Soviet Union, and the United States) and the majority of other signatories.[19]

On June 15, 1946, the United States presented the Baruch Plan for the international control of atomic weapons to the United Nations. The proposal provided "for international control and inspection of nuclear production facilities, but clearly announced that the United States would maintain its nuclear weapons monopoly until every aspect of the proposal was in effect and working." Not surprisingly, the Soviet Union rejected the plan. Then the US rejected the Soviet counterproposal "for a ban on all nuclear weapons." This resulted "in a dangerous nuclear arms race between the United States and the Soviet Union."[20]

The Universal Declaration of Human Rights was adopted on December 10, 1948. It is considered the foundation of international human rights law and has inspired a body of legally binding international human rights treaties. That same year, the Policy Planning Staff of the US State Department was thinking about what its work should be. It advised that "we have about fifty percent of the world's wealth but only 6.3 percent of its population." In this situation, it charged, "our real task in the coming period is . . . to maintain this position of disparity." To do this, "we will have to dispense with all sentimentality . . . we should cease thinking about human rights, the raising of living standards, and democratization."[21] These are the core principles articulated in the Preamble to the UN Charter (1945), which the US was the first to ratify.

An examination of US foreign policy suggests that maintaining a disproportionate share of global wealth continues to be an important objective, regardless of these principles. This, I suspect, is often the aim behind more general talk about "national interest" or "the American way of life." Historian Melvyn P. Leffler claims that policymakers shifted

19. United Nations, "Charter of the United Nations."

20. History.com Editors, "Baruch Plan." This article also discusses the division within the Truman administration. Some of his advisors, including the secretaries of war and commerce, thought that the US should share their atomic secrets with the Soviet Union. "Otherwise, the continuing US monopoly would only result in growing Russian suspicions and an eventual arms race." Others, including a prominent State Department official, didn't trust the Soviets and thought the United States would be foolish to relinquish its atomic "ace in the hole." Noam Chomsky argues that the development of Intercontinental Ballistic Missiles (ICBMS) armed with nuclear warheads might have been prevented, citing recent scholarship on Stalin's 1952 offer "to allow Germany to be unified with free elections on condition that it not join a hostile military alliance." Chomsky, "National Politics," 92.

21. US Department of State Policy Planning Staff, "Review of Current Trends," 524. Ideals such as human rights, democracy, development—ideals held by many Americans—are dismissed as "sentimental" in this document.

their focus from balancing economic imperatives at home and abroad to a preoccupation "with safeguarding America's core values of democratic capitalism."[22] A review of the foreign policy of both Republican and Democratic administrations in the postwar period suggests that democracy and human rights are often sacrificed in the defense of capitalism.

The Cold War

On March 12, 1947, President Truman addressed a joint session of Congress, saying that a very grave situation had arisen involving "the foreign policy and the national security of the country." He warned that the existence of the Greek state and the security of Turkey were at risk and requested 400 million dollars in aid, acknowledging that this entailed risks. He asserted, "I believe that it must be the policy of the United States to support free peoples who are resisting attempted subjugation by armed minorities or by outside pressures." "The Truman Doctrine," as this was called, "became the basis for US foreign policy for several decades."[23]

Truman had been told by a Republican Senator that if he wanted support for aid like this, he would have to "scare the hell out of the American people." Jarecki thinks that the rising fear of war was "both real and manufactured." On the one hand, the Cold War was fueled at times "by exaggerated estimates of Soviet strength." On the other hand, "Stalin's progress across Europe between 1945 and 1946 . . . was an undeniable cause for concern." Jarecki contends that the Truman Doctrine "committed America to a hegemonic global posture" and "effectively called for permanent military preparedness."[24]

Military spending had fallen dramatically after World War II. This concerned not only government officials but also private companies, especially aircraft companies. Lockheed president Robert Gross began lobbying for peacetime support of the aircraft industry by the government through subsidies soon after the war ended. On July 18, 1947, President Truman set up the Air Policy Commission, which interviewed 150 witnesses. "None came from outside the circle of business, military, and government officials who had a direct stake in the expansion of air power."

22. Leffler, *Safeguarding Democratic Capitalism*. From an announcement of an event at the Woodrow Wilson Center, featuring Dr. Leffler and his book.

23. Jarecki, *American Way of War*, 74–77.

24. Jarecki, *American Way of War*, 74, 77, 31. The US State Department says that the Truman Doctrine "established that the United States would provide political, military and economic assistance to all democratic nations under threat from external or internal authoritarian forces." Office of the Historian, "NSC-68, 1951."

The commission stated that "this country . . . must be ready not for World War II but for a possible World War III." It recommended a major increase for Navy and Air Force combat planes and called for an overall 80 percent increase in military spending.²⁵

The Korean War

There was no dramatic increase in defense budgets until the Korean War, however. The US intervened soon after the war broke out in June 1950, when North Korean troops invaded South Korea.²⁶ Gross drafted an address stating that "for the first time in recorded history, one nation has assumed global responsibility." He posed this question: "Are we committed to deal with all future armed aggressions against the peace of the world?" If so, the US would need the means to provide transport of "huge quantities of men, food, ammunition, guns, tanks, gasoline, and thousands of other articles of war to a number of widely separated places on the face of the earth." He contended that it should be "transport from the air." Aircraft purchases by the military tripled by 1952 from their post-WWII low. Industry employment went from 192,000 in 1947 to 600,000.²⁷

---

25 Hartung, *Prophets of War*, 52–59. This book is a landmark investigation of the role of Lockheed Martin in the making of the military-industrial complex up to 2012. Hartung is quoting Wayne Biddle in the quotation about the people who were interviewed by the Air Policy Commission. David Harvey's comment on the role of the military-industrial complex in the development of capital is relevant: "The foundational interests of the state in, for example, the case of national security can be subverted by capital and turned into a permanent feeding trough for capitalist ambitions." Harvey, *Seventeen Contradictions*, 157.

26. "In April 1950, a National Security Council report known as NSC-68 had recommended that the United States use military force to 'contain' communist expansionism anywhere it seemed to be occurring, 'regardless of the intrinsic strategic or economic value of the lands in question'" (History.com editors, "Korean War"). According to the State Department, "National Security Council Paper NSC-68 (entitled 'United States Objectives and Programs for National Security') was a Top-Secret report completed by the US Department of State's Policy Planning Staff on April 7, 1950. *The 58-page memorandum is among the most influential documents composed by the US Government during the Cold War and was not declassified until 1975*. Its authors argued that one of the most pressing threats confronting the United States was the 'hostile design' of the Soviet Union. The authors concluded that the Soviet threat would soon be greatly augmented by the addition of more weapons, including nuclear weapons, to the Soviet arsenal. They argued that the best course of action was to respond in kind with a massive build-up of the US military and its weaponry." Office of the Historian, "NSC-68, 1950," emphasis added.

27. Cited in Hartung, *Prophets of War*, 59–60. The endnote states that the location and audience of the address were not specified. Lockheed was at the forefront of

Negotiations for an armistice in the Korean War started in April 1951. Eventually a ceasefire was agreed upon, and negotiations were spurred by the death of Joseph Stalin in March 1953. An armistice was signed on July 27, 1953. The war cost the US thirty billion dollars (341 billion in 2011 dollars), 4.2 percent of US GDP overall, 13.2 percent in the peak year of the war.[28] Historian Bruce Cumings writes that "North Koreans emerged from this war into a living nightmare, after three years of 'rain and ruin' by the US air force."[29]

"Few Americans realize that at the root of the present US-North Korea crisis is the unresolved Korean War," writes Christine Hong, "a remarkably dirty war that set the paradigm for subsequent US wars of intervention." As Hartung and Jarecki suggest, she too charges that Korea played a key role "in consolidating US war power by justifying the creation of a formidable crisis-generating, self-perpetuating, institutional architecture—the national security state, the military industrial complex, and the perpetual war economy."[30]

---

industry diversification. It received a naval contract for the Polaris submarine-launched ballistic missile, which put the company at the center of nuclear buildup in the 1950s, when Eisenhower threatened "massive retaliation" with nuclear weapons for any attack on the US. Lockheed also made spy planes for the CIA. Hartung, *Prophets of War*, 60. (The Korean War was significant in the fact that it was the first war in which the newly independent United States Air Force was involved and US jet aircraft entered into battle.)

28. All estimates are of the costs of military operations only and do not reflect costs of veterans' benefits, interest on war-related debt, or assistance to allies. See Daggett, "Costs of Major US Wars."

29. Cumings, "Americans Once Carpet-Bombed North Korea." Cumings teaches at the University of Chicago and is the author of *The Korean War: A History*. The US dropped a total of 635,000 tons of bombs, including 32,557 tons of napalm, on Korea, more than during the whole Pacific campaign of World War II. Almost every substantial building in North Korea was destroyed as a result. More than four million people died; more than half were civilians. (About three-quarters of the estimated two million Korean civilians killed came from the North.) This rate was higher than either World War II or Vietnam (Walkom, "North Korea's Unending War"). The US had also considered the use of nuclear weapons during the Korean War.

30. Hong, "Learn to Love the Bomb." The reference is to Ben Kiernan and David Simon, "Donald Trump Just Threatened to Commit Genocide." "If warfare between nuclear powers has emerged as a virtual affair—as cultural theorist Rei Chow states, in order to 'terrorize the other, one specializes in representation, in the means of display and exhibition'—the fact remains that the line between the show of force and the use of force is all too thin" (Hong, "Learn to Love the Bomb").

The Eisenhower Years

On November 1, 1952, the United States successfully detonated "Mike," the world's first hydrogen bomb, on the island of Elugelab, formerly a part of the Enewetak Atoll in the Marshall Islands. The 10.4-megaton thermonuclear device instantly vaporized the island and left behind a crater more than a mile wide.[31] General Dwight D. Eisenhower was elected president on November 4, 1952, by a landslide. He had campaigned on a promise to end the Korean War. In his inaugural address on January 20, 1953, he spoke about atomic technology, declaring that "science has conferred upon us, as its final gift, the power to erase human life from this planet."[32]

On April 16, just a month after Stalin's death, he delivered his first foreign policy address, "The Chance for Peace." He spoke about the costs of the Cold War. Postwar defense expenditures, which had shrunk to nine billion dollars in 1948, had grown to forty-six billion by 1952. But expenses for human resources had remained at around ten billion dollars. "Every gun that is made, every warship launched, every rocket fired," Eisenhower said, "signifies, in the final sense, a theft from those who hunger and are not fed, those who are cold and are not clothed. This world in arms is not spending money alone. It is spending the sweat of its laborers, the genius of its scientists, the hopes of its children. . . . This is not a way of life at all." He concluded that "under the cloud of threatening war, it is humanity hanging from a cross of iron."[33]

After the Korean Armistice was signed in July 1953, Eisenhower introduced his "New Look" policy. It proposed to reduce the amount spent on conventional weapons by emphasizing nuclear weapons. He thought that these would act as a deterrent to conflict with the Soviet Union. The policy was criticized by members of both houses of Congress concerned about cuts in conventional forces. (These reactions helped shape Eishenhower's

---

31. A hydrogen (or thermonuclear) bomb can be up to *one thousand times more powerful* than an atomic bomb, according to nuclear experts. See Dickerson and Mosher, "Fission vs. Fusion". The Soviet Union had developed thermonuclear bombs by 1955.

32. Quoted in Jarecki, *American Way of War*, 139.

33. Quoted in Jarecki, *American Way of War*, 140–41. Eisenhower gave specifics of the trade-offs: "The cost of one modern heavy bomber is this: a modern brick school in more than thirty cities. It is two electric power plants, each serving a town of 60,000 population . . . two fine, fully equipped hospitals . . . some fifty miles of concrete highway" (Eisenhower, "The Chance for Peace"). His granddaughter, Susan Eisenhower, says that the speech was "very prophetic." She told Jarecki that her grandfather was raised in a pacifist household. His mother was devastated when he chose to enter the military. But, Susan says, "he took much of his mother's strong [pacifist] impulses with him into his adult life." Jarecki, *American Way of War*, 125.

misgivings about what he later called the military-industrial complex.) Eisenhower implemented the program, which did reduce conventional defense forces and spending for those forces. But spending on the Air Force grew from a high of 15.6 billion to 16.4 billion dollars.[34]

Eisenhower was also instrumental in approving and establishing precedents for covert actions by the Central Intelligence Agency (CIA) during his presidency. In *The Brothers*, Stephen Kinzer states that Eisenhower "combined the mind-set of a warrior with a sober understanding of the devastation that full-scale war brings. That led him to covert action."[35] John Foster Dulles served as Eisenhower's secretary of state from 1953 to 1959. Allen Dulles was director of the CIA from 1953 to 1961. John Foster ordered the 1953 coup in Iran, "which was intended in part to make the Middle East safe for American oil companies." In 1954, he ordered another coup, in Guatemala, "where a nationalist government had challenged the power of United Fruit, a company his old law firm represented."[36] The US role in these and later coups in the Congo, Indonesia, and Chile, among others, was as much—if not more—about protecting the interests of US capital and corporations as it was about fighting communism.

According to Kinzer, the Dulles brothers were shaped by missionary Christianity and American history, and later, as adults, "by decades of work defending the interests of America's biggest multinational corporations." They also helped shape the US confrontation with the Soviet Union, stoking fear of communism as "Godless terrorism." Kinzer writes that "their view of freedom was above all economic: a country whose leaders respected private enterprise and welcomed multinational business was a free country."[37]

---

34. Jarecki, *American Way of War*, 142–44.

35. Kinzer, *Brothers*, 114. Jarecki thinks that for Eisenhower and John Foster Dulles, "these CIA actions were an effort to gain geostrategic ground in the larger struggle against communism." But he notes, "with increasing frequency, the economic interests of corporations were involved." Jarecki, *American Way of War*, 156.

36. Kinzer, *Overthrow*, 4. See also Dower, *The Violent American Century*. On the coup in Guatemala and other US interventions in Latin America, see Matthew Whelan's essay in this volume.

37. Kinzer, *Brothers*, 115–16, 312, 324–25. Both John Foster Dulles and Allen Dulles were lawyers who became partners at Sullivan & Cromwell (the largest law firm in the US at the time). They and other founders of the Council on Foreign Relations called their policy "liberal internationalism"; Kinzer aptly calls it "corporate globalism." Allen had significant experience in the Middle East and sent millions of dollars as cash bribes to further what he saw as US interests there. This failed in Egypt and Jordan but was successful in Saudi Arabia. He passed tens of millions of dollars to Saudi leaders, which solidified a partnership that gave the US "access to a seemingly unlimited supply of oil." This strengthened "a deeply radical regime devoted to promoting forms of anti-Americanism that would ultimately prove [to be] devastating." Kinzer, *Brothers*, 189. See also Bacevich, "Blood for Oil," 175–204.

In his 1961 Farewell Address, President Eisenhower warned that "in the councils of government, we must guard against the acquisition of unwarranted influence, whether sought or unsought, by the military-industrial complex. The potential for the disastrous rise of misplaced power exists and will persist." Eisenhower feared that this complex "threatens to dominate politics through its pervasive influence and to pursue its own narrow interests by exaggerating threats and manipulating external crises so as to construct a *permanent war economy* that would render it even more powerful."[38] William Hartung contends that "nuclear weapons and nuclear vehicles drove Eisenhower to give" this speech. The air force and the industry wanted a new nuclear bomber. "Eisenhower thought it was a waste of money and redundant."[39] He won this battle, but talk of a "missile gap" with the Soviet Union helped John F. Kennedy win the election. Soon after he took office, "it became apparent that any missile gap that might exist" favored the US.[40]

Conclusion

"A hyper-interventionist, highly militarized foreign policy has defined Washington since at least the days of President Harry Truman," charges Danny Sjursen in a 2018 essay examining the military-industrial complex today. This has led to "bloated budgets for which exaggerated threats, if not actual war, remain a necessity." He points out that even today President

---

38. Eisenhower, "Farewell Address"; emphasis added.

39. Hartung, "Nuclear Politics," 111. "The US included so many nuclear weapons in its first missile-age plan for nuclear war that top military commanders called it a 'hazard to ourselves as well as our enemy,' according to newly declassified documents posted today by the National Security Archive at George Washington University. Under the first Single Integrated Operational Plan, prepared during 1960, a Russian city the size of Nagasaki—devastated in 1945 with a twenty-kiloton bomb—would receive three 80 kiloton weapons. President Dwight D. Eisenhower, then leaving office, along with Navy leaders and White House Science Adviser George Kistiakowsky, was deeply critical of the SIOP's overkill. Eisenhower was later reported to have said that the plan 'frighten[ed] the devil out of me.' Incoming Secretary of Defense Robert McNamara soon decried the 'fantastic' levels of fallout that attacks on a multitude of Soviet targets would produce. Some evidence exists that after the Cold War ended, Strategic Air Command commander-in-chief General Lee Butler tried to curb what he saw as the SIOP's 'grotesque excesses' by paring down the huge target lists. Security classification, however, hides whether General Butler's reforms took hold or whether the SIOP remains an instrument of overkill." Burr, "The Creation of SIOP-62."

40. Hartung contends that at the end of the Cold War "the Pentagon focused on smaller potential adversaries" to keep "the Pentagon budget much higher than it needed to be to defend the country" ("Nuclear Politics," 110–12).

Trump's national defense strategy claims that the US is threatened by the rise of Russia and China, but "it asserts the need for favorable 'balances of power' just about everywhere!" That, says Sjursen, is "*by definition . . . an urge for hegemony, not defense!*"[41] He quotes Eisenhower's "Chance for Peace" speech, noting that it is still salient today: "As Americans experience acute income inequality, the rising cost of a college education, and ongoing deindustrialization in the heartland, the country's runaway spending continues to rise precipitously." The proposed 2019 Pentagon budget is "more than much of the rest of the world's defense spending combined."[42]

In April 2018, The New Poor Peoples Campaign released an audit by the Institute of Policy Studies that compares US military spending to other spending, as Eisenhower did. "The current annual military budget, at 668 billion dollars, dwarfs the 190 billion dollars allocated for education, jobs, housing, and other basic services and infrastructure. Out of every dollar in federal discretionary spending, fifty-three cents goes towards the military, with just fifteen cents on anti-poverty programs."[43]

The military-industrial complex (also called the corporate-military complex[44]) is essential to militarized globalization, but it is costly. Some

---

41. Sjursen, "Trump's National Defense Strategy"; emphasis added. Sjursen is a US Army officer who served tours with reconnaissance units in Iraq and Afghanistan and a former history instructor at West Point. In the National Defense Strategy the objectives of the Department of Defense are "to be prepared to defend the homeland, remain the preeminent military power in the world, ensure the balances of power remain in our favor, and advance an international order that is most conducive to our security and prosperity." United States Department of Defense, "Fiscal Year 2019."

42. Sjursen, "Trump's National Defense Strategy." With regard to military spending, the Stockholm International Peace Research Institute (SIPRI) maintains a Military Expenditure Database. "World military expenditure is estimated to have reached $1739 billion in 2017, the highest level since the end of the cold war," SIPRI reports. At $610 billion, US military spending accounted for more than a third of the world total in 2017. The US's spending was 2.7 times greater than the next highest spender, China; indeed, the US spent more than the next seven highest spenders combined. While US military expenditure had fallen each year since 2010, in 2017 it was unchanged from 2016. However, the US military budget for 2018 has been set at a substantially higher level ($700 billion). The higher spending is to support increases in military personnel and the modernization of conventional and nuclear weapons. See Tian et al., "Trends in World Military Expenditure."

43. Institute for Policy Studies, "The Souls of Poor Folks," 15.

44. "In the twenty-first century, the [national security state] has put special effort into subsidizing warrior corporations ready to join it on the global battlefield. In the process, it has privatized—that is, corporatized—its global operations. It has essentially merged with a set of crony outfits that now do a significant part of its work. . . . War and profit had long been connected in complicated ways, but seldom so straightforwardly. Now, win or lose on the battlefield, there would always be winners among the growing class of warrior corporations." Engelhardt, *Shadow Government*, 7, 81.

argue that military spending produces jobs, but research has shown that it produces fewer jobs than other areas of the economy. According to Heidi Garrett-Peltier, a University of Massachusetts economist, "Over the past sixteen years, by spending money on war rather than in these other areas of the domestic economy, the US lost the opportunity to create between one million and three million additional jobs."[45] These could be jobs in education, healthcare, infrastructure, and clean energy. Other aspects of this complex also have harmful impacts on people, planet, and peace. Two crucial ones are the international arms trade and climate change

Part Two: Threats from Militarized Globalization

International Arms Trade

After World War II, there was a "tremendous growth in the volume of arms traded worldwide."[46] It became another aspect of militarized globalization. The export of weapons is often necessary to support a domestic arms industry for national defense. David Harvey points out that "to survive economically, the defense industries needed a thriving export trade in arms. *This came to have a fundamental role in US capital accumulation, but it also resulted in the excessive militarization of the rest of the world.*"[47]

President Richard Nixon elevated arms transfers to a prominent position in foreign policy. On July 25, 1969, he "suggested that internal security problems in Asia and elsewhere should be handled internally, but the US would provide military and economic assistance to friendly regimes in order to support them." This became known as the Nixon Doctrine. It led to a huge rise in supply of weapons around the world.[48]

During the Cold War, the US and the Soviet Union "transferred billions of dollars' worth of weapons to their respective client states." The US became the dominant arms exporter after the Cold War ended, even when demand for arms fell. The defense industry lobbied to keep arms production, national procurements, and exports up.[49] In 1994, President

---

45. Garrett-Peltier, "Job Opportunity Cost of War," 2. See also Alpert, "The Continuing Cost of War." The Costs of War website at Brown University's Watson Institute for International and Public Affairs is an excellent source for more information (https://watson.brown.edu/costsofwar/). It covers three areas: human economic, social, and political, which includes environmental costs.

46. Stohl and Grillot, *International Arms Trade*, 15.

47. Harvey, *New Imperialism*, 60; emphasis added.

48. Stohl and Grillot, *International Arms Trade*, 17–19.

49. "As of early 2011, Lockheed Martin employed ninety lobbyists at a cost of over

Clinton's Conventional Arms Transfer policy added that "'the impact on US industry and the defense industrial base whether the sale is approved or not' would also be taken into consideration." This portrayed the arms trade "as a money-making industry in the post-Cold War economy." Although the legal arms trade is a very small percentage of total world trade, "it is big business and continues to reflect new security challenges."[50]

In terms of value, the United States was the largest supplier of weapons globally, counting for nearly half of all arms sales between 2007 and 2014.[51] In 2016, US sales again counted for about 50 percent of global sales. Furthermore, many of the major weapons systems went to hotspots like Yemen. The US sold weaponry to at least one hundred countries between 2012 and 2016.[52]

A significant issue with arms transfers is that the supplying state has no assurance about what will happen with the weapons after they are transferred.[53] The most recent case demonstrating this danger is the transfer of

---

$7 million per year. . . . Company lobbyists work on a wide range of issues, from NASA appropriations to homeland security. But most of them work on defense appropriations. . . . Lockheed Martin donated over $3 million to candidates in the last election cycle." Hartung, *Prophets of War*, 262–63. "Lockheed Martin made fifty-nine percent of its total sales ($47.2 billion) in 2016 from just the Department of Defense. That's $27.9 billion from the Pentagon. . . . And that same year they made $5.1 billion in profits." Miles, "Congress Went Bigly."

50. Stohl and Grillot, *International Arms Trade*, 10, 26, 28, 30–31, 39. "The volume of international transfers of major weapons has grown continuously since 2004 and increased by 8.4 per cent between 2007–11 and 2012–16, according to new data on arms transfers published today by the Stockholm International Peace Research Institute (SIPRI). Notably, transfers of major weapons in 2012–16 reached their highest volume for any five-year period since the end of the cold war. The flow of arms increased to Asia and Oceania and the Middle East between 2007–11 and 2012–16, while there was a decrease in the flow to Europe, the Americas, and Africa. *The five biggest exporters—the United States, Russia, China, France and Germany—together accounted for 74 percent of the total volume of arms exports. . . . With a one-third share of global arms exports, the USA was the top arms exporter in 2012–16. Its arms exports increased by 21 percent compared with 2007–11. Almost half of its arms exports went to the Middle East. 'The USA supplies major arms to at least 100 countries around the world—significantly more than any other supplier state,'* said Dr Aude Fleurant, Director of the SIPRI Arms and Military Expenditure Programme. 'Both advanced strike aircraft with cruise missiles and other precision-guided munitions and the latest generation air and missile defence systems account for a significant share of US arms exports.'" India was the largest importer of arms, followed by Saudi Arabia. SIPRI, "Increase in Arms Transfers," emphasis added.

51. Dower, *Violent American Century*, 121.

52. Hartung, "Arms Bonanza."

53. Due to the efforts of nongovernmental organization, in 2009 the United Nations committed to pursue an international Arms Trade Treaty (ATT) with the goal of it

weapons to the Islamic State of Iraq and Syria (ISIS/IS). "Unauthorized re-transfer—the violation of agreements by which a supplier government prohibits the re-export of materiel by a recipient government without its prior consent—is a significant source of IS weapons and ammunition. Most of this materiel was supplied by the US and Saudi Arabia, without authorization, apparently to Syrian opposition forces. The diversion of these weapons 'has eroded the trust that exporting authorities placed in the recipient governments.'" This diverted materiel, recovered from IS forces, comprises purchases by the United States and Saudi Arabia from European Union (EU) member states in Eastern Europe. These weapons "significantly augmented the quantity and quality of weapons available to IS forces—in numbers far beyond those that would have been available to the group through battlefield capture alone."[54]

In *The Shadow World: Inside the Global Arms Trade*, Andrew Feinstein concludes that "the arms industry receives unique treatment from governments," whether companies are state-owned or privatized. Both companies and individuals exercise "*a disproportionate and usually bellicose influence on all matter of policy-making, be it on economic, foreign or national security issues.*" He contends that "the formal and clandestine worlds interact and intersect far more regularly than they would admit. And their dependence on each other is profound. Both form, in effect, the shadow world."[55] The case of weapons transfers to ISIS illustrates this.

Climate Change

The US intelligence community has alerted policymakers to the security implications of climate change every year since 2008. On February 13, 2018, Director of National Intelligence Dan Coats released the most recent Worldwide Threat Assessment during a hearing before the Senate Select Committee on Intelligence. The report discusses a wide range of threats. In the section titled "Environment and Climate Change" it is stated that "*the*

---

being negotiated and signed by 2012. Feinstein, *Shadow World*, 529. The treaty entered into force in December 24, 2014. It aims to "establish the highest possible common international standards for regulating or improving the regulation of the international trade in conventional arms; and prevent and eradicate the illicit trade in conventional arms and prevent their diversion." United Nations, "Arms Trade Treaty," 2. Of the five largest exporters, France and Germany have signed and ratified the Treaty; the US signed in 2013 but hasn't ratified; China and Russia have not signed, nor have the two largest importers, India and Saudi Arabia.

54. Conflict Armament Research, "Weapons of the Islamic State."
55. Feinstein, *Shadow World*, 522–24, emphasis added.

impacts of the long-term trends toward a warming climate, more air pollution, biodiversity loss, and water scarcity are likely to fuel economic and social discontent—and possibly upheaval—through 2018."[56]

When viewed through a national security lens, Nafeez Ahmed suggests that "climate change becomes not a springboard for much-needed social transformation to save the planet." Rather, it is used to justify "innovative new ways to save the profits of the few who run the planet."[57] He cites a 2014 report from the Center for Naval Analyses (CNA) Military Advisory Board as an example. Climate change is "not just a 'threat multiplier,' but now—even worse—a 'catalyst for conflict.'" One of its foci is Africa, "*an increasingly important source of US oil and gas imports*," which experiences tension and stress from "weak governance" and "food and water shortages" that will be exacerbated by climate change. The new Africa Command developed by the Pentagon "reflects Africa's emerging strategic importance to the US." They caution that a "worsening of conditions" due to climate impacts "could prompt further US military engagement."[58]

President Jimmy Carter "began a period of expansion" of military operations "unmatched in the postwar era," after declaring the Persian Gulf was vital to US interests. In his last State of the Union Address (January 23, 1980), he identified "the overwhelming dependence of the Western democracies on oil supplies from the Middle East" as one of three international challenges. "Let our position be absolutely clear," he said. "An

---

56. Coats, "World Wide Threat Assessment," 16; emphasis original. It adds that "extreme weather events in a warmer world have the potential for greater impacts and can compound with other drivers to raise the risk of humanitarian disasters, conflict, water and food shortages, population migration, labor shortfalls, price shocks, and power outages." See also Werrell and Femia, "Impacts of Climate Change."

57. Ahmed is referring to the May 2014 Conference on Inclusive Capitalism, held in London. I analyze this conference and the notion of inclusive capitalism in my chapter in *Globalization and Economic Justice* (Brubaker, "Neo-liberalism and Economic Development"). In an op-ed in the *New York Times*, Benjamin Y. Fong of Arizona State University writes that "the real culprit of the climate crisis is not any particular form of consumption, production or regulation but rather the very *way* in which we globally produce, which is for profit rather than for sustainability.... It should be stated plainly: It's *capitalism* that is at fault.... From a political standpoint, something interesting has occurred here: Climate change has made anticapitalist struggle, for the first time in history, a non-class-based issue." Fong, "The Climate Crisis?"

58. Ahmed, "Climate Warfare Is Here." Ahmed is an international security journalist and academic. He also reports that in 2009, Lord Drayson, then British Minister of State for Strategic Defence Acquisition Reform, said, "I think climate change is a real opportunity for the aerospace and defense industry." The CNA report was written and endorsed by a dozen or so senior retired US generals. Barry Sanders suggests that "by 'threat multiplier,' they mean a threat to the comfortable way of American life so many of us know so well." Sanders, *Green Zone*, 119.

attempt by any outside force to gain control of the Persian Gulf region will be regarded as an assault on the vital interests of the USA, and such an assault will be repelled by any means necessary, including military force."[59] This came to be called the Carter Doctrine. In *The New American Militarism*, Andrew Bacevich contends that "each of President Carter's successors has expanded the level of US military involvement and operations in the region."[60]

Given the amount of oil that the military uses, it is conceivable that "with the exception of a handful of countries, the U.S. military probably produces more greenhouse gas emissions and other forms of pollution than almost any other organization, corporation, or entity on earth," suggests David Vine in *Base Nation*.[61] The National Renewable Energy Laboratory reports that "the DOD [Department of Defense] is the nation's single largest energy user, and one of the largest energy consumers in the world.... Its average daily oil use is over 12,000,000 gallons. Its total annual costs are about $17 billion a year."[62] The transparency of this and other reports is

---

59. David Vine observes that this led to one of the greatest base construction efforts in history (*Base Nation*, 41). Engelhardt points out that President Carter stated that "the crises in Iran and Afghanistan also have dramatized a very important lesson: Our excessive dependence on foreign oil is a clear and present danger to our Nation's security." He called for developing alternative sources of energy to oil, but President Reagan reversed this policy when he took office. (He also removed the solar panels which Carter had installed on the White House.) Engelhardt, *Shadow Government*, 140–41. See also Dower, *Violent American Century*, 53–54, 140.

60. Bacevich, *New America Militarism*, 181, 183. Bacevich is a West Point graduate and Vietnam veteran and professor of international relations at Boston University. He remarks that although "on the surface the exchange might entail blood-for-oil ... the aim was to guarantee the ever-increasing affluence that underwrites the modern American concept of liberty." This raises important questions about the cost of this conception of liberty that are beyond the scope of this chapter. Michael Klare contends that President Trump has militarized our energy policy. "The final step in the president's strategy to become a major exporter involves facilitating the transport of fossil fuels to the country's coastal areas for shipment abroad. In this way, he would also turn the government into a major global salesman of fossil fuels.... Such energy moves have generally been viewed as part of a pro-industry, anti-environmentalist agenda, which they certainly are, but each is also a component in an increasingly militarized strategy to enlist domestic energy in an epic struggle—at least in the minds of the president and his advisers—to ensure America's global dominance." Klare, "Militarizing America's Energy Policy."

61. Vine, *Base Nation*, 137. There have been efforts to have the cost of securing foreign oil added to EPA calculations of climate change. About "20 percent of the conventional DOD budget ... is attributable to the objective of oil security." Liska and Perrin, "Securing Foreign Oil."

62. "Operational energy accounts for 70 percent of DOD's total energy use. Most of this energy comes from liquid fuel used to transport, train, and sustain personnel

commendable. But as Nick Buxton charges, "there is no critical examination of the military's own role in enforcing a corporate-dominated fossil-fuel economy that has caused the climate crisis."[63]

In "Ten Years On: Katrina, Militarization, and Climate Change," Buxton and Ben Hayes write,

> Where we see a future climate crisis, many companies see only opportunity: oil firms looking forward to melting ice caps delivering new accessible fossil fuels; security firms touting the latest technologies to secure borders from "climate refugees"; or investment fund managers speculating on weather-related food prices—to name but a few.[64]

Raytheon, one of the world's largest defense contractors, announced in 2012 that "*expanded business opportunities*" were arising from "security concerns and their possible consequences" due to the "effects of climate change" in the form of "storms, droughts, and floods."[65]

Buxton and Hayes warn that "the implications of a militarized and profit-making approach to climate adaptation and crisis-management are very disturbing," especially for those concerned about "environmental justice, civil liberties, and democracy." Not only does a security-led approach to climate change and complex emergencies fail to address the fundamental causes of these crises, "it will often exacerbate them."[66]

Conclusion

In 2017, the Women's International League for Peace and Freedom declared that "there are about 14,900 nuclear weapons in the world. The detonation

---

and weapons" (https://www.nrel.gov/workingwithus/defense-partnerships.html). This website has other information on the DOD, including reports on initiatives to reduce this use. For official information on US energy use, see the website of the US Energy Information Administration (EIA), https://www.eia.gov.

63. Buxton, "The Elephant in Paris." Buxton also points out that "military climate change strategies focus on securing borders, protecting trade supply-routes for corporations, controlling conflicts around resources and instability caused by extreme weather, and repressing social unrest. *They turn the victims of climate change into 'threats' to be controlled or combated.*"

64. Buxton and Hayes, "Ten Years On." Hayes and Buxton are coeditors of the book *The Secure and the Dispossessed: How the Military and Corporations Are Shaping a Climate-Changed World*.

65. The information on Raytheon was first reported in *Mother Jones*. Schulman, "Defense Contractor," emphasis added.

66. Buxton and Hayes, "Ten Years On."

of even a fraction of these weapons would destroy the planet and end human civilization as we know it."⁶⁷ Both nuclear weapons and climate change "threaten the survival of life on earth as we know it and both are of our making," warned the World Future Council in 2015. After a thorough exploration of the linkages, they concluded that "preventing the dangers of climate change and nuclear war requires an *integrated set of strategies* that address the causes as well as the impacts on the natural and social environment." Furthermore, there is a need for institutions "that strengthen common, ecological and human security, build and reinforce conflict-resolution mechanisms, low-carbon energy alternatives and sustainable lifecycles that respect the capabilities of the living world and create the conditions for viable and sustainable peace."⁶⁸ At this time though, militarized globalization is rampant. Its threats to people, planet, and peace are greater than ever.

---

67. Acheson et al., "Assuring Destruction Forever."

68. Scheffran et al., "The Climate-Nuclear Nexus," 6–7. The document offers concrete proposals for moving forward, providing stepping stones for going from conflict to cooperation.

4

Free Souls, Free People, Free Enterprise

Business, the Cold War, and American Evangelicalism

DAVID R. SWARTZ

Introduction

The crowd of 75,000 at Soldier Field was in a celebratory mood. Three weeks after victory over Germany and three months before victory over Japan, the religious gathering on May 30, 1945—Memorial Day—spilled over with patriotic fervor. Attendees sang the national anthem. The United States Marine Corps Color Guard marched down the center of the field and posted American flags around the stadium. Lieutenant Robert Evans of the US Navy appealed to the crowd to buy war bonds; reports later claimed sales greater than "any other large meeting in the history of the United States." The throng sang "Anchors Aweigh," "As the Caissons Go Rolling Along," "The Marines' Hymn," and "Army Air Corps." Everything about the moment suggested the successful completion of a messianic mission. Americans had freed the world from Japanese totalitarianism, German Nazism, and Italian fascism.[1]

1. Draft of rally program, c. April 1945, Collection 285, Box 27, Folder 14, Billy

But now another threat loomed. The Soviet Union, though still an ally in World War II, featured a Marxist ideology that threatened free enterprise. The fifty entrepreneurs who funded the Memorial Day rally called themselves "The Business World Committee." They manufactured glass, roofing supplies, insulation, iron, and appliances—and they preached against planned economies. Franklin Roosevelt's New Deal, declared many of them, had veered too closely to socialism. For Herbert Taylor, president of Club Aluminum and speaker at the rally, true citizenship meant integrity, entrepreneurship, and interest "in the freedom and welfare of all the world's peoples," especially those within the iron grip of totalitarian communism.[2]

On this Memorial Day in Chicago, freeing people and enterprise from totalitarianism was inextricably linked to Christian faith. Youth for Christ, an important evangelical organization still in its infancy, organized the rally. The patriotic homages were sacralized by an hour-long pageant to a different set of conquering heroes: American missionaries. Their locations—China, India, Russia, Mexico, multiple countries in Africa, and the United States—represented critical sites in the emerging Cold War. After a tender rendition of "Just As I Am," attendees triumphantly sang "All Hail the Power of Jesus' Name." Then a spotlight was thrown on the American and Christian flags as a deep bass voice sang the words to "God Bless Our Boys." Celestial and worldly symbols mixed in a striking spectacle of tanks, planes, jeeps, three huge living white crosses, and an enormous neon sign that blazed "Jesus Saves." The perimeter featured angelic figures blowing golden trumpets upon the colonnades of Soldier Field. These apocalyptic images from John's Book of Revelation inspired hundreds to make "decisions for Christ." Many more pledged to carry the "good news" of the gospel to the ends of the earth. "Where He leads," one of the hymns intoned, "I will follow."[3]

The three-hour display ended with a dramatic rehearsal of this great commission. All the lights at Soldier Field were extinguished, except for a piercing beacon light on an elevated lighthouse at the center of the field. As a choir of five thousand youth sang "We Shall Shine as the Stars," the lone light slowly scanned the stands, illuminating tens of thousands of young evangelicals eager to share their faith. As the stadium lights flickered back on to enthusiastic exclamations and deafening applause, these youths

---

Graham Center Archives (BGCA), Wheaton, Illinois; Torrey Johnson Interview, August 14, 1985, Collection 285, Audio tape 6, BGCA.

2. Taylor, *God Has a Plan*, 124.

3. Victory Youth Rally program, Folder 1, Box 72, Herbert J. Taylor Collection; William F. McDermott, "Bobby-Soxers Find the Sawdust Trail," *Collier's* (May 26, 1945), 23, copy in Photo Album I, Torrey Johnson Collection, Billy Graham Center Archives, Wheaton, Illinois.

rededicated to Christ were released to free souls, people, and enterprise around the world in the service of Christian Americanism. This ideological matrix has persisted into the twenty-first century despite trenchant critiques from the evangelical left in America and from evangelicals across the globe.[4]

Nationalist Consensus

The rising neo-evangelical movement of the 1940s nurtured cultural and social ambitions. Building evangelical institutions to compete with secular institutions, locating *Christianity Today* just down the street from the White House, and conducting crusades in the heart of liberal cities such as Los Angeles and New York City reflected bold aspirations. Indeed, the first presidential address of the National Association of Evangelicals (NAE) rivaled the grandiosity of Henry Luce's "American Century" rhetoric. Harold John Ockenga, pastor of the venerated Park Street Church in Boston, declared, "The NAE is the only hopeful sign on the horizon of Christian history today. If we who are gathered here meet our responsibility this week it may well be that the oblique rays of the sun are not the rusty red of its setting but are the golden rays of its rising for a new era."[5] Emboldened by their own contributions to American successes in World War II, these new evangelicals sought to accelerate an ambitious global vision.[6]

That vision emphasized liberty—not only of freeing souls from atheistic communism and freeing people from authoritarian tyranny but also freeing markets from Marxism. In protecting economies from central control, evangelicals hoped to unleash an entrepreneur-driven prosperity. This capitalistic impulse, however, did not follow a straight path from Adam Smith's notion of laissez-faire economics. Interspersed before and between nineteenth-century evangelical Whigs and twentieth-century corporate capitalists were Jeffersonians concerned about concentrations of wealth and power. Southern and Western populist evangelicals fulminated against big business as much as big government. Under the weight of bank foreclosures and eastern stock exchanges, these populists criticized unfettered capitalism in their calls for economic reform. Even decades later, the Ham and Eggs movement in California did not see the free market as attractive. Activists, according to historian Darren Dochuk, "combined calls for Christian revival and morality with a critique of capitalism and economic injustice."[7]

4. Supple, "Patriotic Note."
5. Ockenga, "Christ for America," 6.
6. On neo-evangelical cultural ambition, see Carpenter, *Revive Us Again*.
7. Dochuk, *From Bible Belt to Sunbelt*, 10, 123.

The coming of the Cold War, however, checked these critiques and tightened the alliance between religious conservatism and capitalism. As the Soviet Union extended its orbit, selling arms and protection to nations in Eastern Europe, Asia, Africa, and Latin America, the United States did the same. Evangelicals, who narrated geopolitical developments by linking Marxism to atheism and a command economy, boosted American efforts. Tying Christian faith to democracy and free enterprise, they promoted military growth in order to protect American economic interests. In fact, George Pepperdine, the founder of Western Auto Supply, started Pepperdine College in order to support the expansion of Christ and capitalism. Through the 1940s, 1950s, and 1960s, the college opposed the nationalization of the American economy, its students debated Cold War issues, and the World Affairs Lecture Series addressed international developments. Numerous other parachurch organizations, including the Business Men's Evangelistic Clubs and Christian Business Men's Committee International, according to Sarah Hammond, tried "to steer the masses to Christ and free enterprise from the top down." The success of World War II and the missions surge of the postwar years seemed to give evangelicals an exhilarating chance to spread the gospel of economic liberty in the tense Cold War environment.[8]

Herbert Taylor, a key organizer of the Soldier Field rally, embodied this entrepreneurial spirit. Concerned that liberal ministers in Chicago were not preaching "a real gospel message," yet criticized by fundamentalists for being "a Methodist do-gooder" and "not sufficiently a Bible-banger," Taylor traversed the middle path of the neo-evangelical movement. A veteran of the navy, he helped distribute food and water in France. When the war concluded, he was offered two jobs: a ministry position with the YMCA or a sales job with the Sinclair Oil Company. Taylor chose business. "God presented me with a plan," he said. "His particular plan for me." The plan called for making a fortune in business by the age of forty-five, then donating his time and money to ministry and philanthropy.[9]

This is precisely what happened. In Oklahoma, Taylor thrived as a lease broker in the oilfield business, an insurance salesman, and a real estate broker. The *Daily Oklahoman* called him "Sign-'em-up Taylor" for his efforts in spearheading a drive for paved roads in the county. Taylor then moved to Chicago, where he worked his way up the corporate ladder to the vice presidency of the Jewel Tea Company, one of the largest direct-sales tea companies in the US. He then took over the Club Aluminum Products

---

8. Dochuk, *From Bible Belt to Sunbelt*, 128–31; Hammond, "'God's Business Men,'" i.

9. For "Methodist do-gooder" and Taylor's ecclesiastical location, see Heidebrecht, "Pragmatic Evangelical," 111. For more on Taylor, see Grem, *Blessings of Business*, 13–48.

Company, which sold high-end cookware, rescuing it from bankruptcy in the bleak years of the Great Depression. His command of debt restructuring and new method of direct sales to department stores and grocery chains proved wildly successful. The young CEO saved 250 jobs and canceled Club Aluminum's $400,000 debt within five years.[10]

Taylor credited his disciplined workforce for Club Aluminum's success. He sought to cultivate good character and good products through a series of questions—Is it the truth? Is it fair to all concerned? Will it build goodwill and better friendships? Will it be beneficial to all concerned?—he dubbed the "Four-Way Test." At base, Taylor sought to imbue good moral habits in his employees. Citing Jeremiah 9:23–24, he explained that the Test was a way of "pointing people to God and to a responsible, satisfying way of life."[11] It promoted eternal values of honesty, faith, and high principles. According to his biographer, the Test was "a visible symbol permeating every nook and cranny of the company."[12] It appeared on annual reports to stockholders, the backs of salesmen's calling cards, and car window stickers. Employees were required to memorize and recite it. It worked so well that national and international levels of the Rotary Club adopted the Test in the 1950s as its organizing principle and mantra.[13] Taylor, rewarded handsomely for his managerial and entrepreneurial genius, accumulated (and gave away) fantastic personal wealth and considerable public praise. *Newsweek* magazine featured Taylor on its cover in 1955.

Evangelical corporate paternalism required as much of the corporation as the workers. Taylor sought direct contact with his employees to learn their frustrations and desires. According to historian Paul Heidebrecht, Taylor was "an old-fashioned businessman who treated his employees like family members." Dispensing more than friendship and moral advice, he also distributed profits. He incentivized ingenuity, high character, and service with profit-sharing. In fact, stockholders sometimes criticized Taylor for being more generous with employees than stockholders. To be sure, Taylor opposed labor unions in principle, but he nevertheless made contributions to the welfare funds of unions. Taylor and other evangelical industrialists saw themselves as paternalistic saviors that could bridge management and labor.[14]

10. On his early career, see Taylor, *God Has a Plan for You*, 21–44.
11. For "satisfying way of life," see Heidebrecht, *God's Man*, 58.
12. Heidebrecht, *God's Man*, 65, 96–98.
13. Heidebrecht, *God's Man*, 49–57. See also *Newsweek*, "Rotary President Taylor," 25–32.
14. On Taylor's paternalism, see Heidebrecht, *God's Man*, 40–41, 67–71; Taylor, *God Has a Plan*, 16, 27–28.

The National Association of Evangelicals called this important task "industrial chaplaincy." In an age of bitterly antagonistic labor battles, its Commission on Industrial Chaplaincy suggested that employer generosity could eliminate antagonistic relationships by balancing pastoral care and free-market principles. One of its early brochures pictured a Bible beaming warm rays over a factory full of workers. The vision—as theological as it was social and economic—included the CEO as a benevolent god who showered fair and attentive interest upon the lowliest assembly-line worker. Sin was depicted as humans on strike against God. As historian Sarah Hammond recounts, "Evangelical business men believed, with no sense of contradiction, that God's grace was unearned, yet a sign of virtue; spiritual, yet manifested in money; everlasting, yet easily lost; a joy, yet a yoke to bear. The 'man of leadership' could never stop working for God, lest he fall from grace." Industrial chaplaincy could reconcile warring parties and transform the hard edges of capitalism into a benevolent and prosperous system of free enterprise.[15]

The paternalistic energies of God's businessmen extended beyond the corporation. Taylor launched community service projects on the deprived Near North Side of Chicago. He served bread and soup at a storefront mission and claimed to have reduced recidivism by 40 percent by placing delinquents in Rotary homes. At the age of forty-seven, only two years late, Taylor set up a major philanthropic organization. The Christian Workers Foundation (CWF), funded through the sale of 25 percent of Club Aluminum's stock, contributed to hundreds of neo-evangelical organizations including InterVarsity Christian Fellowship, Young Life, Christian Service Brigade, Child Evangelism Fellowship, and Fuller Theological Seminary. Taylor provided significant outlays at first and then tried to wean them from dependency. He also served on forty-five boards and committees during his life, including being the founding treasurer of the NAE, which functioned like a modern corporation. Taylor's entrepreneurial vision, which emphasized individualistic, ground-level solutions to social problems over government solutions, sought to serve the twin mandates of profit and paternalism.[16]

Taylor's libertarian philosophy fell outside the mid-century liberal consensus. Excepting the military buildup of WWII, most neo-evangelicals opposed government centralization. To evangelical philanthropists George Pepperdine and R. G. LeTourneau, owner of an earthmoving company, the

15. For the Commission on Industrial Chaplaincy and "man of leadership," see Hammond, "'God's Business Men,'" 252–53, 273.

16. On Taylor's community work, see Heidebrecht, *God's Man*, 47–48, 61, 67–68. On the NAE as a modern corporation, see Hammond, "'God's Business Men,'" 243.

New Deal was a "most benevolent dictatorship... but a dictatorship it is, all the more impressive in that it has been forced upon a great nation, not by the force of arms, but by the force of circumstances." Harold John Ockenga condemned Roosevelt's "managerial revolution" as one cause of the "breakup of the moral fiber of the nation." Taylor, who made small but regular donations to Republican candidates, was sympathetic to these critiques. As such, Taylor and his capitalist colleagues were important constituents of a broader conservative coalition that included Ayn Randian libertarians, small-government Hayekians, and anti-Keynesian economists. Their sense of citizenship was strong, and they wanted to spread the gospel of spiritual, political, and economic liberty through the nation and the world.[17]

Taylor's behind-the-scenes role in the NAE underscored the significance of business and free enterprise to the neo-evangelical project. Responsive to market forces, Taylor's Club Aluminum sponsored *Club Time* broadcasts on ABC that incorporated both spiritual emphases and evangelical networks. Soloist George Beverly Shea starred, leading hymns and Scripture readings to impressive radio ratings of 3.4. Taylor's role at the Soldier Field event was likewise simultaneously hidden and significant. He did not headline the event, as the flashier Torrey Johnson and Billy Graham did, but he did lead "The Business World" committee that financed the event. Programs noted that Taylor, president of the Club Aluminum Corporation of America, had been "in full charge of the US Government aluminum program after the outbreak of World War II." They also thanked dozens of other Christian businessmen: Philip Benson, president of the Dime Savings Bank of Brooklyn; William Erny, a Chicago paper box manufacturer; Carl Gunderson, a Chicago construction contractor and leader of the Christian Business Men's Committee; Freelin Carlton, manager of the Sears department store on State Street; and Cornelius Ulrich, director of the Central Broadcasting Agency in Chicago. They gave money, arranged for savvy marketing, organized the event, and served as ushers. These Christian businessmen embodied the evangelical testimony for Christ and capitalism.[18]

17. For "most benevolent dictatorship" and Taylor's flexible conservatism, see Hammond, "God's Business Men,'" 179. Ockenga quoted in Hammond, "'God's Business Men,'" 203. On his conservative advocacy in Washington, see Taylor, *God Has a Plan*, 43. On the contributions of evangelical corporatism to Christian Americanism, see Kruse, *One Nation Under God*.

18. On *Club Time*, see Heidebrecht, *God's Man*, 74–78. On members of "The Business World" committee, see Victory Youth Rally program, in Folder 1, Box 72, Herbert J. Taylor Collection, BGCA; Hammond, "'God's Business Men,'" 124; Heidebrecht, *God's Man*, 96–97. On YFC's marketing savvy, see Hefley, *God Goes to High School*, 25, 28; Johnson and Cook, *Reaching Youth for Christ*, 18.

Growing hotter in the years after World War II, the Cold War became a point of preoccupation. The NAE's *United Evangelical Action* newsletter carefully observed developments in China and the Soviet Union, condemning Marxist atrocities of religious and political persecution. "When God is out," intoned one representative article, "the tragic sequel is Bureaucracy, Dictatorship and Regimentation. Then the individual exists for the State and not the State for the individual." A popular Vacation Bible School curriculum produced by Scripture Press in Wheaton, Illinois, boasted that it could make "our youth . . . strong in the Lord and the power of His might." "Our answer to Khrushchev," the ad copy read, "is Patriots for Christ for '62 VBS." This felt urgency was rooted in fear that Marxists might win out in Western Europe as France, Britain, and Italy struggled to recover from the devastation of Germany's invasion.[19]

In the immediate postwar years, then, evangelicals set out to save Europe all over again. They had fought off German Nazis and Italian fascists, but now the Soviet Marxists threatened. Youth for Christ's Torrey Johnson wired a German pastor, "If Germany goes communistic, then you can write France, Italy, Spain, and Portugal off . . . and you can shove England down the road of socialism." Hoping that spiritual conversion could fend off communist incursions, Youth for Christ sent dozens of "invasion teams" to Great Britain, Scandinavia, France, the Netherlands, Germany, Greece, and Italy; the Caribbean and South America; and India and China. These touring evangelists, alongside a relief program launched by the nascent NAE, essentially functioned as spiritual relief workers supporting an evangelical Marshall Plan for susceptible nations. General Douglas MacArthur, though not an orthodox Christian himself, encouraged the partnership. He invited Youth for Christ and Southern Baptist evangelists to come to Japan to help "provide the surest foundation for the firm establishment of democracy."[20]

The war for democracy, then, offered resources for evangelism. At a 1945 conference in Winona Lake, Indiana, Merv Rosell argued that the intensity of warfare should be similarly utilized by missionaries. He preached that just as soldiers expect to win their wars in one generation and spare no expense to do so, so should Christians act in their efforts to convert the world in one generation. Indeed, even if the cost is blood it would be worth "the sweetness of world-wide victory." Similarly, another minister,

---

19. For "when God is out," see Bradbury, "Christianity and Democracy," 8; *United Evangelical Action*, "Churches Gain Freedom, but Communists Still Anti-Religious," 6. For VBS curriculum, see *Christianity Today*, "Patriots for Christ," 23.

20. On evangelical material and spiritual relief, see *United Evangelical Action*, "NAE Commences Shipments of Relief Goods," 1; Wright, "Park Street Church," 1. MacArthur quoted in Pierard, "*Pax Americana*," 174.

Robert Hall Glover, suggested that World War II was "an exact parallel to the missionary enterprise" and that therefore missionaries should have munitions and supplies on par with soldiers in war in their own worldwide conflict—the conflict to win souls. The martial language and strategies learned from World War II could be applied to the spiritual realm.[21]

The vibrant display in Chicago reflected a widespread Christian Americanism. Religious organizations such as the National Association of Evangelicals and the Business Men's Evangelistic Clubs encouraged this ideology, as did numerous "Christian" corporations such as Chick-fil-A, Wal-Mart, and the Western Auto Supply Company. American successes in World War II—coupled with the threats of an emerging Cold War—emboldened these activist evangelicals to accelerate an ambitious global vision willing to use both business and war to achieve liberty for all. They meant to free people from tyranny and would do so through cultural relevance, Christian virtue, and entrepreneurship. This grand narrative of Christian Americanism animated evangelical activism in postwar America.[22]

Internationalist Dissent

This potent fusion of faith, business culture, and nationalism dominated, but it was not universal. Not all evangelicals shared the intensity of Christian Americanism displayed by Herbert Taylor, Billy Graham, and Harold John Ockenga. Even in the NAE's *United Evangelical Action*, A. C. Snead cautioned, "We must go to the mission field, not as Americans or Canadians, or those of any other land, but as representing the Lord Jesus Christ. We are to go, not to demand that those of Africa or the East should take our western civilization, but rather that we may present to them the living Christ, who Himself was born in Asia and became the Savior of all men." Even true believers in Christian Americanism emphasized the imperative of mission more than the burden of civilization. Given the power and urgency of the Cold War narrative, this ambivalence generally remained below the surface in the 1950s and 1960s. By the 1970s, however, the new postcolonial environment encouraged more significant opposition

---

21. Rosell, "God's Global 'Go,'" and Glover, "Strengthening the Stakes of the Missionary Tent," quoted in Pierard, "*Pax Americana*," 168.

22. On Christian corporations, see Moreton, *To Serve God and Wal-Mart*; Dochuk, *From Bible Belt to Sunbelt*; Gloege, *Guaranteed Pure*; Grem, *The Blessings of Business*. On the significance of grand evangelical narratives, see Worthen, *Apostles of Reason*, 191.

within diverse evangelical communities of New Left theorists, missionaries, and converts from the Majority World.[23]

First, a small but loud evangelical left marshaled strident critiques of a neoliberal consensus committed to economic growth. Young radical evangelicals objected to the levels of consumption required for sustained economic growth. They prophesied a dire economic future, citing scarcity of resources, energy dependence on other nations, the staying power of poverty, and environmental degradation. They worried most of all, however, about the moral deficiencies of economic growth. In the first newsletter of the Post-Americans, a small intentional community made up of evangelical seminarians in Chicago, Jim Wallis wrote, "We protest the materialistic profit culture and technocratic society which threaten basic human values." At its base, they maintained, unlimited growth (and capitalism in general) merely justified corporate greed. The American profit culture elevated corporations to a too-powerful role in economic structures. Jack Sparks of the Christian World Liberation Front (CWLF), an evangelical commune in Berkeley, California, wrote, "We are controlled . . . by an economic bureaucracy which has been a long time building and which rolls inexorably along, constantly increasing our alienation from ourselves, from freedom and from each other." More than one hundred articles on the disenfranchised (which included the poor, oppressed, Blacks, women, and the tortured) appeared in the *Post-American* from 1973 to 1978, many of them explicitly blaming consumptive culture and big business for their economic plight.[24]

Objections to faith in science and to the "spirit-deadening assembly-line routine" of technology pervaded the evangelical left's skepticism of unlimited growth. "The spiritual revolutionary is not enamored with either social or physical sciences," stated CWLF's "Revolutionary Catechism." "He knows only one true science: the science of the application of God's love to people." In contrast, technology—new ideas, materials, machines, and products—gave the "powers and principalities," as Jim Wallis called governments, corporations, and other brokers of power, an even more insidious means of wielding control over "the people" than traditional uses of power. Infant formula, by all appearances, seemed like a technology that could help dry mothers or orphaned babies. Instead, it led to costly

---

23. Snead, "Foreign Missionary," 3–4.

24. For "materialistic profit culture," see "Peoples Christian Coalition—Newsletter No. 1" (July 1971), in Box VII7, Folder "People's Christian Coalition—Trinity," Sojourners Collection, Wheaton College Special Collections, Wheaton, Illinois. For "we are controlled," see Sparks, "The End of Affluence," 7; and Sparks, "The American Condition," Box 2, CWLF Collection, Graduate Theological Union Archives, Berkeley, California.

dependence on American companies, which remained intent on increasing their consumer base abroad. The ties between technology and big business led an egalitarian, anti-liberal movement of New Leftists to despair about "the technocracy," a term used with regularity on several evangelical campuses and in the Post-American and Other Side communities. Fed by New Left sociology (and by a fundamentalist distrust of big government; skepticism of science and rationality; and faith in the efficacy of prayer, healing, and other divine interventions), young evangelicals preached against what most observers have seen as elements universally supported by evangelicals and the New Right: big business and technology.[25]

These two elements, contended evangelical radicals, necessarily resulted in a third: American imperialism. Though fortified by a booming economy and new technologies, the tremendous appetites of corporations required ever-expanding markets that spilled outside American borders. The United States, Wallis contended, nurtured an "expansionist thrust." He drew this connection between economic growth and American imperialism from the scholarship of New Left historians, especially William Appleman Williams. Some evangelical radicals read Williams' *Tragedy of American Diplomacy*, a revisionist history that characterized American internationalism as empire-building more than the spread of freedom. The Post-Americans added Gabriel Kolko's *Roots of American Foreign Policy* and M. J. Pusey's *USA Astride the Globe* to their assigned readings for community seminars. American attempts to contain communism and spread democracy around the world, they maintained, did not truly democratize the world but rather betrayed an attempt to solidify imperial dominance.[26]

Richard Barnet, a State Department official in the Kennedy administration who attended Church of the Savior in Washington and served as a contributing editor to the *Post-American*, offered evangelicals a glimpse into the maneuverings of high-level diplomacy. He described how American-dominated multinational corporations favored non-democratic regimes because of "the good investment climate" that strong military dictators often delivered. In fact, Barnet argued, the US government, when American investments were at stake, explicitly preferred authoritarian over

---

25. *Right On*, "The Revolutionary Catechism," 2; Pannell, "Evangelicals and the Social Crisis," 11. On the "technocracy," see Dennis, "The Counterculture," 15–19, 36–37; Dennis, *Reason for Hope*, 126–53.

26. For "expansionist thrust," see Wallis, "Invisible Empire," 1; Williams, *The Tragedy of American Diplomacy*. For young evangelical citations of Williams, see "Bibliography: People's Christian Coalition, November 1971," Box VII7, Folder "Peoples Christian Coalition Trinity," in Sojourners Collection, WCSC; Moore, "Mission as Subversion," 6; Carlson, "Angola: Caught in Between," 6; and Reese, "Structure of Power," 8–9.

unstable democratic governments. In its efforts to expand markets overseas, the United States turned into a "homicidal menace for millions of innocent people of Indochina." Barnet called the impersonal killing of foreign enemies through new technologies and divisions of labor "bureaucratic homicide." Too many layers of management separated the president in the White House from soldiers in the jungles of Vietnam. Barnet, who contended that an ideological mask of anticommunism obscured an intrinsic capitalist expansionism, later made Nixon's infamous "enemies list." Drinking deep from the wells of revisionist history and New Left sociology, some of the more militant young evangelicals eyed conspiracy at the highest levels of the United States government.[27]

A more conventional evangelical left made inroads into moderate sectors of evangelicalism. Senator Mark Hatfield, a Republican from Oregon, accused the State and Agriculture departments of offering famine relief on the basis of where the US could create future markets to sell American products. After attending a world conference in Rome, he contended that world hunger threatened global stability more than a weapons imbalance with the Soviet Union. Politicians and government bureaucrats still insisted on a massive budget for national defense, Hatfield lamented, presumably under the illusion that military spending could spark a boom economy. For a decade, from the mid-sixties to the mid-seventies, the Wheaton College student newspaper and InterVarsity Christian Fellowship's magazine printed more articles critical of US foreign policy and corporations than articles in support of them. As these statements suggest, instinctive criticisms of American imperialism coalesced around several key international issues— US intervention in Vietnam and Central America, sponsorship of repressive regimes in Latin America, and apartheid in South Africa. Younger moderate evangelicals in the United States comprised a minority political voice that nonetheless sounded often and insistently.[28]

Of the many evangelical statements on global injustice, Ron Sider's 1977 book *Rich Christians in an Age of Hunger* was by far the most influential. Readers of *Rich Christians*, which opened with the sentence "Hunger and starvation stalk the land," found the book a dark one. "Ten thousand persons died today," intoned Sider, "because of inadequate food. One billion people are mentally retarded or physically deformed because of a poor diet. The problem, we know, is that the world's resources are not

27. On Barnet's evangelical connections, see Holley, "Richard J. Barnet Dies," B6; B.B., "Before You Vote," 4; Wallis, "The Issue of 1972," 2–3. For "the good investment climate," see *Wittenburg Door*, "Door Interview," 17. For "bureaucratic homicide," see Barnet, *Roots of War*, 3–23.

28. Hatfield, "On World Hunger," 4; Wallis, "Invisible Empire," 1.

evenly distributed. North Americans live on an affluent island amid a sea of starving humanity." The perpetuation of current American policy, explained Sider, would lead the world toward global economic collapse. Sider's overarching tone, however, carried a moral rather than economic edge. Evangelicals shouldn't merely take action to avoid economic collapse, he wrote; they should take action because Christians have a moral obligation to right injustices. Sider complained that they all too often failed to do so because of an inadequate conception of sin. "Christians frequently restrict the scope of ethics to a narrow class of 'personal' sins," he explained. "But they fail to preach about the sins of institutionalized racism, unjust economic structures and militaristic institutions which destroy people just as much as do alcohol and drugs." "If God's Word is true, then all of us who dwell in affluent nations are trapped in sin," Sider concluded. "We have profited from systematic injustice.... We are guilty of an outrageous offense against God and neighbor." Sider's incorporation of the language of sin offered a uniquely evangelical contribution to broader debates on global poverty. Remarkably, the book also sold well. Despite its depressing tone and scathing indictment, by 1997 it had gone through four editions and sold more than 350,000 copies. It also drew the fire of politically conservative evangelicals such as David Chilton, who wrote a rejoinder entitled *Productive Christians in an Age of Guilt Manipulators*.[29]

International evangelicals contributed to the domestic evangelical left's denunciations of American cultural, economic, and political imperialism. At the Billy Graham–sponsored Lausanne Congress on World Evangelization, René Padilla, a theologian from Ecuador, accused North American Christians of explicitly promoting "the American Way of Life" abroad. Recalling how Christian mission work in Africa and Asia was so closely connected with colonialism, Padilla said, "We have equated 'Americanism' with Christianity to such an extent that we are tempted to believe that people in other cultures must adopt American institutional patterns when they are converted." The conflation of theological orthodoxy with socioeconomic and political conservatism harms the Christian witness overseas, he continued. "At least in Latin America today, the evangelist

---

29. Sider, *Rich Christians*, 172. For "trapped in sin," see Stafford, "Ron Sider's Unsettling Crusade," 18–22. Miriam Adeney similarly contended, "The marvel of the US standard of living, made possible by the systematic rape of the raw materials of developing countries, enforced by unequal trade treaties with a local opulent oligarchy" (*God's Foreign Policy*, 67). For a conservative critique of Sider, see Chilton, *Productive Christians*.

often has to face innumerable prejudices that reflect the identification of Americanism with the Gospel."[30]

The debate over the Panama Canal marked a high point of antipathy toward American imperialism. In a 1977 "Open Letter to North American Christians," Puerto Rican Orlando Costas of the Latin American Theological Fraternity and seven other evangelical leaders lambasted North Americans for their "ignorance, greed, and ethnocentrism." Arguing that the United States had stolen, not bought, the canal, these Latin American critics maintained that the United States had cut fees for American companies at the expense of Panama. They condemned Reagan's rhetoric and persistent colonialism in Latin America, charging that "your precious 'American Way of Life' . . . feeds in no small proportion on the blood which gushes 'from the open veins of Latin America.'" Members of InterVarsity's International Fellowship of Evangelical Students in Costa Rica wrote,

> Panama has waited patiently while you procrastinated in the renegotiation of the treaty through the years of Vietnam, Watergate, and the recent elections. You condemn the relics of colonialism in Rhodesia and South Africa. Why are you so slow to see the "beam in your own eye"? During the construction of the canal more than 25,000 poor laborers from the Third World laid down their lives on the altar of the First World economic development—yet your politicians have the gall to boast "we built it"! Your senators have been swamped with letters from citizens blinded by ignorance, greed, and ethnocentrism. We exhort you as brothers and sisters in Christ to write your senators today, indicating your support for the new treaty as a step toward justice for Panama and better relations with all Latin America.

In a similar "Letter of Tears to North American Christians," evangelical leaders across Latin America complained that "your precious 'American way of life,' the opulence of your magnates, and your economic and military dominion, feeds on the blood which gushes from the open veins of Latin America." Moderate and progressive leaders in North America published these letters in many of the most prominent evangelical magazines.[31]

30. Padilla, "Evangelism and the World," 125.

31. "An Open Letter to North American Christians," *Vanguard* (January-February 1977) 4–5. A similar statement came from a Chilean student: "As a Chilean Christian I have cried many times out of disappointment at the lack of interest and active concern of American Evangelical Christians here in the USA for what this country's foreign policy has done, and is doing, in other countries in the name of justice." Buastavino, "Letters to the Editor," 2. For another criticism of US policy regarding the Panama

American missionaries, seeing their home country in the context of the world, also pushed back. Barbara Benjamin, a young missionary from New York City, encountered the vagaries of American economic markets and foreign policy in Ecuador. Her neighborhood in the grimy port city of Quito was stricken with poverty after US-owned fruit giants United Brands and Chiquita pulled out of the region. American attempts in the 1960s to strengthen the Latin American economy through the Alliance for Progress, she observed, "never touched the masses." Benjamin explained, "They had a ridiculous policy of working only through government channels, so the money was greedily devoured by opportunists. Political expedience determined how money flowed." Inept US policy, she concluded, had resulted in 50 percent unemployment for men in her neighborhood, naked children whose families could not afford clothing, and hostility toward the United States.[32]

Encountering evangelical apathy to these conditions upon her return to the United States in the mid-1970s angered Benjamin. "You cannot separate social concerns and evangelism," she wrote in an article read by tens of thousands of InterVarsity students. Railing against "middle-class gentry out in suburbia-land [who] talk about illegal aliens," she urged students to move to cities where they could follow "God's mandate to take the Gospel to the poor." She also urged political activism: "Christian churches must become centers of action. We need to exercise a stronger prophetic voice to our culture, speaking up against the sins and shortcomings of our society. When I read the Old Testament, I become convinced that our churches need to be addressing the president, the Congress, and all those in high places." She continued, "The prophets spoke out loudly and plainly. We must too—more than we do. We can't just sit and mutter, 'But they'll call me a liberal.' Let them call you a liberal—let them call you a Communist if they have to—but speak up! I believe there's a real moral majority out there that will hear us and respond."[33]

Benjamin's notion of a "moral majority" did not materialize in the way she expected. She expected internationalist dissent to build. Indeed,

---

Canal from a professor at Seminario Biblico Latinamericano in San Jose, Costa Rica, see Leggett, "Panama Canal: Three Myths." The United States, wrote Leggett, did not buy the canal; rather, it "imposed its will on the new republic of Panama by means of a treaty in which the peoples affected had no say." For more examples of anti-American literature from Seminario Biblico Latinamericano, see Tamez, *Bible of the Oppressed*. For "Panama has waited patiently," see "Letter from Central America," *Sojourners* 6 (November 1977) 9. See Bonilla et al., "A Letter of Tears to North American Christians," Folder "Discipleship Workshops," Evangelicals for Social Action Archives.

32. Benjamin, "Immigrant Love," 13.

33. Benjamin, *Impossible Community*, 33–35; Benjamin, "Immigrant Love," 13.

in a political environment before below-the-belt issues pushed evangelicals toward the Republican Party, it seemed possible to critique American consumption and capitalist beneficence, especially as moderate American evangelicals joined international evangelicals to question the notion that freeing souls and people required free enterprise.

In the late 1970s, however, Jerry Falwell and Pat Robertson emerged. Disenchanted with Jimmy Carter's presidency, they engineered an alliance with Ronald Reagan and the Republican Party. Though internationalist dissent would not disappear, the Moral Majority represented a reenergized Christian Americanism that sought to win Cold War sites around the world. Falwell, for example, denounced opponents of apartheid in South Africa. He called Desmond Tutu a "phony" and suggested that Nelson Mandela might be a communist stooge. In 1985, he urged Americans to reinvest in South African business, not sanction it. This was an approach, said Robert Walker, a US representative from Pennsylvania, that fit the Cold War context. He said, "You have a longstanding position among American conservatives in support of South Africa, nearly a carte blanche attitude that says, 'Whatever they do is acceptable because it is a nation that is friendly to the West and has great strategic value to us.'" Dodging issues of race, the Moral Majority promoted an expansionist economics and strong national security as a way of promoting Christian interests abroad.[34]

A burgeoning prosperity gospel movement also contributed to the persistence of Christian Americanism. Incurable Pentecostal optimism and individualism meshed with the consumer culture of advanced capitalism to feed expansion. Adherents maintained that God chooses people and nations, most especially Israel and the United States, as instruments of divine purpose. As Richard Pierard writes, they felt a "deep sense of national 'chosenness' that was part and parcel of American civil religion, which during its postwar revival was being linked in a transcendent fashion to the world Christian mission." The Cold War, which fused evangelical missionary activity, global neoliberal capitalism, and US military engagement, set the American agenda until the Soviet Union's demise in 1989. Victory in the war against Marxism fueled America's sense of chosenness even more. Material wealth and success, after all, are signs of God's blessing. The entrepreneurial legacy of Christian Americanism, newly invigorated by the prosperity gospel, has continued well into the twenty-first century.[35]

---

34. For Falwell and Walker, see Pear, "Falwell Denounces Tutu." On the evangelical turn from Carter to Reagan, see Swartz, *Moral Minority*, 213–32.

35. Bowler, *Blessed*; Pierard, *"Pax Americana,"* 164–65.

Conclusion

In 2017, Donald Trump was inaugurated as president of the United States. Polls showed that 81 percent of White evangelicals voted for him. Even considering evangelical antipathy toward the despised Hillary Clinton, even considering numerous cultural Christians who self-identify as evangelical but do not practice traditional standards of piety, even considering high concern for below-the-belt domestic issues like abortion, the numbers were stark—and frankly threatened the notion that progressive American and Majority World evangelicals had successfully redirected the movement away from Christian Americanism. White evangelicals voted for "America first." Public liturgies—such as Robert Jeffress' anthem "Make America Great Again," performed on the stage of the Kennedy Center in 2017—continued to implicate evangelicalism's complicity in empire.

These poll numbers, however, tell only part of the story. They do not count African-American evangelicals or large numbers of Latino, Asian, and African immigrants. Nor do they include many younger evangelicals, who typically are underrepresented in polls. Robert P. Jones describes high numbers of older evangelicals who sound the "death rattle of a white Christian America"—but also high numbers of younger evangelicals opposing Trump's candidacy. Moreover, most White evangelical elites resisted the Trump wave. In addition to historic peace churches, dozens of evangelical groups seek to disentangle strands of business, the church, and the military. Despite its superpatriotic, corporate-friendly reputation, evangelicalism also contains a pacific germ. It is possible that the dominant strain of Christian Americanism that has pervaded evangelicalism over the last eighty years may be seen someday as a historical anomaly. Evangelical ethicists who proffer trenchant critiques of the military-industrial complex, however, do not represent a vast grassroots subculture. There is a fundamental divide between cosmopolitan evangelicals associated with *Christianity Today*, the National Association of Evangelicals, many mission agencies, and evangelical universities and seminaries, and those who have had less opportunity to be shaped by global encounters and educational opportunities.[36]

Whatever the future of evangelical discourse over business and war, the persistence of Christian Americanism reflects what Scott Appleby calls "the ambivalence of the sacred." Drawing from Rudolph Otto, who describes the experience of the sacred as *"mysterium tremendum et fascinans,"* Appleby suggests that some religious people respond to soul-shaking encounters with

---

36. On nonwhite opposition to empire, see Padilla and Scott, *Terrorism and the War in Iraq*; Noll, *The Scandal of the Evangelical Mind*. For "death rattle," see Jones, *End of White Christian America*, 248.

the divine by seeking reconciliation, compassion, and martyrdom. Others are moved toward violence. Evangelicalism marshals each impulse in its use of redemptive violence to free souls, free people, and free enterprise from tyranny.[37]

---

37. Otto, *The Idea of the Holy*; Appleby, *The Ambivalence of the Sacred*.

5

The Business of War in Latin America

MATTHEW PHILIPP WHELAN

By their eloquent and attractive example of a life completely transfigured by the splendor of moral truth, the martyrs and, in general, all the Church's Saints, light up every period of history by reawakening its moral sense.

—POPE ST. JOHN PAUL II, *VERITATIS SPLENDOR*

Introduction

This chapter looks for clues regarding the functional and ideological interdependence of economics and warfare by examining Latin America's Cold War and the US's involvement in it. That the region is still reckoning with the legacy of this period can be seen, among other places, in the proliferation of truth commissions since,[1] as well as ongoing debates

1. Truth commissions are official bodies tasked to investigate human rights violations, war crimes, or other abuses. They try to identify causes and consequences and tend to conclude with an official report. The truth commission for El Salvador, for instance, was mandated by the UN-brokered peace agreement that ended the civil war, and it presented its report, *From Madness to Hope: The 12-Year War in El Salvador; Report of the Commission on the Truth for El Salvador*, in 1993. For more on

about amnesty for perpetrators of war crimes.[2] For example, in early 2016, a US judge approved the extradition of Inocente Orlando Montano Morales, a former colonel, to face charges in Spain for his role in the slaying of six Jesuit priests, their housekeeper, and her daughter in El Salvador in 1989.[3] Later that same year, El Salvador's supreme court struck down an amnesty law enacted after the civil war, making possible prosecutions for crimes committed in that country during the war.[4]

Because the history of the US's interventions in Latin America runs so deep, a thoroughgoing examination of this subject is well beyond the scope of this essay. As Greg Grandin notes, between the mid-nineteenth and early twentieth century alone, "Washington had sent gunboats into Latin American ports over six thousand times, invaded Mexico (again), Guatemala, and Honduras, fought protracted guerilla wars in the Dominican Republic, Nicaragua, and Haiti, annexed Puerto Rico, and taken a piece of Colombia to create both the Panamanian nation and the Panama Canal." Moreover, US corporations were intimately involved in this process, exercising a powerful influence upon economies throughout Latin America.[5] The historians Steven C. Topik and Allen Wells refer to this time as "the second conquest of Latin America," a phrase they use to describe the impact of the region's integration into the world economy through the export of raw materials and the role of US and other corporations in this process of extraction and integration.[6]

After an interlude beginning in the early 1930s, during which time the US briefly abandoned its militarism, with President Franklin D. Roosevelt famously assuring his neighbors to the south that the US would heretofore be a "good neighbor" and respect their sovereignty, forswear unilateral interventions, and make concessions, US militarism resumed with a vengeance. But during the Cold War, it appeared under a different guise: it was especially employed in the fight against communism. Indeed,

---

truth commissions in Latin America, see May, "'La verdad' y comisiones de la verdad," 494–512.

2. Ratner and Abrams, *Accountability*; Kornbluh, *The Pinochet File*.

3. See Associated Press, "US Judge Approves Extradition." See also Reuters, "El Salvador Will Cooperate." Most of the priests were originally from Spain, which is the reason the trials are there.

4. Maslin, "El Salvador Strikes Down Amnesty." Relatedly, Matt Eisenbrandt, a lawyer for the San Francisco–based Center for Justice and Accountability, has recently detailed the extraordinary difficulty and risk involved in finding and trying those involved in the killing of Archbishop Óscar Romero in March 1980. Eisenbrandt, *Assassination of a Saint*.

5. Grandin, *Empire's Workshop*, 3.

6. Topik and Wells, *The Second Conquest*.

from the vantage of US policymakers and others, Latin America became a crucial front in the battle between the US and the USSR, capitalism and communism, freedom and tyranny, Judeo-Christian civilization and atheism.

With the hindsight of nearly thirty years, it now seems that perhaps the biggest problem with the US's "reading" of Latin America through the lens of its war against the communists was a misapprehension of the threat the USSR posed there. To be clear, the USSR certainly did pose a threat to US geopolitical interests, especially in Cuba, and the standoff over nuclear-armed Soviet missiles on the island brought the world to the brink of nuclear war. "Marxism and the Cuban example were very influential; that was no figment of the US State Department's imagination," writes John Charles Chasteen. The problem, as Chasteen points out, is that the US tended to view reformers of all sorts, whether Marxist or not in inspiration, as Soviet proxies. Moreover, it is also important to note that even those reformers who were truly Marxists were not organized or financially supported by the USSR. "There simply were no Soviet proxy guerilla forces in Latin America," Chasteen concludes.[7]

What also seems clearer in retrospect is that this misapprehension led to intractable difficulties on the part of US leaders and policymakers in distinguishing between the USSR's presence and influence, on the one hand, and popular and homegrown movements of social reform, on the other. During the Cold War, Latin America was among the most unequal regions in the world (and still is),[8] and elites often fought to retain privilege and property by branding opponents communist and courting US support against them in the form of armaments and military training. Consequently, as Lesley Gill observes, "fighting 'communists'" became "an enormously elastic category that could accommodate almost any critic of the status quo."[9] The category was so elastic, as we will see below, that it expanded to

---

7. Chasteen, *Born in Blood*, 275. As Stephen G. Rabe and others have documented, the USSR tended to regard Latin America, and the Western Hemisphere as a whole, as the US's sphere of influence. Other than in Castro's Cuba, then, the USSR's involvement in the region was limited—or, at least, far less involved than the overblown rhetoric of civilizational war and falling dominoes would seem to suggest. See Rabe, *Killing Zone*, xxxvi. Along these same lines, Piero Gleijeses' archival research in Cuba recently uncovered how communist leaders in that country focused on inciting revolution in Africa rather than Latin America for fear of coming face to face with US military might. See Gleijeses, *Conflicting Missions*.

8. Güereña, "Unearthed: Land, Power and Inequality in Latin America."

9. Gill, *School of the Americas*, 10. As Benjamin Cowan persuasively argues, anticommunism in Brazil and elsewhere extended far beyond ideological opposition to Marxism, subsuming anxieties about gender and sex as well (Cowan, *Securing Sex*).

include proponents of the social teaching of the Catholic Church, who in El Salvador and elsewhere advocated for better access to private property in land on the part of the landless and land-poor.[10]

Reflection upon this period, during which time the US formed alliances with dictators, organized coups, and supported security forces that unleashed violence on a massive scale, is important for understanding contemporary Latin America and many of its struggles. As I argue in this chapter, it also offers insight into linkages between economics and warfare—linkages that endure and that are crucial for learning to see the region as what Grandin calls "a workshop for empire."[11] The focus of this chapter, however, is more limited still, exploring two pivotal episodes in the formation and hardening of these linkages: first, the covert coup d'état orchestrated by the CIA in Guatemala in 1954, which deposed a democratically elected leader, installed the first in a long series of authoritarian rulers in his place, and established a new pattern for the US's presence in the region; and second, the founding of the Alliance for Progress and its vision of progress, which fused economic development and warmaking against communism.

In both cases, we see the business of war at work—and not only in the use of war, or the threat of war, to protect business, that is, trade, commerce, profitmaking, and so on. We also see subtler forms of this business that emerged in the fight against communism and the building up of an apparatus of repression that was systematically employed against the Latin American people. At the same time, as we explore the business of war and its contribution to a deeply rooted pedagogy of death,[12] we will also encounter signs of resistance and the presence of a counter-pedagogy of peace and life. To this end, the epigraph above from Pope St. John Paul II

10. For more on this point, see Whelan, *Blood in the Fields* (forthcoming).

11. In Grandin's words, "Reagan's Central American wars can best be understood as a dress rehearsal for what is going on now in the Middle East [the book was published in 2007]. It was in these wars where the coalition made up of neo-conservatives, Christian evangelicals, free marketers, and nationalists that today stands behind George W. Bush's expansive foreign policy first came together." Grandin, *Empire's Workshop*, 5. Additionally, the products of this workshop would later be exported elsewhere, for instance, in the application of the so-called Salvadoran Option—an approach to counterinsurgency warfare during the civil war in El Salvador in the 1980s, which utilized death squad terror—to the quagmire in Iraq. See Mahmood et al., "From El Salvador to Iraq"; Buncombe and Cockburn,"Iraq's Death Squads."

12. The phrase *pedagogía de la muerte* ("pedagogy of death") is from Escobar Alas, *Veo en la ciudad violencia y discordia*. In his pastoral letter, Escobar Alas, the sitting archbishop of San Salvador, describes this pedagogy as a process whereby people are taught by example "how to kill, whom to kill, by what means and for which reasons to kill" (24). He traces its roots to the so-called conquest of the Americas and its ramifications over subsequent centuries.

points to a criterion for the evaluation of history and the illumination of its moral sense, which is the lives of the martyrs. Following this suggestion, this chapter concludes with a reflection upon the fact that there are now martyrs of the church among the countless victims of this period, which presses the question, how should we approach the business of war in Latin America given that one of its products is martyrdom?

The Business of War in Guatemala

In many ways, we can discern a turning point in US attitudes toward Latin America beginning in 1950, with the Department of State's declaration that "the cold war is in fact a real war in which the survival of the free world is at stake." This declaration undergirded the "containment" strategy inaugurated under President Truman and carried through to the end of the Cold War. As a result, Congress substantially increased direct military assistance to the region over the ensuing decade and began to foster and strengthen regimes that opposed communism, even authoritarian ones.[13] Around this same time, George Kennan, one of the architects of US containment policy, by which the US sought to stop the spread of communism, enumerated US interests in Latin America in the following terms: "(1) The protection of our raw materials, (2) The prevention of military exploitation of Latin America by the enemy . . ."[14]

The list continues, but these two objectives top it, and they are closely tied. Kennan's use of the plural possessive for the first is as important as it is indicative. Observe how it is the raw materials of the US that need protecting, with Latin America figured as the field for their production. Kennan's words signal the US's considerable economic interests in the region as an export market and a site of investment.[15] They also point to the US's role in a much longer story in which, in the words of Eduardo Galeano, Latin America "continues to work at the service of others' needs, as a source and reserve of oil and iron, of copper and meat, of fruit and coffee, the raw materials and foods destined for rich countries that profit more from consuming them than Latin America does from producing them."[16]

The sentiment Kennan expresses is commonplace in the US's policy toward and popular imagination of Latin America. What heightens anxiety about communism's spread, as well the extremity of the measures

13. Smith, *Talons of the Eagle*, 126; Bethell and Roxborough, *Latin America*, 25–27.
14. Smith, *Talons of the Eagle*, 126.
15. Smith, *Talons of the Eagle*, 123–24.
16. Galeano, *Open Veins of Latin America*, 1.

taken to defeat it, is not just the nature of the enemy and the ideological and existential threat it poses but also its presence—or, more accurately, the fear of its potential presence—in "our own backyard," as the political scientist William LeoGrande puts it.[17] Throughout his book of the same name, LeoGrande primarily uses this idiom to signal the proximity of the communist threat to US shores. It was one thing to take the fight to the enemy, as the US did in Vietnam, when the enemy was twelve thousand miles away in a foreign and mysterious land. But Latin America, he writes, "was our backyard."[18] Observe here, too, a subtler but still unmistakable sense of possession signaled by the phrase, which expands to include both the raw materials and also the territory as a whole. The threat, after all, is not in our neighbor's backyard, but ours. The logic points to how a sense of possession over raw materials and the territory of their production merge with warmaking—in this case, to stop communism's infiltration of Latin America. In short, we see the conjunction of economics and warmaking in the sense of their simultaneous occurrence, as well as their profound ideological interpenetration.

An examination of what happened in Guatemala in 1954, when the CIA initiated its first, full-scale covert operation in Latin America in order to unseat the Guatemalan president Jacobo Árbenz, offers a microcosm of this problematic. Catholic Christians who were engaged in a concerted effort to implement the church's social doctrine regarding agrarian reform were misconstrued as communists. But first, some background. During the Cold War, the rationale behind US support of right-wing military dictatorships was that they were best equipped and most willing to confront and defeat the communist menace. Another reason was to protect US investments and business interests. With openings to democracy came calls for better wages and working conditions through the formation of labor and other protective organizations.

Throughout the region, agrarian reform in particular became a flashpoint. It sought to address the problem of vast inequalities in landholdings through a more just distribution of land. However, to the eyes of US policymakers, labor unrest and communism proved difficult to disentangle. Such unrest was either a sign of communism's presence or it cultivated the conditions for its spread. To the eyes of US corporations with holdings in the region, it threatened the bottom line.[19]

17. LeoGrande, *Our Own Backyard*.
18. LeoGrande, *Our Own Backyard*, 10.
19. Grandin, *Empire's Workshop*, 41–42.

When Árbenz assumed the presidency of Guatemala in 1951, the centerpiece of his reform agenda was an agrarian reform law, known as Decree 900, which called for the elimination of *latifundia* (large landed estates); the redistribution of unused land; and the provision of land, credit, and technical assistance to the landless and land-poor, with previous owners indemnified.[20] Its purpose was to break the hold of the oligarchy on Guatemalan rural life and return land to those who farmed it. At the time, 2 percent of landowners controlled 72 percent of Guatemalan land, with 88 percent holding only 14 percent.[21] Although Árbenz was not communist himself, his collaborators in the design and implementation of the reforms were members of the Communist Party of Guatemala.[22]

Among the lands targeted for expropriation were some held by the United Fruit Company (UFC—present-day Chiquita Brands International), the Boston-based corporation involved in banana production on Central and South American plantations. The UFC was the largest landowner and employer in Guatemala at the time, but with only a small fraction of its extensive landholdings under cultivation.[23] The company was known locally as *El Pulpo* (The Octopus) because its tentacles infiltrated all aspects of Guatemalan life. The company also had close ties to powerful figures in President Eisenhower's administration. Secretary of State John Foster Dulles and the director of the CIA, Allen Dulles, had a long-standing relationship with the UFC, doing legal work for them and even possessing substantial stock options in the company.[24] The Eisenhower administration regarded Árbenz's reform as a plot to align Guatemala with the Soviet bloc and to further what John Foster Dulles called "the communist infiltration in Guatemala."[25]

In what unfolded in Guatemala, we encounter the business of war in Latin America in both the senses described above. First, the US employs war to protect the interests of the UFC. Of course, this sense of war's business is not unique but part of a much older story, which long predates

---

20. Piero Gleijeses has called the reform the most successful in the history of Central America. Gleijeses, "Agrarian Reform," 453.

21. Rabe, *Killing Zone*, 39. As Rabe points out, at the time Louis Hale of the State Department's Latin American Division challenged the notion that the Árbenz administration or its reform was communist.

22. Gleijeses, "Agrarian Reform," 453; Rabe, *Killing Zone*, 44.

23. Wittman and Saldivar-Tanaka, "Agrarian Question in Guatemala," 29, citing statistics from Deere and León, *Mujer y tierra*.

24. Kinzer, *Brothers*, 101–2, 148–51.

25. On the close ties between UFC and the Eisenhower administration, see Schoultz, *Beneath the United States*, 337–38.

the Cold War. Its roots sink deep into the first conquest of the Americas and ramify through the second, and it will continue long after the Cold War ends.[26] But in Guatemala, a new and consequential variant begins to emerge, which complexly relates to the US's fight against communism and the logic of Eisenhower's "falling domino principle" as it is extended to Latin America.[27] This implies another sense of war's business: an activity and its rationale. In this case, the business of war is stopping communism from spreading to the US's backyard, along with the panoply of tools employed to ensure it does not.

In response to the expropriation of UFC lands, the Eisenhower administration tasked the CIA with organizing, arming, and training the opposition to Árbenz in neighboring Honduras, an operation known as PBSUCCESS.[28] In June 1954, forces under the command of Colonel Carlos Castillo Armas crossed into Guatemala, deposed Árbenz and sent him into exile. They installed Castillo Armas in his place, the first of a long series of US-backed military regimes that would govern Guatemala for four decades. Among the first tasks of Castillo Armas was to reverse the agrarian reform and annul the expropriations. Less than two years into his time in office, Castillo Armas had successfully evicted almost all the beneficiaries under Árbenz's agrarian reform from their lands.[29] For his part, Eisenhower continued to look to what had happened in Guatemala with pride, which, as he once put it to CIA operatives, "averted a Soviet beachhead in our hemisphere."[30]

The US's intervention in Guatemala in 1954 was a watershed, solidifying the linkages between both senses of the business of war and also establishing an enduring pattern for subsequent US involvement in the region and in the world.[31] In Guatemala, we also see the considerable elasticity of the label communist as well as the cost of reading Latin America through the lens of the fight against it. For in this case, the label included those who argued

---

26. Grandin traces in considerable detail how a "militarized and moralized" version of capitalism that develops during Latin America's Cold War is deployed after it ends. Grandin, *Empire's Workshop*, 159–95.

27. As Eisenhower himself explained in a famous 1954 press conference about Indochina, "You have a row of dominoes set up, and what will happen to the last one is the certainty that it will go over very quickly." Quoted in Schoultz, *Beneath the United States*, 343.

28. For more on Operation PBSUCCESS, see Cullather, *Operation PBSUCCESS*; Cullather, *Secret History*; Schlesinger and Kinzer, *Bitter Fruit*.

29. Schlesinger and Kinzer, *Bitter Fruit*, 221; Alarcón, *Problemática de la tierra*.

30. Rabe, *Eisenhower and Latin America*, 60–61.

31. Blum, *Killing Hope*.

not for the abolition of private property, which is the orthodox communist view,[32] but who were drawing on Catholic social teaching to argue for its proliferation. To be sure, Archbishop Rossell y Arellano and much of the church's visible leadership articulated concerns about the reform being communist and anti-Christian—a threat to the right to private property and part of the introduction of impiety and licentiousness into the nation.[33] Rossell y Arellano reportedly claimed that the devil himself "was stalking the countryside" disguised as an agrarian reformer.[34]

But as Anita Frankel has documented, the Árbenz administration did not respond to these accusations by opposing the church, whose members, after all, populated the government itself. Instead, the government responded to the charge that the agrarian reform was communist by advocating for it on the basis of church teaching itself. The highly skewed distribution of property in Guatemala and the effort to address it through Decree 900 was an attempt, the government argued in an extensive media campaign, to implement church teaching. The implication was clear: it was not the government but the most visible representatives of the church that had misconstrued church teaching.[35]

Along these lines, a book by Tulio Benites is especially noteworthy. Entitled *Meditaciones de un católico ante la reforma de Guatemala* (*Meditations of a Catholic in the face of the agrarian reform of Guatemala*; hereafter *Meditations*), the book was published in 1952 as part of a series put out by the Ministry of Public Education. It was written to address the misunderstandings of those like Rossell y Arellano who presented the agrarian reform as "a war against religion," or those like the president of the Asociación General de Agricultores (General Association of Agriculturalists [AGA]) who thought that in response to Decree 900, it was necessary to rally in defense of "God, Nation, and Family."[36] Over the course of *Meditations*, Benites argues that in labeling the reform communist, its opponents demonstrate a profound misunderstanding of communism.[37]

32. Marx and Engels, *The Communist Manifesto*.

33. Benites, *Meditaciones de un católico*, 11. All translations of quotations from Benites' *Meditaciones* are my own.

34. Gleijeses, *Shattered Hope*, 211.

35. Frankel argues along these lines in Frankel, "Political Development in Guatemala," 233–35. Benites does the same in Benites, *Meditaciones de un católico*.

36. Benites, *Meditaciones de un católico*, 11.

37. Decree 900 differs in important ways, Benites thinks, from Lenin's understanding of agrarian revolution. For instance, lands in Guatemala are being expropriated with indemnification, not confiscated. According to Lenin, indemnification was contrary to agrarian communist revolution. Moreover, Decree 900 has been designed to help those that work the land own it. Benites, *Meditaciones de un católico*, 15, 91–101.

More fundamentally still, they also contradict "the teachings of Holy Mother Catholic Church."[38] In short, they do not defend church teaching but rather defend "the landholders who hold the vast majority of the cultivable lands of Guatemala."[39] For, according to Benites, Catholicism does not condone the defense of the established disorder but, above all, stands for "compassion for the dispossessed and defenseless, charity for the needy, love of neighbor."[40]

Much of *Meditations* examines Catholic social teaching and its understanding of "access to property for all, a better distribution of land."[41] Benites focuses especially on Leo XIII's *Rerum Novarum*, Pius XI's *Quadragesimo Anno*, and the thought of the Belgian Cardinal Désiré-Félicien-François-Joseph Mercier. As Benites suggests, the real problem is the church in Guatemala's inadequate understanding of its own social teaching. Rather than seeing the evident resonances between it and Decree 900, church leaders have instead construed Decree 900 and agrarian reform more generally as the work of the anti-Christ.[42]

Among the most interesting features of *Meditations* is the way Benites situates the concerns underlying agrarian reform in relation to the Spanish colonization of the Americas, what Walter Mignolo calls "the colonial wound."[43] This is a much older story of war's business in this region of the world. Benites begins and ends *Meditations* with an extended reflection upon the sixteenth-century Dominican friar Bartolomé de las Casas and his Dominican confrères—Antonio de Montesinos, Pedro de Córdoba, Bernardo de Santo Domingo, and Domingo de Villamayor—and their opposition to the *encomienda* system.[44] Of the original inhabitants of these lands, those who were not decimated were dispossessed and then entrusted (*encomendada*) to the Spanish *encomenderos*.[45] Las Casas therefore worked for the abolishment of the *encomienda* system itself, which he viewed as a kind of slavery under the guise of Christian catechesis, and for the return of the usurped lands to those to whom they belonged. "Although they [the indigenous inhabitants of these lands] be outside the faith of Christ," he reasoned, "neither are nor ought [they] to be deprived of their freedom or dominion over their goods. Indeed, they may freely and licitly use, possess,

---

38. Benites, *Meditaciones de un católico*, 12.
39. Benites, *Meditaciones de un católico*, 12.
40. Benites, *Meditaciones de un católico*, 101.
41. Benites, *Meditaciones de un católico*, 79.
42. Benites, *Meditaciones de un católico*, 61–91, 104–5.
43. Mignolo, *The Idea of Latin America*.
44. Benites, *Meditaciones de un católico*, 15–16, 20–61, 101.
45. Benites, *Meditaciones de un católico*, 18, 29–35.

and enjoy freedom and such dominion and must not be reduced to slavery."[46] Las Casas, Benites observes, was also considered an anti-Christ in his own day for relentlessly advocating that the Spaniards "return the lands, goods, mines, and treasures they robbed in an unjust war."[47]

According to Benites, Guatemala's contemporary landscape is a palimpsest, bearing the traces of the past. To read it rightly is to see it in relation to the history whose marks are still visible upon it. For instance, in many estates, Benites observes, the current landowners are the heirs of the Spanish *encomenderos* themselves, and the *campesinos* are the descendants of those who were once entrusted to them. Moreover, the injustices denounced by Las Casas suffuse the Guatemalan countryside. Benites references the commonly held view that *campesinos* are naturally born to be servants. Because their needs are minimal, it is often reasoned, campesinos can be paid in kind, or with meager wages, or with rental plots of marginal land—all of which are insufficient to support workers and their families.[48]

On Benites' narration, then, the story of Las Casas' struggle continues in present-day Guatemala, overshadowing the conflict over Decree 900. Those working for a more just distribution of land are in fact the true successors to Las Casas. Moreover—and this is pivotal—Benites argues that the church's social teaching itself is a contemporary articulation of the Lascasian position. To paraphrase Leo XIII only slightly, those who are concerned about the conditions in the Guatemalan countryside and are advocating agrarian reform are trying to find some opportune remedy for the misery and wretchedness pressing down so unjustly on the majority of the *campesinado*, who have little protection against the violence of the existing order—an order that pressures them for the sake of gain and that gathers profit from the perpetuation of their need.[49]

We have been examining Guatemala at such length because it presents *in nuce* the problematic under examination in this chapter. We see how the US's involvement in the region relates to a much older story of war's business and also how that involvement undergoes important alterations in the face of communism and the perceived threat it poses, not only to the US's raw materials and territory but also to its very being and way of life. Indeed, the threat was so existential that it had to be stopped, even if its cost was overthrowing governments, establishing dictatorships, and embracing terror and brutality. But in Guatemala, we also see the collateral damage of

---

46. Quoted in Gutiérrez, *Las Casas*, 305.
47. Benites, *Meditaciones de un católico*, 6–7, 101.
48. Benites, *Meditaciones de un católico*, 62.
49. Leo XIII, *Rerum Novarum*, 3, 20.

this business, which only continues to mount as the century progresses, as faithful members of the church—landless, land-poor, and their advocates—are construed as communists and suffer greatly as a consequence.

The Business of War across Latin America

The overthrow of Árbenz was significant for reasons besides the ones we have been considering. For instance, it contributed to a process of radicalization. In Guatemala, the US destabilized the government of an OAS member state, whose democratically elected and popular president sought to raise the standard of living of his impoverished people by, among other ways, offering them access to land to farm. Consequently, the coup fueled animosity toward the "Colossus of the North" throughout Latin America—a hostility then-Vice President Richard Nixon famously encountered in his 1958 South American tour.[50]

What happened in Guatemala also bolstered the growing sentiment that revolution rather than reform was the only path toward real change for the impoverished. Ernesto "Che" Guevara was in Guatemala at the time of the coup, which only contributed to his view of the US as an imperialist power that would topple any government that sought to address the vast and entrenched inequalities that plagued the region.[51] Among the lessons Guevara drew was that Árbenz made a fatal error in seeking a peaceful solution to injustice in Guatemala.[52] As Hilda Gadea Acosta, Guevara's first wife, later recalled, "It was Guatemala which finally convinced him of the necessity for armed struggle and for taking the initiative against imperialism. By the time he left, he was sure of this."[53] This revolutionary vision found fertile soil in Cuba, where Guevara became a central figure in Fidel Castro's 26th of July Movement, which toppled the regime of President Fulgencio Batista in 1959 and replaced it with a revolutionary socialist state.

These events sent shockwaves throughout the Americas. While the fears of US policymakers about the spread of communism preceded the Cuban Revolution, they reached a new level of intensity after it, precipitating

---

50. Nixon continually encountered demonstrations against US imperialism, culminating in his motorcade being surrounded by a mob in Venezuela, which spat on and rocked his car, threatening to overturn it. The Eisenhower administration denounced the demonstrations as communist.

51. Lynch, *Aquí va un soldado*, 26.

52. Dosal, *Comandante Che*, 23–43.

53. Quoted in Sinclair, *Che Guevara*, 12.

a dramatic escalation of anxiety regarding the USSR's presence.[54] One way the Kennedy administration sought to stem the spread of what it called "Castro-Communism" was through the Alliance for Progress. At the outset of his presidency in March 1961, John F. Kennedy announced this bold, ten-year initiative that sought to promote economic growth, development, and democracy. Its purpose was to strengthen diplomatic ties and promote cooperation between the US and Latin America. It was also, of course, to counter the effects of the Cuban Revolution of 1959—an attempt to widen the space between this fallen domino and all those perceived to be teetering around it.

Interestingly enough, to stem the spread of communism, the US was at least initially prepared to accept agrarian reform. Just as in Guatemala, land concentration and landlessness throughout the region were acute. By the early 1960s, approximately half the population in Latin America was rural and so largely dependent upon land or wages from work on land for their livelihood. Rates varied from country to country, but estimates are that 5 to 10 percent of the people owned 70 to 90 percent of the land.[55]

At an inter-American conference in Punta del Este, Uruguay, in 1961, which established the Alliance, agrarian reform was among the first reforms mentioned in the charter signed by all participant nations. "The representatives of the American Republics hereby agree to establish an Alliance for Progress," the charter states, and "to encourage, in accordance with the characteristics of each country, programs of comprehensive agrarian reform, leading to the effective transformation, where required, of unjust structures and systems of land tenure and use; with a view to replacing latifundia and dwarf holdings by an equitable system of property."[56] Such reform was understood by the Alliance to be an essential, precipitating policy for growth and development, and its pursuit was situated squarely within a vision of modernization. The goal of agrarian reform was, to cite the charter once more, "to accelerate economic and social development, thus rapidly bringing about a substantial and steady increase in the average

54. Brands, *Latin America's Cold War*, 3.
55. Smith, *Talons of the Eagle*, 150.
56. "Declaration of Punta del Este, 1961." The charter depicted the manifest injustice of predominant land tenure arrangements throughout Latin America primarily as a barrier to development, construing comprehensive agrarian reform as a prerequisite for economic growth—a way to bring about greater production and rural employment. It therefore recognized a functional relationship between structural and institutional transformation, on the one hand, and growth and development, on the other. After Punta del Este, most of the member nations attempted to enact some form of agrarian reform legislation, but now, with the blessing of the US government. Feder, "Land Reform," 656.

income in order to narrow the gap between the standard of living in Latin American countries and that enjoyed in the industrialized countries."[57]

From these considerations, it might seem as though the US was now prepared to take a fundamentally different approach vis-à-vis Latin America. However, to understand why this was not the case, we need to take a closer look at modernization theory, a socioeconomic approach arising in the 1950s and associated with figures like W. W. Rostow, which was central to the Alliance's vision.[58] Modernization theory's understanding of socioeconomic development was lodged squarely within the geopolitical framing we have been examining. Its fundamental animating questions were these: How did the nations of Africa, Asia, and Latin America emerging from European colonialism (the so-called Third World) fit into the worlds of the Western and Eastern blocs (the so-called First and Second World, respectively)? Were these new Third World nations potential sites for the spread of communism? Or could they move toward capitalist development and defend against communism's advance? As both the hierarchical classification scheme and these questions suggest, modernization theory offered a stadial account of societal development, in which countries progress through uniform and successive stages of economic growth. Eventually, they "take off" into advanced capitalism with self-sustaining growth, ongoing improvement of conditions, and flourishing democratic institutions. Modernization theory set about to explain why so many societies remained mired in what it characterized as traditionalism and backwardness, and it fashioned specific interventions to remedy the situation.

According to those like Rostow, lack of economic progress made Latin America susceptible to the infiltration and spread of communism. To counter this threat, Rostow and others proposed foreign aid, policy measures, and technical assistance to safely and smoothly guide nations through the stages of development.[59] But because communism posed such a grave risk to a country's progression through these stages and to eventual take off, modernization theorists often advocated harsh tactics to counter communism—an approach Bradley Simpson alludes to in his suggestively titled study, *Economists with Guns*.[60] Héctor Lindo-Fuentes and Eric Ching describe this dynamic with respect to El Salvador: "Because of the threat

57. "Declaration of Punta del Este, 1961."
58. Our analysis of modernization theory draws heavily upon Lindo-Fuentes and Ching, *Modernizing Minds*, 78–83.
59. Lindo-Fuentes and Ching, *Modernizing Minds*, 56, 60.
60. Simpson, *Economists with Guns*.

of communist conspiracy, societies experiencing the transition [to capitalism] needed to be closely monitored and . . . assisted with money and weaponry."[61]

There were important differences between the Kennedy administration and the US administrations that followed, but as Peter Smith persuasively shows, what united them all was this "two-track" strategy: the war against communism combined with the promotion of socioeconomic development.[62] That the former priority reigned supreme and bent all the others to its demands was especially clear in the case of agrarian reform, the promise of which the Alliance increasingly abandoned, among other reasons, because of the fierce resistance to it by traditional elites, who fashioned themselves anti-communists and whose collaboration was necessary to the US in the war against the USSR.[63] In El Salvador, for instance, the basic premise of elites like Napoleón Viera Altamirano was that communism and measures like agrarian reform were identical, such that opposition to one entailed opposition to the other.[64] As Smith observes, in the face of such resistance from elites, "Washington lost its nerve and backed off from its promises [of agrarian reform]. Agrarian reform, the US government believed, might stir up radical sentiments and play into the hands of communist subversives. Better to leave things as they were."[65]

By the late 1960s, national security was firmly at the forefront of the Alliance's concerns, which involved increased military aid and training to member governments. The Kennedy administration also marked an important shift in the US's military presence in the region in other ways as well, underwriting a resurgence and expansion of Special Forces that could operate with more flexibility. In addition to covert interventions, as in Guatemala, then, the Kennedy administration turned to counterinsurgency and police training, approving vast increases in military aid, based on the rationale that it would be used against communist subversion.[66] Advisors from the State Department, Department of Defense, and the CIA supported, trained, and reinforced local intelligence operatives, teaching them interrogation and counterinsurgency techniques and providing technology and equipment. National intelligence agencies throughout the region were supported (and sometimes established) by the US and became

61. Lindo-Fuentes and Ching, *Modernizing Minds*, 80.
62. Smith, *Talons of the Eagle*, 147.
63. Feder, "Land Reform"; Smith, *Talons of the Eagle*, 153–54.
64. Lindo-Fuentes and Ching, *Modernizing Minds*, 66–67.
65. Smith, *Talons of the Eagle*, 154.
66. Rabe, *Killing Zone*, 57.

important precursors to the *esquadrones de la muerte* (death squads) that would operate with impunity in the 1970s and 1980s.[67]

In El Salvador, for instance, the US sent ten green berets to El Salvador to help set up *Organización Democrática Nacionalista* (National Democratic Organization [ORDEN]) in the mid-1960s, an infamous paramilitary group that not only gathered intelligence but also carried out assassinations in coordination with the military.[68] The US also helped found the *Agencia Nacional de Seguridad Salvadoreña* (National Security Agency of El Salvador [ANSESAL]), which Paul Almeida describes as "a clearinghouse for intelligence information deriving from the National Guard, treasury police, ORDEN, customs police, national police, and the army" and which worked closely not only with these entities but likewise with private landowners as well. The increased centralization and bureaucratization of government intelligence meant a major improvement in the state's ability to monitor and target those involved in what it deemed subversive activity.[69] For the next three decades, the US military and CIA continued to provide funding and support, and Salvadoran officers received training either in the School of Americas in the Panama Canal Zone or at military bases in the US.[70] As Murat Williams, the US ambassador to El Salvador during the Kennedy administration, explained in a 1980 op-ed piece, support for security forces in El Salvador and throughout the region as a whole stemmed from fear of "Castroism."[71]

What is especially crucial for our purposes is that the Alliance's increased emphasis on national security, while certainly representing a shift from previous policy and the promotion of socioeconomic development, did not represent a break from it. This is because the various forms of assistance on offer—foreign aid, technical assistance, military support, and so on— were all compatible and mutually reinforcing. They were all aimed at guiding nations successfully along the path to modernization without succumbing to communism along the way.[72] The title of Rostow's most famous work communicates this compatibility: *The Stages of Economic Growth: A Non-Communist Manifesto*.[73] Once again, we are encountering tight, ideological linkages between economics and warmaking. But with modernization

---

67. Grandin, *Empire's Workshop*, 48. See also Gill, *The School of the Americas*.
68. Nairn, "Behind the Death Squads," 20–29.
69. Almeida, *Waves of Protest*, 121; Stanley, *Protection Racket State*, 98.
70. Lindo-Fuentes and Ching, *Modernizing Minds*, 51.
71. Williams, "Still More Arms."
72. Lindo-Fuentes and Ching, *Modernizing Minds*, 81.
73. Rostow, *The Stages of Economic Growth*.

theory, warmaking is not simply to protect raw materials or territory, nor can it be understood solely in terms of the war against communism. Rather, it comes clothed with idealism. This is a form of warmaking for the good of the countries themselves and their own interests, for the sake of their own economic progress and freedom.

Therefore, although these two discernible tendencies in US foreign policy during Latin America's Cold War—touting reforms meant to bring development and freedom, on the one hand, and forming alliances with brutal military regimes and supporting terror, on the other—seem to be in tension, if not in outright contradiction with one another, they are in fact closely linked. Throughout Latin America's Cold War, the rationale behind US support of authoritarian rule was that such regimes were best equipped and most willing to do what was necessary to defeat communism. The political reasoning thus mirrored the economic reasoning we have just been examining: just as modernization theorists hoped for a takeoff into the freedom of capitalism, US officials similarly hoped for the eventual freedom of democracy.[74] But on both counts, communism proved such a grave threat that it was necessary to embrace warmaking to stop it. The result proved paradoxical and tragic, as the US simultaneously worked with Latin American regimes to implement reforms meant to improve the lives of ordinary people, while at the same time fashioning the machinery of repression that crushed them when they spoke out against injustice or organized to remedy it.[75] As Archbishop Óscar Romero observed in one of his final homilies, "They are massacring the organized sector of our people for the mere fact of gathering in the streets to ask for justice and freedom."[76]

Twelve years before Romero himself was shot and killed by a sniper as he celebrated mass in neighboring El Salvador, Viron P. Vaky, deputy chief of mission in Guatemala City, described the brutal consequences of this logic in a memo to his colleagues in the embassy and in Washington, DC, in 1968, which is well-worth quoting at length:

> We have not been honest with ourselves. We have condoned counterterror; we may even in effect have encouraged or blessed it. We have been so obsessed with the fear of insurgency that we have rationalized away our qualms and uneasiness. This is not only because we have concluded we cannot do anything about it, for we never really tried. Rather we suspected maybe it is a good tactic, and that as long as Communists are being killed

---

74. Rabe, *Killing Zone*, 52 (see also xxxvii, xxxix).
75. Lindo-Fuentes and Ching, *Modernizing Minds*, 78.
76. Romero, *Homilías (VI)*, 243; translation mine.

it is all right. Murder, torture and mutilation are all right if our side is doing it and the victims are Communists. After all, hasn't man been a savage from the beginning of time so let us not be too queasy about terror[?] I have literally heard those arguments from our people.

Have our values been so twisted by our adversary concept of politics in the hemisphere? Is it conceivable that we are so obsessed with insurgency that we are prepared to rationalize murder as an acceptable counter-insurgency weapon? Is it possible that a nation which so reveres the principle of due process of law has so easily acquiesced in this sort of terror tactic? ... The record must be made clearer that the United States Government opposes the concept and questions the wisdom of counter-terror ... otherwise we will stand before history unable to answer the accusations that we encouraged ... these things.[77]

In this passage, Vaky suggests that the answer to each of the questions he poses is a troubling "yes." For in Central America and throughout Latin America, much worse violence was yet to come. During the hottest years of Latin America's Cold War, and with the massive escalation of bloodletting in the late 1970s and the 1980s, the US chose not to oppose the wisdom of counter-terror but to embrace it—and to do so again and again. The country still stands before history and its accusations.

The Martyrs of Latin America as Models of Resistance to the Business of War

The epigraph to this chapter, from John Paul II's 1993 encyclical *Veritatis Splendor*, claims that the martyrs display before all people lives transfigured by the splendor of moral truth. What is more, in their lives, and especially in their deaths, martyrs even illumine history itself, enabling the restoration of its moral sense, which often lies buried in the rubble, as it were. As John Paul continues, "By witnessing fully to the good, [the martyrs] are a living reproof to those who transgress the law [Wis 2:12], and they make the words of the Prophet echo ever afresh, 'Woe to those who call evil good and good evil, who put darkness for light and light for darkness, who put bitter for sweet and sweet for bitter' [Isa 5:20]."[78] John Paul is suggesting a theological narration or re-narration of history itself, with the martyrs now emerging as history's true protagonists. This approach amounts to a

77. Quoted in Wilkinson, *Silence on the Mountain*, 325.
78. John Paul II, *Veritatis Splendor*, 93.

kind of retrospective reexamination and reevaluation of history, now seen in relation to the splendor of martyrs' witness to Christ. For in their lives, and especially in their willingness to lay them down for the sake of others, martyrs bear witness to the love of God revealed in Christ—an imitation so close that martyrs have traditionally been seen as other Christs.[79]

Doing justice to John Paul's suggestion is well beyond the bounds of this chapter. But by way of conclusion, I want briefly to examine it with respect to the business of war in Latin America, specifically in terms of the cost of doing business in this way. As mentioned above, truth commissions across the region have been documenting this cost for some time now, joining the countless others who have tirelessly worked to remember the victims, to resist the distortion of memory and to hold the perpetrators of terror accountable. But even this work of remembrance and truth-telling has brought much suffering—even martyrdom—in its train. Bishop Juan Gerardi, auxiliary bishop of Guatemala City, who was founder and director of the Archdiocesan Human Rights Office, was also active in the Recovery of Historical Memory Project (REMHI), which sought to tell the truth about the violence that took place there. Two days after the publication of the results of REMHI's work, *Guatemala: Nunca Más* (*Guatemala: Never Again*), he was found bludgeoned to death in the garage to his home, his face unrecognizable. He was seventy-five years old.

There has been relatively less reflection upon the extraordinary fact that, now in the church's discernment, there are martyrs and saints among the victims of the period we have been considering in Latin America. In one sense, this is not news. Many of the victims of the violence have been venerated as martyrs for some time now. Saint Archbishop Óscar Romero of El Salvador was shot and killed by a sniper as he said mass on March 24, 1980, in San Salvador and was immediately considered a martyr, even despite the incredible danger of showing esteem for him in public.[80] While not as well known as Romero, Blessed Stanley Rother of Oklahoma City in the US was killed on the grounds of his church in the rural highlands of Guatemala on July 28, 1981, and was similarly seen as a martyr from early on. However, the church formally recognized their martyrdoms only recently, with Romero beatified on May 25, 2017, and then canonized on October 14, 2018, and Rother beatified on September 23, 2017. Moreover, as we consider martyrs like Romero and Rother, it is important to keep in mind that, as Pope Francis said in a press conference prior to Romero's beatification, "After him [Romero], there is Rutilio Grande [Romero's Jesuit

---

79. See Moss, *The Other Christs*.
80. Andrés, *Dios pasó por El Salvador*, 193, 179–244.

friend gunned down in 1977], and there are others, too. There are others who were killed."[81] There were many, many others, who are only now beginning to be recognized as the martyrs they undoubtedly are. Romero and Rother are only two of a great cloud of witnesses.[82]

These are important developments, and they contribute to the clarification of and reflection upon the past and the business of war in Latin America. As José Luis Escobar Alas, the sitting archbishop of San Salvador, writes in his 2017 pastoral letter, *Ustedes también darán testimonio, porque han estado conmigo desde el principio* (*You are also to testify because you have been with me from the beginning*), the church in El Salvador has also failed to do its part to remember its martyrs and hold up their witness before the world. "I want to recognize—as I must out of justice, truth, and charity," he begins the letter, "that we in the archdiocese have crossed the threshold of the third millennium without having acknowledged all the men and women who were victims of persecution, torture, repression, and who were ultimately martyred for following Christ and incarnating the Gospel in this country."[83] It is a remarkable admission. If these men and women are, as Escobar Alas says later in the letter, the *piedras fundamentals* (fundamental stones, or building blocks) of the church in El Salvador and witnesses to the faith for members everywhere, it is a status they have mysteriously possessed all the while the credibility of that witness has been unacknowledged—and sometimes even questioned—by the very church that is now raising them to the altars.[84]

The pastoral letter—more than two hundred pages in length—compiles the testimonies of twenty-four martyrs of the church in El Salvador and Guatemala (including Romero, Gerardi, and Rother), presenting biographies, circumstances surrounding their deaths, and reflecting upon them in light of a comprehensive theology of martyrdom. Moreover, the story Escobar Alas tells about martyrdom parallels and even intersects with the one about agrarian reform we have touched upon at various points in this chapter, and more generally, with the long, ongoing story of measures to defend against, in Ignacio Martín Baró's words, "the war *campesinos* suffer in their own flesh."[85]

81. Pope Francis, "In Flight Press Conference."
82. Escobar Alas, *Ustedes también darán testimonio*, 146, 160.
83. Escobar Alas, *Ustedes también darán testimonio*, 3. All translations of quotations from Escobar Alas' *Ustedes también darán testimonio* are my own.
84. Escobar Alas, *Ustedes también darán testimonio*, 146.
85. Escobar Alas, *Ustedes también darán testimonio*, 124, 23, 28, 39, 58, 124, 171, 178, 181, 187, 198.

Admittedly, part of the reason it has been difficult to speak of martyrdom in El Salvador and elsewhere in Latin America is that it took place in predominantly Christian countries, often at the hands of other professing Christians and with the help of a nation that represented its violence as on behalf of Judeo-Christian civilization. Roberto D'Aubuisson, the mastermind of the plot to kill Romero, not only received US training in intelligence and security operations, but he was even honored in a ceremony on Capitol Hill for his "continuing efforts for freedom in the face of communist aggression which is an inspiration to freedom-loving people everywhere."[86] Jesse Helms defended him before his detractors as "a free enterprise man and deeply religious."[87] As Escobar Alas observes, many in El Salvador were encouraged to believe—precisely as faithful Christians— that "massacres, genocides, disappearances or assassinations were a necessary evil to prevent the entry of communism."[88] They were similarly encouraged to believe that those who peacefully proposed a different path forward—by calling for the establishment of stable sources of employment, payment of just wages, promotion of access to education and healthcare, implementation of true agrarian reform, and legalization of cooperatives and other labor organizations—were communists and therefore a threat to the nation and Christianity.[89]

Romero's life and death, however, tell a different story. Late in 1979, as Romero analyzed the crisis his country was enduring, one of the principal tasks of the church, as he saw it, was to dethrone the idols that ruled El Salvador. Significantly, Romero identified the root of the violence affecting the predominantly Catholic El Salvador, not as communism, but as the worship of wealth and property, which prevented the vast majority of the Salvadoran people from accessing the land and other goods God had created for all. "In our country," Romero claims, "this idolatry is at the root of structural and repressive violence."[90] Those in thrall to it, Romero argued, willingly maintained their privilege at the expense of the basic human dignity of others, both through the perpetuation of structures and institutions (structural violence), as well as through the use of repressive measures to prevent any challenge to these structures and institutions (repressive violence). In the process, they refused to acknowledge what John Paul II called property's social mortgage—a reference to property's purpose

86. Omang, "D'Aubuisson Honored by Conservatives."
87. Bates, "Jesse Helms."
88. Escobar Alas, *Ustedes también darán testimonio*, 196.
89. Escobar Alas, *Ustedes también darán testimonio*, 196–97.
90. Romero, "Church's Mission," 45.

to serve the needs of the whole human community, in addition to the needs those who possess it.[91] This vision of property, which demands justice in the distribution of goods like land and involves community organizing in order to attain access to it, points toward an alternative pedagogy of life and peace.

Early the following year, in 1980, as the violence in El Salvador continued to escalate, Romero personally wrote President Jimmy Carter—addressing him as a Christian whose foreign policy was known for its emphasis on the promotion of human rights—regarding the US's plan to resume military aid to El Salvador. Doing so, Romero argued, would not promote justice and peace, or help to defend human rights, as was the stated intention, but only exacerbate the repression against those whose only crime was asking that basic human rights be respected.[92] In March 1980, the same month Romero himself was slain by men who had received US anti-communist counterinsurgency training at the School of the Americas, US military aid to El Salvador resumed.

In hindsight, it is now much clearer that so many of those killed, like Romero himself, were not communists but simply engaged in the task of trying "to illumine the reality of pain, of suffering, of poverty, of violence, of injustice, of oppression, of torture, of marginalization, and of death with the light of faith," as Escobar Alas puts it.[93] Yet that did not stop, Escobar Alas continues, countless "lay men and women integrated into the Church as pastoral agents, catechists, members of the ecclesial base communities, members of choirs and other groups, from being killed for celebrating the Word or carrying a Bible—a book that, ironically, made them suspect of communism."[94] Escobar Alas goes so far as to write of a *ruta martirial* (route or path of martyrdom) upon which the church in El Salvador and Latin America continues to walk, which is "permeated with the sanctity of those men and women who gave their blood for the love of Christ personified in the faces of the impoverished."[95]

On this view, these martyrs bear witness to the love of God in Christ, but they do so while also bearing witness to Christ's ongoing love of and identification with the impoverished (see especially Matt 25:31–46). As Romero himself observed, during his tenure of less than three years as archbishop in El Salvador, more than fifty priests and nuns were attacked, threatened, slandered, tortured, or expelled from the country, and six priests

---

91. Romero, "Church's Mission," 42–45.
92. Romero, *Homilías (VII)*, 293–94.
93. Escobar Alas, *Ustedes también darán testimonio*, 176.
94. Escobar Alas, *Ustedes también darán testimonio*, 146.
95. Escobar Alas, *Ustedes también darán testimonio*, 160.

were brutally killed. The archdiocesan radio station and other institutions associated with the church were bombed and parish communities raided. At least in one case, soldiers entered a church and shot the tabernacle, strewing the consecrated hosts everywhere. "If all this has happened to the Church's most visible representatives," Romero says, "imagine what has happened to ordinary Christians, to *campesinos*, catechists, lay ministers, and to the ecclesial base communities. There, the threats, arrests, tortures, and murders number in the hundreds and thousands. . . . The true persecution has targeted the poor, who are today the body of Christ in history. They are the crucified people, like Jesus."[96] According to Romero, there is a form of atheism endemic to his predominantly Christian country, which affects all those who fail to see and attend to Christ in his suffering and needy flesh.

Conclusion

Acknowledging martyrs like Romero among the victims of this time helps illumine what was at stake in Latin America's Cold War, enabling a different story to be told about what actually took place. For as Romero saw it, a whole people was being crucified, and martyrs were being made simply for pointing to this reality and for standing with the wounded. As Stanley Rother wrote in a letter to his brother over worries about his safety in returning to Guatemala, "The shepherd cannot run at the first sign of danger."[97] In this case, the price of Rother's not running was laying down his life, following in the way of the good shepherd (John 10:11). In so doing, Rother along with the other martyrs of this period continue to offer us not only an icon of Christ in their own persons but also a sign of Christ's ongoing passion in the world in the body of a whole people. Together, their witness "lights up" what has often been represented as a struggle on the part of Judeo-Christian civilization against godless communism, testifying that this business was actually something quite different altogether.

96. Romero, "La dimensión política," in *La voz de los sin voz*, 188.
97. Monahan, *The Shepherd Cannot Run*.

6

The Business of War on the Korean Peninsula

WONCHUL SHIN

Introduction

The Korean Peninsula has suffered. Not long after embracing its independence from the thirty-five years of Japanese colonial occupation in August 1945, the Korean Peninsula was cut into two bodies at the thirty-eighth parallel by the United States and the Soviet Union. The two divided bodies became two Koreas as the result of the extension of the Cold War: the Republic of Korea (ROK) in the south was established in August 1948 under the supervision of the US and the United Nations, and the Democratic People's Republic of Korea (DPRK) in the north was founded in September 1948 under the sponsorship of the Soviet Union.[1] Then the tragedy of a fratricidal war, the Korean War, began on June 25, 1950, and the Korean Peninsula was smeared with the blood of countless civilians and combatants until the two Koreas signed the armistice agreement in July 1953. The armistice agreement marked the temporal end of the Korean War, but also the beginning of the history of conflict, mistrust, and hatred between the

1. Kwak et al., *US-Korean Relations*, 223.

two Koreas. From the Cold War era to the recent post-Cold War era, they have identified each other as the archenemy and maintained a high level of military expenditure and preparedness to the extent that both can be called "garrison states."[2] The militarization in the Korean Peninsula has been maintained and even intensified, and this continued military threat and tension has been a significant stumbling block to promoting positive peace there.[3]

In this chapter, I critically examine the issue of the competitive militarization—the arms race—between the two Koreas. First, this chapter debunks the myth of the DPRK's military superiority, which the US and the ROK have used to justify the ROK's increasing defense expenditure, through empirical analysis of defense spending of the two Koreas. Second, this chapter argues that the US-ROK alliance is the key factor in the growth of the ROK's defense spending, although the so-called North Korea threat has been used to legitimate the intensification of the arms buildup. Third, this chapter examines the greatest beneficiaries of the ROK-DPRK's militarization: the South Korean military-industrial complex (MIC) and the US MIC rather than citizens in the Korean Peninsula. Fourth, I contextualize the critical analysis of this militarization through the recent case of the controversial deployment of a Terminal High-Altitude Area Defense (THAAD) system on the Korean Peninsula. Finally, I present a theological response to the continued militarization of the Korean Peninsula and call for moral imagination, liberating people from fear and envisioning the peace of Christ, reflected in the peace movement led by the National Council of Churches in Korea.

The Myth behind the Militarization of the Korean Peninsula

Since the armistice agreement in July 1953, the two Koreas have made notable progress toward peace. For example, the July 4th Joint Communique in 1972 focused on the peaceful reunification of the two Koreas, and the Agreement on Reconciliation, Nonaggression, Exchanges and Cooperation in 1991 and the June 2000 Pyongyang summit between President Kim Dae Jung and

---

2. Hamm, *Arming the Two Koreas*, 1.

3. It is important to clarify the concepts of peace in this chapter. Positive peace is different from negative peace, "the absence of violence (e.g., a cease-fire or similar circumstance keeping enemies apart)." Rather, it involves "moving from indifferent to positive, harmonious relations, intentional or unintentional, direct or structural, or both." This approach to peace eschews "offensive deterrence" based on "the threat of using [military] capabilities" that can be used as aggressive offense, including preemptive attacks, and defensive offense as well. Galtung, "Peace, Negative and Positive."

DPRK National Defense Commission Chairman Kim Jong Il further paved the way to peace.[4] However, regardless of this political progress, the two Koreas have failed to reduce and stop "the competitive arms buildups" and the militarization of the Korean Peninsula.[5]

Since the armistice agreement, the ROK's defense expenditure comprises 5 to 6 percent of the gross national product, although it has varied over time, and it is approximately 30 percent of the ROK's national budget.[6] The ROK's defense spending is the tenth largest in the world in terms of the absolute amount.[7] In the recent post-Cold War era, the ROK's defense budget has increased fourfold, from 6.6 trillion won in 1990 to 26.6 trillion won in 2008.[8] This trend of a high level of militarization has even intensified given the Ministry of National Defense's (MND) Defense Reform 2020: it plans "an annual average increase [in the defense budget] of 7.6 percent to 53.3 trillion won by 2020, another doubling over the next decade."[9] Concerned with national security, the ROK has officially claimed two main reasons for maintaining its high level of defense expenditure and arms buildup: (1) catching up to the DPRK's military superiority, and (2) defending against the DPRK's threat. According to the first edition of the ROK Defense White Paper (*Kukpang baeckseo*), the biannual governmental report on national defense issues started in 1988, the DPRK still possesses "military superiority in both bean counts and cumulative investments," although the ROK has outspent the DPRK since the mid-1970s.[10] This has been the main justification for increasing the ROK's defense spending: "Seoul must defend against the North Korea threat."[11]

However, through his critical examination of the ROK's official position and the empirical analysis of defense expenditures of the two Koreas, Taik-young Hamm demonstrates that the DRPK's military superiority

4. Hamm, *Arming the Two Koreas*, 90; Shin, *One Alliance, Two Lenses*, 15.
5. Hamm, *Arming the Two Koreas*, 90.
6. Heo, "Political Economy," 483.
7. Heo, "Political Economy," 483.
8. Suh, "Allied to Race?" 101–2. At the time of publication, 6.6 trillion won would be worth about 5,871,233,148.00 US dollars, and 26.6 trillion won about 23,662,848,748.00 US dollars.
9. Suh, "Allied to Race?," 102.
10. Hamm, *Arming the Two Koreas*, 91. The "bean counts" methodology as "the most simple and elementary form of balance assessment" is "the comparison of numbers of the visible components of military might: the order-of-battle, manpower, number of tanks, artillery tubes, ships, aircraft, missiles, special forces, or whatever is available for an armchair general or a (security) concerned scholar." Hamm, *Arming the Two Koreas*, 43.
11. Suh, "Allied to Race?," 103–4.

claimed by the ROK is a myth rather than a fact. He argues for using cumulative defense expenditures as "the best single measure of the 'actual' military capabilities" of the two Koreas, which is more accurate than the ROK's official position based on "the 'bean-counting' methodology" that does not include "qualitative factors of weapons, organizational effectiveness, and manpower."[12] Comparing the cumulative defense expenditures of the two Koreas, Hamm concludes that the ROK's official claim about the DPRK's military superiority should be rejected for the following reasons: (1) the ROK's estimate of the DPRK's defense expenditure has been exaggerated; (2) the ROK's official defense budget does not include the considerable US military aid to the ROK; and (3) the ROK's official data does not reflect "the depreciation factor."[13] Although the DPRK outspent the ROK in total defense expenditures from 1964 to 1975, the ROK achieved its military superiority in the 1980s in terms of cumulative defense expenditures and has further widened the gap up to the present.[14] This critical analysis suggests that the claim of the military superiority of the DPRK is quite misleading. However, it has served as an effective myth disseminated by the ROK for justifying its continued expansion of defense expenditures and the intensification of the militarization of its territory.

The US-ROK Alliance as the Powerful Driver of the Militarization on the Korean Peninsula

Jae-Jung Suh has critically analyzed the process of constituting the DPRK's identity—the social reality of constant threat—by the ROK and the US in the post-Cold War period. Since Pyongyang launched a rocket in August 1998, the DPRK has been identified as a "country now threatening the South with its missiles, nuclear weapons, and even fragility."[15] Suh argues that the social realities of the DPRK as a "missile threat," "nuclear threat," and "time bomb" have been constituted and maintained by "an intense effort [of the ROK and the US] to discipline the production of social understanding," and that this understanding is not "an automatic, objective reflection of the material reality."[16] This image of the DPRK as constant threat has been reinforced by the South Korean private media, specifically those associated with the conservative parties. *Chosun Ilbo*, one of the most influential newspapers,

12. Hamm, *Arming the Two Koreas*, 61.
13. Hamm, *Arming the Two Koreas*, 113.
14. Hamm, *Arming the Two Koreas*, 112–15.
15. Suh, *Power, Interest, and Identity*, 153.
16. Suh, *Power, Interest, and Identity*, 153–64.

having the largest circulation of all Korean newspapers representing conservative views of the ROK-DPRK relationship, devoted more than 20 percent of its coverage (editorials and columns) to reaffirming the identity of the DPRK as a threat to the ROK and East Asia from 1992 to 2003.[17] In addition to the myth of the DPRK's military superiority, the social reality of the constancy of threat by the DPRK has been another main explanation for increasing defense spending and continued militarization of the ROK.

Although "the North Korea threat" is a powerful justification, it fails to account for the expansive growth of the ROK's defense expenditure into the early 2000s, increasing fourfold between 1990 and 2008: "Why did it [the ROK] feel compelled to keep increasing its defense budget to widen the gap to a 10:1 ratio by 2002?"[18] As discussed above, the ROK had achieved military superiority over the DPRK in terms of cumulative defense expenditure in the 1980s. Also, most military analysts agree that the ROK's military capabilities (i.e., "the state-of-the-art system of the South") qualitatively exceed the DPRK's "1950s-vintage weapons systems."[19] Hence, it is hard to argue that the DPRK's constant threat is the main driver of the ROK's increasing military spending and continued militarization.

Following this critical analysis, Suh argues that the US-ROK military alliance is indeed the main driver of the ROK's increasing defense budget. He highlights "the costs of interoperability," which include "hardware, software, and human resources" that make allied militaries interoperable.[20] For the ROK's military to achieve and maintain interoperability with the US military, it has to constantly build and update interoperable weapons systems (US-made weapons) and platforms for reducing friendly fire and coordinating joint exercises and operations with the allied military. For example, in 1994, reflecting a US official's critique of the interoperability of the ROK's attack helicopter system, the ROK agreed to upgrade its weapons system by purchasing "an array of sophisticated US-made gear," including Apache attack helicopters made by McDonnell Douglas Corporation and Maverick antitank missiles made by Raytheon Company and General Motors Corporation's Hughes Aircraft Company.[21] In addition to the hardware expenditures, the ROK has had to bear the defense burden of customizing the software infrastructure (i.e., military planning, standard operating procedures, rules of engagement, etc.) and moving or training human assets

17. Shin, *One Alliance, Two Lenses*, 69–71.
18. Suh, "Allied to Race?," 105.
19. Suh, "Allied to Race?," 104.
20. Suh, "Allied to Race?," 117.
21. Ricks, "South Korea Agrees," A10.

(i.e., the US-ROK joint military exercises) for the sake of interoperability with the US military.[22]

Although it is hard to deny the fact that the ROK has received considerable military and economic assistance from the US since the 1950s, the ROK, as the "weaker" partner (given the asymmetric power balance in the US-ROK alliance), is under heavy pressure to maintain interoperability and continue to upgrade its military capabilities by purchasing US-made weaponry as "a way to signal its commitment to the alliance or buy the ally's interest."[23] The ROK's Defense Reform 2020 emphasizes the concepts of "jointness" and "Network Centric Warfare," adopting the core concepts of the recent US military transformation. By doubling its defense budget, the ROK aims to realize these goals of enhanced interoperability.[24] In addition, statistical data on US arms sales to the ROK suggests the ROK's heavy burden in maintaining the alliance, which comprises the largest portion of the increasing defense budget. According to a congressional budget evaluation, the projected 1.2 billion dollars in arms sold to the ROK in 2007 represented a threefold increase from 2005. This figure is quite considerable since it represented almost one-third of the 3.4 billion dollars in arms sold to the entire East Asia and Pacific region and was nearly equal to the projection of arms sales for all of Europe.[25] Based on this projection, the US sold 4.4 billion dollars of weapons to the ROK from 2007 to 2010, which put the ROK into sixth place among recipients of US weapons.[26] Therefore, as Suh argues, regardless of the North Korea threat, the ROK has increased its defense spending and intensified the militarization of the Korean Peninsula in order to maintain the US-ROK alliance.

The ROK's increasing defense spending and the continued militarization of the Korean Peninsula under the US-ROK alliance have been sustained and undergirded by two kinds of fear: (1) fear of abandonment and (2) fear of "the North Korea threat." The ROK (particularly its conservative element) fears that it may be "abandoned by its allies," specifically the US, just when its security is jeopardized.[27] This "abandonment fear" has increased with the recent serious changes to the US-ROK alliance, such as the projected return of wartime operation control to the ROK, the projected disbandment of the Combined Forces Command, and the relocation and reduction of

22. Suh, "Allied to Race?," 118.
23. Suh, "Allied to Race?," 119.
24. Suh, "Allied to Race?," 122.
25. BBC Monitoring Asia Pacific, "US Military Sales," 1.
26. Asia News Monitor, "South Korea/United States."
27. Suh, "Allied to Race?," 119.

United States Forces Korea in the ROK.[28] The fear of abandonment pushes the ROK to increase its defense spending and intensify its militarization as a "remedial action" for tightening the US-ROK alliance.[29] The increased spending and further militarization have been justified by appealing to the fear of the so-called North Korea threat. As discussed above, the social reality of DRPK's constant threat has served as the ROK's effective justification for increasing its defense spending and purchasing US-made weapons. In other words, the seemingly endless militarization of the Korean Peninsula has been grounded in the fear of abandonment under the US-ROK alliance and fear of "the North Korea threat."

The Military-Industrial Complex as Beneficiary

It has been commonly argued by the South Korean government that South Korean citizens ultimately benefit from the national security that results from the ROK's increased defense spending. However, this argument is quite misleading in light of the outcomes of the continued arms buildups. The ROK's increasing defense expenditure contributes to the seemingly endless cycles of militarization of the Korean Peninsula. While the ROK has increased its defense spending fourfold in recent decades, it has only prompted the DRPK to intensify its development of nuclear weapons technology and to continue to test its nuclear tech and satellites. Given the increasing military tension between the two Koreas, how can one say that South Korean citizens, who live in the garrison peninsula, are beneficiaries of the ROK's increasing defense expenditures? Rather, it would seem to be the military-industrial complex that benefits most from the further militarization of the Korean Peninsula, specifically in terms of the direct economic value.

Chung-in Moon warned in the 1980s of "a potential for the gradual formation of a military-industrial complex" in the ROK—a dense network of alliances among the ROK government, the military, and the defense industry—although whether it constitutes a military-industrial complex as dense as the US MIC is debatable.[30] In any case, the South Korean defense industry was intensively developed in the seventies and eighties with a

---

28. Suh, "Allied to Race?," 123. For more information on the recent relocation and reduction of the United States Forces Korea, see Yeo, "US Military Base Realignment," 113–20.

29. Suh, "Allied to Race?," 119.

30. Suh, "Allied to Race?," 107. See also Everett, *Third World Military Industrialization*, 258.

substantial amount of aid from the US, including "a wide range of defense-related technology transfer through technical data packages, manufacturing license agreements, and co-production."[31] In addition to the US aid, the development of the South Korean defense industry has been significantly supported by a series of government-driven Force Modernization and Improvement Plans with extensive incentives, such as exemption from import tariffs, governmental procurement pledges, and research-and-development support through governmental agencies.[32] In other words, from the beginning, South Korean military-industrial companies have maintained close ties with the ROK government.[33]

The ROK's Ministry of National Defense generally assigns one-third of its defense budget for arms buildup.[34] Because of its close ties with South Korean military-industrial companies, the MND spent 2.9 trillion won to purchase weapons from them in 1991.[35] In addition, the MND provided defense contractors with 52.3 billion won as research and development assistance by establishing the "Defense Industry Promotion Fund" in 1996.[36] It is clear that the South Korean military-industrial sector will benefit increasingly as the defense budget expands.

There is another direct beneficiary of the continued militarization of the Korean Peninsula: the US MIC. As noted above, the ROK has been a loyal client of US weapons producers and accounts for a quite considerable portion of US foreign military sales (FMS). In 1991 alone, the MND spent 590 billion won to purchase weapons made by foreign companies, and more than 60 percent of the total amount was spent on US-made weapons. Under the pressure of maintaining interoperability with the US military, grounded in fear of abandonment, the ROK needs to keep upgrading their weapons systems as the US MIC develops new hardware and adopts new software. As long as the US-ROK alliance continues, the US MIC will assign a considerable amount of FMS to the ROK. It is apparent that the US MIC

31. Lee, McLaurin, and Moon, *Alliance Under Tension*, 82.

32. Lee, McLaurin, and Moon, *Alliance Under Tension*, 83.

33. Generally, these military-industrial companies belong to South Korean industrial conglomerates (*jaebol*), such as Hyundai Precision Industry, Samsung Aviation, Korean Airlines, Daewoo Heavy Industry, etc. Some scholars argue for the role of US military offshore procurements and the MIC as a hidden but significant factor in the successful development of the South Korean *jaebol*. See Glassman and Choi, "The Chaebol and the US," 1160–80.

34. Suh, "Allied to Race?," 108.

35. Suh, "Allied to Race?," 108. At the time of publication, 2.9 trillion won would be worth about 2,581,565,500.00 US dollars.

36. At the time of publication, 52.3 billion won would be worth about 46,557,198.50 US dollars.

will be a major beneficiary of the ROK's increasing defense spending and further militarization of the Korean Peninsula.

Critical Reflection on the Deployment of THAAD on the Korean Peninsula

On July 8, 2016, the ROK and the US released a joint statement saying that "in response to the evolving threat posed by North Korea" they had "made an Alliance decision to deploy a Terminal High-Altitude Area Defense (THAAD) system to United States Forces Korea (USFK) as a defensive measure to ensure the security of the ROK and its people and to protect Alliance military forces from North Korea's weapons of mass destruction and ballistic missile threats."[37] The joint statement argues that the deployment of THAAD will contribute to "a layered missile defense that will enhance the Alliance's existing defense capabilities against North Korean missile threats."[38]

The ROK and the US have officially proclaimed the effectiveness of THAAD's defense capabilities against "the North Korea threat," a threat involving North Korea's fourth nuclear test and the ballistic missile launch in 2016. However, since this joint announcement, the effectiveness of THAAD to defend the ROK's territory against the DPRK's ballistic missiles has come under question. As its name represents, THAAD is designed to "detect and shoot down ballistic missiles in their reentry [terminal] phase."[39] Those favoring the THAAD deployment emphasized that it would create "a multilayered defense shield" given its "superior maximum range [125 miles] and altitude [93 miles]" and potential to intercept ballistic missiles "launched at high trajectories" in conjunction with the Patriot missile system (PAC-2/3) already deployed in the ROK, which covers short ranges (15–21 miles) and altitudes (9–20 miles).[40] Given THAAD's specifications, it is true that it would contribute to the multilayered missile shield. However, the question remains whether it is actually effective in defending the ROK against various types of North Korean ballistic missiles.

Bruce Klingner argues that the DPRK has deployed "at least 400 Scud short-range tactical ballistic missiles, 300 No-Dong medium-range missiles,

---

37. United States Forces Korea, "ROK-U.S. Alliance Agrees to Deploy THAAD."
38. United States Forces Korea, "ROK-U.S. Alliance Agrees to Deploy THAAD."
39. Lee, "THAAD Deployment," 35.
40. Klingner, "THAAD Missile Defense," 28–30. See also Sankaran and Fearey, "Missile Defense and Strategic Stability," 321–44.

and 100 to 200 Musudan intermediate-range ballistic missiles."[41] When we consider the relatively short distance between Pyongyang and Seoul (approximately 194 kilometers), the Scud missile and No-Dong missile may be the most effective weapons for attacking the ROK. However, many scholars and military analysts argue that THAAD is not suitable for intercepting Scud missiles launched at low trajectories.[42] In addition, it may "not be efficient against missiles with an irregular and unstable trajectory" such as that of the No-Dong missile.[43] In other words, the multilayered missile shield based on the THAAD deployment would arguably not be at all effective in defending the ROK's territory against the North Korean missile threats.

The alleged enhanced defense capabilities achieved by the THAAD deployment appear to be another myth for justifying further militarization of the Korean Peninsula. If THAAD gives no direct advantage in defending the ROK's territory, why has the ROK agreed to deploy it? As we explored above, the real driver of this deployment would be the pressure of maintaining interoperability with the USAF under the US-ROK alliance. For decades, the US government and military have pushed the ROK to join "a comprehensive, interoperable, and multilayered ballistic missile defense (BMD) system."[44] The THAAD deployment on the Korean Peninsula has to be understood as a part of the US military strategy on comprehensive and interoperable theater missile defenses (TMD) throughout the world.[45] Since the 1990s, the ROK has officially maintained its position of "strategic ambiguity" on the issue of participation in the TMD system,[46] but it ended up deploying THAAD in Seongju County, located approximately 300 kilometers southeast of Seoul, as a sign of its commitment to the US-ROK alliance under the intensified military aggression of the DPRK. In other words, the THAAD deployment may be considered another cost of interoperability under the US-ROK alliance.

Considering the DPRK's reactions after the ROK-US joint announcement, it is apparent that South Korean citizens are not benefiting from the deployment of THAAD on their land. National security has actually been jeopardized rather than enhanced, since the deployment of THAAD has encouraged further isolation of the DPRK and intensified the arms race

41. Klingner, "THAAD Missile Defense," 23.

42. Lee, "THAAD Deployment," 35.

43. See Institute for Security and Development Policy, "THAAD on the Korean Peninsula."

44. See Klingner, "THAAD Missile Defense," 22. See also Sankaran and Fearey, "Missile Defense and Strategic Stability," 323–25.

45. Ahn, "[Why does the US hasten to deploy THAAD?]," 82–83.

46. Sankaran and Fearey, "Missile Defense and Strategic Stability," 322.

between the two Koreas.⁴⁷ Many critics point to a likelihood of pushing the DPRK to increase the sophistication of its submarine-launched ballistic missiles (SLBMs); it is estimated that the DPRK has an SLBM able to travel more than one thousand kilometers, and thus it could be fired outside the radar range of THAAD.⁴⁸ In response to this likely scenario, the ROK now seeks to build "a nuclear-powered submarine" to defy the DPRK's SLBM system; even conservative lawmakers in the ROK have called for "a nuclear balance" on the Korean Peninsula by urging the redeployment of US nuclear weapons.⁴⁹ The deployment of THAAD has indeed resulted in aggravating military tension and heating up the arms race between the two Koreas, blocking the road to peace on the Korean Peninsula.

If South Korean citizens are not benefiting from the deployment of THAAD, then who is? The direct beneficiary would be the US MIC, specifically the Lockheed Martin Corporation as the main contractor of THAAD and subcontractors such as Raytheon and Boeing.⁵⁰ The cost of deploying a full battery of THAAD (six launchers and forty-eight interceptor missiles) is an estimated 1 billion US dollars. Although United States Forces Korea has agreed to foot the bill, it is likely that we will see the deployment of more THAAD batteries in order to cover the entire territory of the ROK. The initial THAAD deployment in Seongju County cannot cover the ROK's capital region and metropolitan area but only protects the southern region, including the cities of Busan and Pohang.⁵¹ To cover the whole territory of the ROK will require at least three more full batteries, at an estimated cost of 3 billion dollars, plus an additional 1 billion dollars of maintenance expense per year, which has to be paid out of the ROK's defense budget.⁵² In addition, the precedent of THAAD sales to Korea will encourage the US MIC to persuade other nations in East Asia such as Japan and Taiwan to purchase THAAD systems.⁵³ To sum up, THAAD deployment on the Korean Peninsula seems to be an initial step toward the expansion of the US MIC's economic benefit guaranteed in the comprehensive global TMD system.

47. Lee, "THAAD Deployment," 35.
48. Institute for Security and Development Policy, "THAAD on the Korean Peninsula."
49. Kim and Yang, "Experts Warn North Korea."
50. Ahn, "[Why does the US hasten to deploy THAAD?]," 84.
51. Ahn, "[Why does the US hasten to deploy THAAD?]," 84.
52. Ahn, "[Why does the US hasten to deploy THAAD?]," 84.
53. Ahn, "[Why does the US hasten to deploy THAAD?]," 85.

Conclusion: Calling for Moral Imagination beyond Fear

The Korean Peninsula still suffers. It suffers from the seemingly endless cycle of competitive militarization between the two Koreas. The ROK has justified its increased defense spending by appealing to the myth of the DPRK's military superiority and the need to defend its citizens from "the North Korea threat." Nevertheless, the real driver of further militarization by the ROK is the US-ROK alliance, specifically the pressure of maintaining interoperability between the allied militaries. Continued militarization directly benefits the ROK MIC and the US MIC, rather than the inhabitants of the Korean Peninsula. The case of the controversial deployment of THAAD on the Korean Peninsula clearly supports the critical analysis of continued militarization presented throughout the chapter.

Tragically, since the Korean War, South Korean citizens have been haunted by two fears: that of being abandoned by the US and that of "the North Korea threat." These fears were manipulated by the authoritarian regimes of the ROK from the 1960s to the 1980s and by conservative administrations from the 1990s onward and have been amplified by the conservative media. It is not accidental that conservative newspapers have published numerous articles and editorials about "the North Korean missile threat" and "the US-ROK alliance crisis" as the controversy over the THAAD deployment has heated up. These manipulated and amplified fears have devastated "the moral imagination" of the South Korean citizens; many of them have lost "the capacity to imagine and generate constructive responses and initiatives that, while rooted in the day-to-day challenges of violence, transcend and ultimately break the grips of those destructive patterns and cycles."[54]

Nevertheless, there have been prophetic communities that have tried to preserve and cultivate the moral imagination beyond fear and toward peace on the Korean Peninsula. Soon after the ROK-US joint statement on the deployment of THAAD, the National Council of Churches in Korea (NCCK) released its official statement titled "Go Away THAAD, Come Peace" and envisioned the moral imagination moving toward "true peace" achieved by "mutual respect and dialogue," not "military weapons."[55] The envisioned moral imagination was practiced through the NCCK members' active participation in the democratic protest against the THAAD deployment in solidarity with residents in Seongju County and the "Peace

---

54. Lederach, *Moral Imagination*, 29.

55. The Reconciliation and Reunification Commission of the NCCK, "[Go Away THHAD, Come Peace]."

Prayer Service" calling for the peace of Christ.[56] This example of the moral imagination presents us with the hope of breaking the destructive cycles of competitive militarization on the Korean Peninsula. This hope is not mere optimism that glosses over the tragic realities in ROK-DPRK relations, but "responsible hope" that "generates and sustains moral agency" to overcome fear and strive for the peace of Christ on the Korean Peninsula.[57]

---

56. The Reconciliation and Reunification Commission of the NCCK, "[Go Away THHAD, Come Peace]."

57. Marshall, *Though the Fig Tree*, xiii.

Part Three

PRACTICING THE BUSINESS OF WAR TODAY

7

Contracting Justice?
Private Military and Security Contractors and the Commodification of War

BRADLEY B. BURROUGHS

Introduction

Over the course of the last generation numerous developments have dramatically changed how wars and similar conflicts are waged. Among the most consequential, yet also among the most invisible, has been the growing role of private military and security contractors (PMSCs). Offering a wide array of services—from logistical support to strategic planning, from armed security to military training—PMSCs have operated in scores of countries around the globe.[1] Their employers include nongovernmental organizations, corporations, and states that range from the comparatively weak to military superpowers. Nonetheless, no party has been more central in the rise of PMSCs than the United States, which has been both a key supplier of PMSCs and the largest consumer of their services.

At times, egregious incidents have drawn attention to the United States' dependence on PMSCs and their presence in the US's wars in

---

1. See Singer, *Corporate Warriors*, 8–17.

Afghanistan and Iraq. For instance, on March 31, 2004, a roadside bomb killed four Blackwater employees in Fallujah before a crowd dragged their bodies through the streets and hung them from a bridge over the Euphrates.[2] Around that same time, news reports were emerging that implicated contractors from CACI International and Titan in the use of torture at Abu Ghraib prison.[3] And most prominently, two years later, on September 16, 2006, Blackwater contractors opened fire in Baghdad's Nisour Square, killing seventeen civilians and injuring at least twenty more.[4]

Such incidents occasionally grab headlines. To the extent that we focus upon the headlines, however, we are liable to miss that these are not isolated incidents but instead part of a broader shift in how the United States staffs and conducts war—and, increasingly, how other states do so as well. Utilization of military contractors is by no means novel in US history, and in fact stretches back to the nation's inception in which colonial forces contracted private individuals and businesses to support the Revolutionary War.[5] And yet the shift to utilizing PMSCs that began in the mid-1990s is remarkable in its size and scope.

The size of the contracting force in recent wars has grown massively. While the Department of Defense (DOD) contracts the majority of PMSCs that the US employs, the State Department and the United States Agency for International Development (USAID) also rely heavily upon them. At its highest point, in March 2010, these three agencies combined to employ over 262,000 contractors in Iraq and Afghanistan.[6] As a result of this reliance, contractors have come to represent an unprecedented proportion of US forces. Throughout US history, regular troops have typically outnumbered contractors in theatre by significant margins—for instance, by ratios of 6:1 in the Revolutionary War, 20:1 in World War I, 2.5:1 in the Korean War, and 60:1 in the Gulf War.[7] In the United States' most recent interventions in the Balkans, Afghanistan, and Iraq, however, that has generally equalized to a ratio of 1:1, and in certain cases DOD contractors alone have outnumbered soldiers by 3:1.[8] The costs to employ those contractors have been significant. Accounted in 2017 US dollars, DOD contracts in Iraq and Afghanistan

2. Gettleman, "Enraged Mob."

3. Merle and McCarthy, "6 Employees from CACI." See also Bina, "Private Military Contractor Liability."

4. Johnston and Broder, "F.B.I. Says Guards Killed 14."

5. Commission on Wartime Contracting, "At What Cost?," 20.

6. Commission on Wartime Contracting, "Transforming Wartime Contracting," 20.

7. Commission on Wartime Contracting, "At What Cost?," 21.

8. See Peters and Plagakis, "Contractor and Troop Levels," 5.

surpassed 25 billion dollars each year for seven consecutive fiscal years, from 2007 to 2013.[9] Among the largest contracts have been a 30 billion dollar multiyear contract with Kellogg Brown & Root (KBR) for logistical support and a 2.1 billion dollar contract with DynCorp for a variety of services, including program management, logistical support, and military training.[10]

In addition to the remarkable size of the contracting force and government expenditures, PMSCs have also been entrusted with an exceptionally broad scope of tasks. Whereas in previous wars contractors were enlisted predominantly to provide services removed from the battle space, such as medical care, food preparation, and transportation, in recent conflicts PMSCs have been charged with armed security, military training, intelligence gathering and analysis, and maintaining weaponry and equipment.[11] They have even been tasked with overseeing other PMSCs. As part of Project Matrix, Aegis Defence Services won a 293 million dollar contract in May 2004 to provide antiterrorism support, tracking PMSCs and reconstruction projects in Iraq, as well as coordinating communication between coalition forces and PMSCs.[12] Moreover, PMSCs have also been responsible for operating and maintaining computing systems at NORAD's Cheyenne Mountain base, which coordinates the US response to nuclear threats, and have flown aerial drones on behalf of the military.[13] Given the critical roles they have come to play, it is understandable that Ashton Carter, at the time the Under Secretary for Defense Acquisitions, Technology, and Logistics, concluded that the US "simply is not going to go to war without contractors."[14] Due to the flexibility and cost savings PMSCs can provide and the legitimation lent to the industry, especially by the US government, the same is likely to be true of an ever-growing number of nations in the years ahead.

And yet, particularly when viewed from a Christian perspective, the current regime of PMSC use, especially as exemplified in the US but also as practiced more broadly, should occasion significant moral reservations and even objections. Transforming war into a capitalist imperative for an increasingly influential industry, the expanded use of PMSCs makes it more difficult to place democratic checks upon the use of military power,

9. Peters and Plagakis, "Contractor and Troop Levels," 12.
10. Commission on Wartime Contracting, "Transforming Wartime Contracting," 212–14.
11. See Schwartz and Church, "Department of Defense's Use of Contractors," 14–16.
12. Stanger, *One Nation under Contract*, 100; Isenberg, *Shadow Force*, 68–69.
13. Singer, *Corporate Warriors*, 16–17.
14. Quoted in Commission on Wartime Contracting, "Transforming Wartime Contracting," 18.

commodifies war in a fashion that obscures its tragedy and misery, and threatens to further constrict the role of justice in determining military engagements.

Military Privatization and the Perils of Power

The wide range of services PMSCs provide and the varied environments in which they operate make a comprehensive ethical analysis of the industry impossible in an essay of this length. DOD contracts with KBR for food services raise markedly different issues than those with companies such as Blackwater (which has since changed its name to Xe and then again to Academi) for armed security. Yet further issues emerge when considering cases such as Executive Outcomes' 1995–96 intervention in Sierra Leone, in which the firm provided the government with soldiers, helicopter gunships, and military training worth roughly 10 million dollars in exchange for approximately 200 million dollars in rights to Sierra Leone's diamond fields.[15] And all of these differ substantially from nongovernmental organizations, such as the World Wildlife Federation, employing PMSCs to provide for security needs. To refine our focus, this essay will concentrate primarily upon the United States government's use of PMSCs while also seeking as possible to illuminate more general industry dynamics.

In the vast majority of instances involving nation-states, a crucial dynamic in the rise of PMSCs is privatization as governments have transferred key functions from public institutions to private enterprises. Hence, while the rise of PMSCs most obviously marks a shift in military affairs, it more broadly constitutes a shift in political, as well as economic, affairs. A number of factors have driven this shift. In the case of the US, the reduction of the active-duty military that followed the end of the Cold War combined with a decline in funding to allied agencies to leave government without "the organic capacity to perform some mission-critical functions," especially in contingency operations, such as the wars in Iraq and Afghanistan.[16] At the same time, PMSCs began tapping into the pool of recently demobilized soldiers, capitalizing upon specialized skills and developing logistical capacities that enabled them to fill such gaps.[17] As a result, government agencies would come to treat private contractors as a "default option" for meeting

---

15. Singer, *Corporate Warriors*, 112–13, 166–67.

16. Commission on Wartime Contracting, "Transforming Wartime Contracting," 2.

17. See, for instance, Singer, *Corporate Warriors*, 53; Godfrey et al., "Private Military Industry," 111.

many needs.¹⁸ This move, which promised to boost efficiency by eliminating redundancies and replacing long-term investments with short-term contracts, also drew momentum from the larger privatizing trend that, from the 1980s onwards, reshaped the operations of many Western governments as utilities, hospitals, transit, airport operations, and many other previously public services were handed over to private firms.¹⁹

Thus, the outsourcing of military and security services to PMSCs by no means stands as the only or even the largest example of privatization; from a Christian perspective, however, it must rank as one of the most worrisome. Such worries should not be premised upon a romanticization of the modern, Westphalian state and the direct monopoly on military violence that has been one of its most salient characteristics. After all, that monopoly only solidified in the last two or three centuries.²⁰ Considered in the longer sweep of history, one might judge the model of political rulers contracting with private forces, such as mercenaries, to be "the rule rather than the exception."²¹ And yet, Christian thinkers voiced no consistent objection to such arrangements. In the few cases where they did object, as in the Third Lateran Council's denunciation of the *routiers*, they generally focused less upon the use of private military forces per se than upon abuses those forces had committed, such as practicing "such cruelty upon Christians that they respect neither churches nor monasteries, and spare neither widows, orphans, old or young nor any age or sex."²² In other words, such denunciations objected not to privately contracting for military services, which they seemed not to regard as inherently evil, but to brigandage and criminality.²³ Any romanticized conception of the modern state dissolves further in view of an honest examination of its history. The Napoleonic Wars, the military-led extermination of the Native Americans, the Armenian genocide, the Japanese subjection of Manchuria, and the horrors of two world wars capped by the nuclear bombings of Hiroshima

18. Commission on Wartime Contracting, "Transforming Wartime Contracting," 2.

19. Godfrey et al., "Private Military Industry," 106–25, especially 110.

20. See Percy, *Mercenaries*, 7, 68–120.

21. Eckert, *Outsourcing War*, 44, 58. See also Singer, *Corporate Warriors*, 19; and Avant, "From Mercenary to Citizen Armies," 41–72.

22. Tanner and Alberigo, *Decrees of the Ecumenical Councils*, 1:224–25; Russell, *Just War in the Middle Ages*, 189. For one of the more notable defenses of mercenarism, see John of Naples, "Should a Christian King Use Unbelievers to Defend His Kingdom?"

23. This is perhaps unsurprising given that King David, one of the most prominent figures in the Christian Bible, could reasonably be interpreted as having served as a mercenary. See 1 Samuel 27:2–11 and Wright, *David, King of Israel*, 32–36. See also Eckert, *Outsourcing War*, 74.

and Nagasaki attest to Westphalian-style militaries' capacity for massive and murderous violence.

Nevertheless, a Christian account of the nature of power provides reason to worry that as the tendency for governments to privately contract military force expands, the prospects for justice contract. A crucial reason for this is that it provides a means for authorities to exert power in ways that become increasingly difficult to check.

Some Christians may fail to recognize or refuse to acknowledge such threats due to assumptions about government derived primarily from chapter 13 of Paul's letter to the Romans. There Paul admonishes "every person" to be "subject to the governing authorities" because such authorities "have been instituted by God" and are "God's servant for your good"; in particular, Paul identifies that service with bearing the sword, which the authorities use "to execute wrath on the wrongdoer" (13:1–4). Interpreted positivistically and in isolation, this passage might be (and often is) read to demand complete, quietistic submission to government, which should be given carte blanche in ordering secular affairs since it will always do so in accordance with God's will. From this perspective, the use of PMSCs appears simply as another way in which government wields the sword to invariably serve our good.

In the larger biblical canon, however, governmental authorities' service to human good and alignment with God's will is far from invariable. Instead, such authorities commonly defy the will of the Lord, who "is a God of justice" (Isa 30:18) and calls human beings to do "righteousness and justice" (Gen 18:19). The Bible contains numerous examples in which governmental authorities employ their power unjustly and, in a reversal of Romans 13:3, terrorize not bad conduct but good. As judges, the sons of Samuel "perverted justice" (1 Sam 8:3). Isaiah denounces rulers "who make iniquitous decrees, who write oppressive statutes, to turn aside the needy from justice and to rob the poor of my people of their right" (10:1–2). The Gospel of Matthew depicts King Herod seeking to secure his power by massacring innocent children (2:16). Revelation foresees the coming of an apocalyptic beast that bears all the hallmarks of government and "make[s] war on the saints" (13:7). And, of course, the Christian story turns upon the person of Jesus Christ, the "Just One" (Acts 7:52) who "knew no sin" (2 Cor 5:21), whom the Roman imperial authorities ignominiously tortured and executed.

Even if governmental power invariably serves human good in some eschatological sense then, Christians should recognize that checks upon such power provide mechanisms that can be used to resist tyranny and advance human beings' temporal good, helping earthly affairs more closely approximate God's will. For this reason, Reinhold Niebuhr concluded that "democracy in politics is a perennial necessity" since "justice will always require that the power of government be checked as democracy checks it."[24] This does not guarantee that democratic governments will necessarily be just, of course. Yet without such checks, humanity's bondage to sin means government power will tend even more strongly toward oppression and injustice.[25] And the desirability of democratic checks is a point on which even Niebuhr's most ardent critics can find themselves agreeing. While cautioning that no democracy is ever truly governed by the people but always by an elite, John Howard Yoder, for instance, identifies democracy as the least oppressive such arrangement "since it provides the strongest language of justification and therefore of critique which the subjects may use to mitigate its oppressiveness."[26]

Viewed through this lens, a central problem with PMSCs is a lack of transparency and the ability this affords them and government leaders to evade democratic checks. Again, one must resist romanticism. Public militaries are themselves frequently opaque and insufficiently subject to democratic controls, as underscored in the Vietnam War era by the Pentagon Papers and more recently by the deaths of US soldiers in Niger as part of operations that even members of the Senate Armed Services Committee claimed they were unaware of.[27] But the use of PMSCs does not resolve such problems and may in fact aggravate them. Given the promiscuous potential of PMSCs, even identifying whose behalf they are acting upon can be difficult. Such problems multiply when taking account of the fact that PMSCs commonly engage subcontractors to fulfill portions of their missions. In the United States, further complications arise from the legal protections accorded PMSCs. Deeming information about contracts, policies, missions, and more to be proprietary, PMSCs for years shielded crucial information about their operations from Freedom of Information Act (FOIA) requests.[28] The FOIA Improvement Law of 2016 may compel greater disclosure. But in regard to PMSCs its efficacy has yet to be truly tested and its loopholes fully discovered.

In the past, US policymakers have exploited such loopholes and similar peculiarities to pursue strategic objectives without public scrutiny

24. Niebuhr, *Christianity and Power Politics*, 85.

25. This argument is made most cogently in Niebuhr, *The Children of Light*.

26. Yoder, *Priestly Kingdom*, 158–59.

27. Haltiwanger, "How Many Troops?"

28. See, for instance, Minow, "Outsourcing Power," 999–1000, 1024–25; Godfrey et al., "Private Military Industry," 119–21; Avant and Sigelman, "Private Security and Democracy," 230–65.

or support. For example, Peter Singer has argued that the administration of George W. Bush utilized PMSCs in Colombia to evade congressional limits on the use of military personnel.[29] Despite worries that such measures amounted to "outsourcing a war," the details of the contracts awarded to the main PMSCs involved, DynCorp and Military Professional Resources Incorporated (MPRI), have proven difficult to obtain.[30] Moreover, as Allison Stanger and Mark Eric Williams explain, procurement procedures for PMSCs can be structured in ways that hide all but the most minimal information from FOIA requests.[31] Among the consequential information generally hidden from view is the number of contractors killed in areas of conflict. During the United States' wars in Afghanistan and Iraq, the Pentagon kept no public tally of PMSC fatalities. When the Commission for Wartime Contracting investigated, it found that from the October 2001 start of the war in Afghanistan and the March 2003 start of the war in Iraq through July 2011, 887 contractor deaths had been reported in Afghanistan and 1,542 in Iraq.[32] While the Commission acknowledged that the full number of contractor deaths was "undoubtedly higher," these figures alone represent over 28 percent of US personnel deaths. As those wars continued, the proportion of contractor deaths rose; between June 2009 and March 2011, for example, the number of contractor deaths exceeded 50 percent of US fatalities.

The opacity that clouds the United States' employment of PMSCs has led to a state of affairs in which citizens—and even their congressional representatives—often find themselves in the dark on key matters of US foreign policy. Not only do they remain oblivious to the true costs of those policies in blood and treasure, but they are often uninformed about the very policies themselves. Such an arrangement does not merely diminish public debate but seeks to obviate it entirely. In the process, it further shifts power from the legislative branch to the executive.[33] Thus, although the reliance upon private parties for military services may seem to signal a weakening of governmental power, this is not necessarily so. Instead, as Saskia Stachowitsch argues, it is a means by which the neoliberal state predicated upon privatization cedes direct control of certain tasks so that the executive branch may

29. Singer, *Corporate Warriors*, 206–11; Singer, "Outsourcing War," 126. See also Pattison, "Legitimacy of the Military," 140.

30. Singer, *Corporate Warriors*, 208. See also International Consortium of Investigative Journalists, "Outsourcing War."

31. Stanger and Williams, "Private Military Corporations," 11.

32. Commission on Wartime Contracting, "Transforming Wartime Contracting," 31.

33. See Avant, "Implications of Marketized Security," 511.

gain "flexibility and independence" in other areas, consolidating its power and the power of the state.[34]

When War Becomes a Capitalist Imperative: Commodification and the Loss of Tragedy and Anguish

Nevertheless, although they can be easily overstated, worries about the enfeeblement of the state do not entirely lack basis. In the United States' employment of PMSCs, this means of consolidating the power of the state—or, more narrowly, the executive branch—simultaneously entails the empowerment of private corporations. Thus, even if the state is currently the dog that wags the tail of the PMSC industry, it is by no means impossible that, should the transfer of power and influence to corporate interests continue, ultimately the tail should wag the dog.

Even to this point the PMSC industry has gained immense power and influence in government policy, perhaps most strikingly represented in the person of Dick Cheney. Following his 1989-93 tenure as US Secretary of Defense, Cheney became the CEO of Halliburton, an oil-services firm that was also the parent company of Brown & Root Services (BRS), which through further mergers soon became KBR. Before Cheney's arrival at Halliburton, BRS had won significant government bids, including the lucrative contract for the Logistics Civil Augmentation Program, known as LOGCAP I. Nevertheless, and in spite of Cheney's attempts to limit his own public involvement in BRS's government contracts, during his time as CEO of Halliburton the amount of government credit guarantees BRS received jumped from 100 million to 1.5 billion dollars.[35] In July 2000, Cheney stepped down as CEO of Halliburton to become George W. Bush's running mate. As vice president, Cheney was instrumental in crafting the United States' response to the attacks of September 11, 2001, which would lead the US to war in Afghanistan and Iraq.

Moreover, Cheney played a salient role in marketing the Iraq War to the American people, though not necessarily on the most honest grounds. Most ominously, Michael Morell, a CIA officer who routinely handled President Bush's daily briefings and later served as acting director of central intelligence, has noted that Cheney continued to assert that a connection between Iraq and al-Qaeda existed even after the CIA judged it doubtful and has also alleged that Cheney's aid, Scooter Libby, attempted to intimidate CIA officers into changing their assessment, describing Libby's actions as

34. Stachowitsch, "Military Privatization," 30.
35. Singer, *Corporate Warriors*, 140.

"the most blatant attempt to politicize intelligence that I saw in thirty-three years in the business."[36] More publicly and indisputably, Cheney blithely assured audiences that when it entered Iraq, the United States would be "greeted as liberators" and that the war would "go relatively quickly, weeks rather than months."[37] This despite the fact that less than a decade earlier he defended President George H. W. Bush's decision not to mount a full-scale invasion of Iraq by saying that such an operation would ensnare the US in a "quagmire."[38]

KBR profited immensely from the United States' decisions to go to war in Afghanistan and Iraq that Cheney influenced. Between 2002 and mid-2011 KBR received contract awards totaling 40.8 billion dollars, a number of which were later flagged for being awarded without sufficient competition.[39] Much of the focus on Cheney's relationship with KBR has centered upon charges of individual corruption, charges against which he sought to defend himself by pledging to donate to charity all deferred compensation from Halliburton.[40] Even if one accepts Cheney's response as sufficient, however, the prospect of a high government official employing false pretenses to grease the skids that lead to war and to a huge payday for his former corporation—which additionally appears to have benefited from preferential treatment and a lack of competition—is troubling. While some may argue that Cheney's case does not fully realize it, it clearly suggests the possibility for governmental and corporate power to coalesce to generate a dangerous inertia toward war.[41]

Hence, another crucial worry Christians should harbor about PMSCs focuses upon the transformation of war into a capitalist imperative essential to the profitability of enterprises possessing significant political power. Such a conception of war not only obviously fails to harmonize with the strong pacifist strand of the Christian faith but resounds cacophonously even with more permissive understandings that allow that the violence of war may be justified under certain circumstances.

In a *locus classicus* of the Christian defense of justified war, Augustine sounds a crucial leitmotif. Meditating upon the conflict of unavoidable ignorance with unavoidable duty, he considers the role of a judge, who at

36. Morell, *Great War*, 87.
37. Thorpe, *Soldier Girls*, 80.
38. Spillius, "Dick Cheney Iraq 'Quagmire.'"
39. Commission on Wartime Contracting, "Transforming Wartime Contracting," 25, 75–77.
40. Murphy, "Cheney's Halliburton Ties Remain."
41. For similar worries, see Minow, "Outsourcing Power," 1022.

times in Augustine's context would have felt compelled to use torture as part of the investigative process. Because torture was regarded as the most reliable means of discovering the truth, its use would have seemed to be a duty of the office. But is the judge happy? To this question, Augustine responds, "Surely it would be more compassionate, and more worthy of the dignity of man, if he were to acknowledge that the necessity of acting in this way is a miserable one: if he hated his own part in it, and if, with the knowledge of godliness, he cried out to God, 'From my necessities deliver Thou me.'"[42] Extending this line of thought, Augustine notes that "wise men, they say, will wage just wars."[43] Nevertheless, if one is truly wise, one will "be readier to deplore the fact that he is under the necessity of waging even just wars." Although it may be necessary, war is tragedy. Moreover, Augustine insists, "this is misery. And if anyone either endures [wars] or thinks of them without anguish of the soul, his condition is still more miserable."

Augustine's insights present poignant questions to PMSCs and their clients, which in a real sense includes all US citizens, as well as citizens of many other countries. Can one fully appreciate the misery and tragedy of war and call out to God for deliverance from war while building companies and industries whose profitability depends upon it or that proactively plan to capitalize upon it? As war becomes a capitalist imperative, at what point is it transmogrified from a tragic necessity thrust upon us, a necessity deplored and accepted only reluctantly, into an apparent good—though finally an illusory good—misguidedly pursued to the ultimate immiseration of ourselves and others? And might such a transmogrification quench the anguish that should accompany our contemplation of war and without which we are, in Augustine's words, "still more miserable" for having "lost all human feeling"?[44]

The current regime of PMSC use, and perhaps the very nature of PMSCs, endangers such wholesome anguish, for as military force becomes commodified it tends simultaneously to become fetishized. Fundamental to commodification is that the commodity, which is intended specifically for exchange, becomes expressed in objective, monetary terms. This directs attention away from the conditions of production and to the price tag, "concealing, instead of disclosing, the social character of private labor" and endowing commodities with a mystical, fetishistic quality such that they appear as if by magic rather than as the products of human labor.[45]

42. Augustine, *City of God* 19.6.
43. Augustine, *City of God* 19.7.
44. Augustine, *City of God* 19.7.
45. Marx, *Capital, Volume One*, 324.

Commodification of military labor conceals many crucial realities. Among them are the lives lost by military contractors. As the Commission on Wartime Contracting in Iraq and Afghanistan observed, "The extensive use of contractors obscures the full human cost of war."[46] Combined with the tendency of contemporary warfare and media outlets to elide civilian casualties and perpetuate the ideology of "surgical strikes," such obscurity contributes to the mythical conception of contemporary warfare as bloodless, or at least free of tragedy, even as lives are lost. Occasional reports of contractor deaths may threaten to puncture such precious illusions. Yet they can be easily dismissed as the unfortunate results of freely chosen market transactions made by individual contractors rather than the upshot of foreign policy decisions in which we as citizens are implicated. When, through commodification and other machinations, war becomes ostensibly non-tragic—its losses generally hidden from public view and rationalized when they appear—true anguish over the horror of war becomes nigh impossible.

The Global Rescaling of Military Recruitment and the Exploitation of Military Contractors

The commodification and privatization of military labor manifested in the PMSC industry has concealed not only the lives lost in war but also a dramatic shift in the identity of those who provide such labor. One might naturally assume that the vast majority of those serving in the United States' wars would be United States citizens, or at least persons on their way to gaining their citizenship. Increasingly, however, such assumptions are mistaken. Rather, local nationals (LNs) and third-country nationals (TCNs)—that is, respectively, persons from the country in which the conflict is taking place and those who hail from neither that country nor the United States—often comprise a large percentage of US forces. For instance, in September 2009, LNs and TCNs together composed 91 percent of DOD contractors in Afghanistan and 56.4 percent of all US personnel, including both contractors and military troops.[47] In Iraq, the United States has depended heavily upon TCNs, whose numbers have consistently surpassed those of US contractors and rivaled the number of US troops. Notably, TCNs have been disproportionately represented among contractors providing security services. In October 2012, for example, TCNs represented 86 percent of

46. Commission on Wartime Contracting, "Transforming Wartime Contracting," 30–31.

47. Schwartz and Church, "Department of Defense's Use of Contractors," 24.

all private security contractors in Iraq.[48] PMSCs have thus effected what Maya Eichler calls a "global rescaling of military recruitment"[49] as well as a redistribution of the accompanying risks to persons on the periphery of the global economic order. The lives of persons from poor countries are often the ones on the line in US wars.

Preference for LNs and TCNs is not accidental; indeed, it may be essential to success in the current PMSC marketplace not only because it redistributes military risk and thus reduces the possibility of political resistance, an attractive quality for governmental officials, but also because it helps PMSCs deliver on what may be their strongest selling point: cost savings. Doug Brooks, founder of the International Stability Operations Association, the leading PMSC trade group, has admitted as much, stating, "If you're running Triple Canopy and you want to protect a warehouse, your basic American [security contractor] is costing you about 30,000 US dollars a month . . . and if company X who is competing against you uses Iraqi [security contractors] which costs them around 700 US dollars a month, who is going to win that contract?"[50]

Beyond earning a fraction of what US nationals make, LNs and TCNs generally lack leverage to push for better treatment or higher wages, making them ripe for exploitation. The Commission on Wartime Contracting recorded a number of such instances from just one fact-finding mission in April 2009, including the story of a Ugandan security contractor for Triple Canopy whose base was so ill-equipped and lacking in cold-weather gear that he ultimately shot and killed himself. Other cases involved firms preventing TCNs from returning home after completing their contract terms, forcing them to work twelve-hour shifts and seventy-two-hour weeks and denying promised time off. A later mission found instances of TCNs lured to Afghanistan under false pretenses.[51] Thus, as Eichler concludes, "inequalities of race, class, gender, and citizenship do not enter" into the discourse of the PMSC industry, and yet they are often "unspoken assumptions." The use of PMSCs has thereby created "new opportunities for the exploitation of vulnerable populations."[52]

Many factors contribute to the vulnerability of LNs and TCNs, including the dynamics of commodification and the remoteness of the

48. Office of the Assistant Secretary of Defense, "Contractor Support of US Operations."
49. Eichler, "Contracting Out of Military Work," 606.
50. Bennett, "Cheap Labor for Private Security."
51. Commission on Wartime Contracting, "Transforming Wartime Contracting," 92–94.
52. Eichler, "Contracting Out of Military Work," 609.

United States' wars in Iraq and Afghanistan, which conspire to assure that details of their plight rarely come into view. Compounding these is the moral myopia that can distort the nation-state system and leaves many US citizens unable to see such persons as members of a common community that entitles them to robust protections and interests us in their just treatment. As the philosopher Michael Walzer keenly observes, when considering questions of justice "the primary good that we distribute to one another is membership in some human community."[53] Without some such sense of common membership, moral questions hardly arise.

Central themes of the Christian faith would correct the myopic vision that so commonly excludes citizens of other nations from our moral concern. It teaches that all persons belong to the community of humanity created by God and that bears the divine image. When that community became riven by divisions, Jesus Christ "broke down the dividing wall" and "create[d] in himself one new humanity . . . thus making peace" (Eph 2:13–15). This new humanity in the body of Christ includes all persons at least as potential members in accordance with Christ's proclamation that "I, when I am lifted up from the earth, will draw all people to myself" (John 12:32). And our citizenship in the municipalities of the world is relativized by the realization that "our citizenship is in heaven" (Phil 3:20). All, then, exist within what should be the ambit of Christians' moral concern. We cannot unfeelingly dismiss the maltreatment of PMSC personnel as the result of freely chosen market transactions any more than we can sterilely write off civilian casualties as mere "collateral damage." To do so is to betray our allegiances to God and God's beloved community. As Martin Luther King Jr. insisted, those possessed by such a vision find themselves "called to speak for the weak, for the voiceless, for the victims of our nation and for those it calls enemy, for no document from human hands can make these humans any less our brothers."[54]

Preventing Military Contracting from Contracting the Role of Justice

As we have seen, the appeal of PMSCs derives substantially from the promise that they might lower the price of war, particularly by making war less financially and politically costly. Simultaneously, the PMSC industry has established political connections and developed lobbying capabilities that, together with the dynamics of privatization and commodification, could

---

53. Walzer, *Spheres of Justice*, 31.
54. King, "Time to Break Silence," in *Testament of Hope*, 234.

contribute inertia toward continuing present military interventions or initiating future ones. As the impediments to war decrease and the possible pressures toward it increase, we face another pressing question: Will our and our nations' wisdom and moral fiber prove sufficient to resist the temptations to fight unjustly? Or will we instead become more liable to pursue military interventions, even when they possess hardly a patina of justice? Put differently, can we prevent the growth of military contracting from further contracting the role of justice in determining military engagements?

Such questions are especially pressing for Christians who defend the possibility of justified war. Few have identified the central difficulty of that strand of thought more succinctly than Paul Ramsey, who posited that within it "the chief problem facing us is not *what* are the moral limits upon the just conduct of war, but *where* are those principles, i.e., *where* are the men [sic] in whose minds and *where* is the community of men [sic] in whose very *ethos* the propelling reason for ever engaging in war also itself lays down intrinsic moral limits upon how the defense of civilized life is to proceed?"[55] The tendency to idolize the Westphalian nation-state, as well as parochial allegiances that predated it, has long presented obstacles to cultivating persons who appreciate the gravity of war and conscientiously limit their support of it to cases that satisfy stringent criteria of justice.

Nevertheless, the increasing use of PMSCs promises to make those obstacles even more difficult to surmount. On the one hand, as Amy Eckert argues, "If they are not calling down the costs of war on themselves, citizens will lose the personal motivation to take the justice of their cause seriously."[56] On the other, even if citizens are keenly interested in such questions of justice, outsourcing military responsibilities to private corporations requires ceding to corporations the ability to select who in fact conducts the war. This is particularly problematic in the case of contractors who provide armed security. Despite the fact that their jobs entail the very real possibility of employing lethal force, a function many regard as inherently public,[57] firms could select employees on grounds that serve narrower private interests—for instance, by choosing to hire persons willing to accept low wages or to work in substandard conditions, or even persons who exhibit an enthusiasm for deadly violence. In light of the many instances of PMSCs hiring unqualified or ill-equipped individuals,[58] as well as examples of

55. Ramsey, *War and the Christian Conscience*, xxii–xxiii, emphasis original.
56. Eckert, *Outsourcing War*, 79.
57. Verkuil, *Outsourcing Sovereignty*, 27.
58. For some examples, see Singer, *Corporate Warriors*, 156–57; Singer, "Outsourcing War," 125; Hagedorn, *Invisible Soldiers*, 245–46. And while by no means conclusive proof of injustice, studies of Blackwater have revealed that their employees shot first

certain firms' insensitivity to the demands of justice in labor relations, such worries are by no means simply theoretical.

Forming persons equipped to recognize and faithfully adhere to moral limitations upon war marks a particular challenge for Christian defenders of just war. As Gerald Schlabach argues, Christianity lacks a "just war *tradition* in the full communal sense of which Aristotelians such as philosopher Alasdair MacIntyre speak, a living tradition with operative practices shaping a community through time."[59] Yet we need such communities of formation and accountability if we are to have Christians who can keep the distinctive motifs of Christian teaching about justified war—and the limitations upon it—from simply blending into the theme played when the drums of war begin to beat. But whether one identifies oneself as a just warrior, a pacifist, or in some other way, all Christians have a stake in vivifying theological and ethical reflection upon war and how we might live faithfully as war becomes increasingly privatized, technologized, and commodified. For in a faith that teaches us that all are our brothers and sisters, war is always an affair of immense gravity and can never be just business.

---

in more than 80 percent of engagements. See Hagedorn, *Invisible Soldiers*, 103; Eckert, *Outsourcing War*, 17.

59. Schlabach, "Warfare vs. Policing," in Schlabach, *Just Policing*, 72, emphasis original.

8

The Military-Educational Complex

KARA N. SLADE

> Accordingly, I think that it is well to warn studious and able young men, who fear God and are seeking for happiness of life, not to venture heedlessly upon the pursuit of the branches of learning that are in vogue beyond the pale of the Church of Christ, as if these could secure for them the happiness they seek; but soberly and carefully to discriminate among them.
>
> —ST. AUGUSTINE, *ON CHRISTIAN DOCTRINE*

> When he saw a dead body, he couldn't even see the wounds.
>
> —GRAHAM GREENE, *THE QUIET AMERICAN*

Introduction

In 2011, members of the American Institute of Aeronautics and Astronautics (AIAA), the principal professional society for engineers in the aerospace industry, were asked to share what can only be described as their aerospace engineering conversion story on the institute's website. As the AIAA's winsomely illustrated online public relations campaign asked,

> When did you know you wanted to work in aerospace? For some it was a specific moment, for others it was a gradual realization that space and flight had captured their imagination and wouldn't let go.[1]

A survey of the responses posted on the site revealed that besides the influence of a beloved family member or teacher, the most common source of motivation for students to enter the profession involved the aesthetic allure of airplanes or spacecraft. One member described the particularities of this aesthetic response in markedly poetic terms:

> I was in Spanish class in the 8th grade, sitting by the window on the third floor. From my seat I could see an F-16 practicing its aerobatic routine for the annual air show, over and over again. . . . I was not so much taken with the pilot inside as with the machine itself. It was a thing of beauty. I thought about the people who created it, and what it must feel like to see your creation dancing over your head. I decided then I wanted to be one of them and bring forth my own beautiful machines.[2]

Upon reading the archive of submissions to this campaign myself, I was reminded of the much more prosaic words of a student in one of my own engineering classes who succinctly described the same sense of attraction: "Dr. Slade, I just think bombs are cool."

As Christians living in America, we are called to clarity of sight and truthfulness of speech about the realities of war, including the technologies of war. And yet that clarity can be elusive, especially for those who are directly involved in the design and manufacture of weapons. How might an attraction to the spectacle of an F-16 "dancing" impede the ability to turn a critical eye on its use as a tool of state violence? How might the intoxicating sense of achievement that comes from seeing a complex project through to its conclusion sever engineers like me from any sense of connection to those it will be used against? This detachment, I believe, is one of the primary stumbling blocks to moral formation for future engineers like my rather unreflective student. While this has heretofore taken a back seat to matters of moral casuistry or policy analysis in Christian moral theological discourse around defense technologies such as drones, I believe the problem

1. AIAA.org, "When Did You Know?"
2. AIAA.org, "When Did You Know?"

of moral detachment from the work of military technology bears further interrogation in greater depth.

Much of this volume is rightly focused on more direct aspects of war and its conduct in the twenty-first century. However, I am interested in a set of questions that originate at a significant remove from the front lines but which still participate—at times, tacitly—in the broader national project that is the contemporary American way of war. How does the "military-educational complex" function in America to recruit and form the designers and builders of weapons, from the aforementioned F-16 to the Predator drone to intelligence satellites? And how might Christian theology be called to speak a word of witness to a process of marketing, recruitment, and education that begins in childhood and extends through engineering schools to the work of professional societies like the AIAA? While this chapter cannot provide a comprehensive and complete answer to these questions, I hope that at least it will spur other Christian thinkers and teachers across the disciplines to ask better questions about the intersections of military technology and education—including those at their own institutions.

Writing as a former engineering educator at the undergraduate and graduate level, as well as a former federal civil servant, I am of course interested in how military priorities, both in terms of research funding and recruitment, are brought to bear on higher education. At the same time, the matter of research funding is perhaps at once the most obvious and the least interesting aspect of how the military and the university converge or collide. Little moral-theological acumen is needed to note the vast amount of grant money funneled from various parts of the Department of Defense and related agencies to American universities. The pipeline of money as such is easy enough to follow. This essay, on the other hand, is concerned with a different pipeline—a conduit of *people*—that begins in K-12 education, extends through engineering schools, and culminates in professional recruitment by corporations and government agencies.

This essay is particularly concerned with three aspects of the intersection of military technology and education. The first is the notion of the "STEM pipeline" and the depth of its tacit relationship to the aerospace and defense industry. Specifically, I am interested in how the rhetoric promoting STEM (science, technology, engineering, and mathematics) education, from the early grades to higher education, works as an alternative soteriology meant both to establish and to maintain the health of the national social body. In other words, how is technological education thought of as a saving necessity for the American economy and for the future of the defense industry? Second, I will address the aforementioned aesthetic appeal of military technology and its role in promoting the defense industry as a career, both to those students considering it as a possible option for specialization, and as a means of reinforcement to professionals already within the system. Third, I will turn to the teaching of engineering ethics as a discipline within the military-educational complex and to the limitations that prevent it from acting as any sort of meaningful check to the ways in which technology is deployed for the purposes of killing. And finally, I hope to offer a theological witness to the possibility of life otherwise, both within and beyond the porous borders of the military-educational complex.

The Pipeline

The path to a career in the aerospace and defense (A&D) industry functions on multiple levels, working to funnel students of all ages into a "pipeline" of human capital. Through public rhetoric in the popular press and strategic plans as it talks among itself, the Department of Defense and associated government agencies, as well as private defense contractors, have established a consistent narrative of incipient national emergency. While the precise nature of this emergency may shift depending on the audience, the key features of the story remain constant. The security of the nation, defined variously as protection from external threats, the maintenance of an adequate industrial base, or the continued preeminence of American defense manufacturers in a global market, depends on a renewed supply of technically educated employees.

Turning first to public discourse, a June 2015 editorial in *US News and World Report* is a typical example of the genre as it is produced for the popular press. The authors describe the technical staffing problem facing the US defense industry in stark, almost apocalyptic terms:

> As students make their decisions about which colleges to attend and contemplate their eventual majors and careers, it may come as a surprise that their decisions are fundamental to our national security. The country's defensive capabilities often depend on brains, not brawn. Development of nuclear weaponry is but one example. And the biggest contemporary threat—one that could surface at any time and on an unfathomable scale—is the likelihood of a massive cyberattack. Study after study warns that our dependence on advanced technology in almost every aspect of communication, commerce, and transportation makes us highly vulnerable to the armies of hackers in countries that wish us harm.[3]

3. Levy and Plucker, "Brains, not Brawn."

National security and safety thus depend on a steady supply of properly educated citizen-engineers to guard the technological frontier. And, in this case, citizenship is a key piece of the argument. Unlike other sectors of the technology economy, the defense industry cannot rely on the preferred neoliberal solution of importing foreign workers on H-1B visas due to security clearance regulations:

> Yet too few students choose to study engineering, physics, computer science, and mathematics, all necessary areas to shore up our cyberdefenses. One traditional solution for our shallow talent pool has been to import talent, but this strategy is showing considerable strain. Even when we still use this strategy—for example, by issuing H-1B visas (85,000 this year) or encouraging foreign university students (just shy of 900,000) to stay in the country upon graduation—it does not improve our national security: government, defense, and aerospace companies can't hire foreign citizens for jobs requiring a domestic security clearance, yet increasing numbers of jobs in these fields require such clearances. It is literally impossible for us to "talent import" our way to a well-defended nation. As long as national security clearance is required for data warriors (and we think it should be), an army of mercenaries can't defend us from a cyberattack.[4]

Perhaps ironically, the defense industry is one sector of the American manufacturing economy that is protected from the forces of globalization. Building American weapons requires workers who, by the usual calculations of personnel security officers, can be trusted to keep America's secrets.

As a result, developing a pool of properly trained and qualified Americans has become a project that necessarily begins in early life. A briefing prepared by ReadyNation, an organization within the Council for a Strong America funded by donors ranging from the Gates, Ford, and Pritzker foundations to Eli Lilly, cited aerospace industry executives in support of its work. In bold print, the president of Boeing Military Aircraft, Shelley Lavender, is quoted as follows: "Through strategic investments of time and resources, the goal is to inspire and prepare children with the skills necessary to be successful in the 21st century—that starts with quality early learning opportunities."[5]

The path to the military-educational complex is thus one that begins in "the first five years of life."[6] According to ReadyNation, early childhood

---

4. Levy and Plucker, "Brains, not Brawn."
5. ReadyNation, "Building the Defense Industry's Workforce."
6. ReadyNation, "Building the Defense Industry's Workforce."

education is useful for the national project insofar as it is a support to and preparation for children's future roles in the technological apparatus of national security:

> While most industry efforts to build a skilled workforce, including STEM careers, address older students, a comprehensive solution requires starting much earlier in life. High-quality early childhood education lays the foundation for a future workforce that has the STEM skills and other qualities the defense industry needs. For this reason, companies need to support efforts to help children start on the path to success well before they enter kindergarten.[7]

Success for American children, it seems, is indistinguishable from fulfilling an expected role in the economy. And in particular, they are expected to take their place in those sectors of the economy that support the defense industry and military technology. Children are human capital, and those with abilities in science and mathematics are capital assets destined for a very particular role in the economy:

> The bottom line is that the future of the defense industry and our nation's national security depend on our success at ensuring our children are prepared for the rigors of college and the workforce. We must start early to put our nation's children on the right path and lay the foundation for a highly skilled future workforce.[8]

For ReadyNation and their likeminded associates, even the youngest children exist within a calculus of utility and worth, tied to an almost existential anxiety over the future contours of the national project.

This process that exists at the nexus of propaganda, education, and corporate recruitment does not end in childhood. The project of recruiting the next generation of aerospace and defense engineers continues and intensifies in undergraduate programs in science, engineering, and related technological disciplines. Here, students are targeted for recruitment not only upon graduation, but also for internships that funnel them toward full-time employment in the industry even as they are still enrolled in school. As one document on defense industry "talent strategies" explains,

> One way to fill the ranks in the A&D industry is to target young talent fresh out of higher education institutions. With a shortage of STEM students, companies are more focused than ever on

---

7. ReadyNation, "Building the Defense Industry's Workforce."
8. ReadyNation, "Building the Defense Industry's Workforce."

identifying appropriate skills early. Internships are a key strategy used within the sector for identifying future employees. It is a "try before you buy" situation for both parties, says Matt Riddle, vice-president and general manager of business operations in BAE's US combat systems division. "We're not making them transcribe and make copies," he adds. "They are literally working with our engineers." Ms. McDonald of SRC says interns are treated the same as other team members. If a unit must travel to conduct field tests, for example, they are brought along. "Don't treat interns like interns," she says. SRC provides stipends of up to 500 dollars per month after the students return to their schools to create loyalty to the company. The students, in turn, seek out potential SRC recruits on campus.[9]

This corporate-led strategy depends on a multifaceted approach that includes not only introducing students to the work environment but also ongoing financial incentives and peer-to-peer marketing of the industry as a career option.

For its part, the government itself named the same difficulties in an earlier study published by the National Academy of Engineering and the National Research Council. The strategy outlined therein relies to some extent on the adjustment of personnel policies that would ostensibly include compensation packages. However, the experience of working with the Department of Defense itself is presented as its own, self-evident enticement:

> The DOD workforce recruitment policies and practices should be reviewed and overhauled as necessary to ensure that the DOD is fully competitive with industry (not simply the "defense industry") in recruiting the highest quality STEM talents. DOD should judge its recruiting competitiveness by the quality of its STEM hires, and it should continue to adjust its policies and practices until it has become fully competitive with overall industry and academia in the quality of its recruitments. Such practices might include . . . more active outreach and recruitment efforts aimed at civilian hires of needed scientists and engineers that emphasize the many exciting technologies that

---

9. Magnuson, "Talent Strategies," 8. BAE is "an international defense, aerospace and security company which delivers a full range of products and services for air, land and naval forces, as well as advanced electronics, security, information technology solutions and customer support services," according to its website (https://www.baesystems.com/en-us/our-company). SRC is "a not-for-profit research and development (R&D) company committed to redefining possible in the areas of defense, environment and intelligence," according to its website (srcinc.com).

are being developed by DOD and their potential contribution to the nation.[10]

This combination of the "exciting" nature of defense technologies with an idealistic approach to government service is strikingly similar to the results of the AIAA survey mentioned in the introduction. It is to precisely this potent mixture of aesthetic attraction and the idealism of national service that this chapter now turns.

The Nuclear Techno-aesthetic as Limit Case

The United States' nuclear weapons research program provides perhaps the most helpful, and helpfully well-documented, example of the role of the aesthetic in weapons technology. Granted, the aesthetic allure of the atomic bomb, rooted in an experience of what has been dubbed the "nuclear sublime" (as a special case of the Kantian sublime), represents an extreme case within the broader defense technology discipline. Yet this limit case illumines the forces at work in the development of more prosaic technologies as well.

In an ethnographic study of the culture of the United States' nuclear research establishment, Joseph Masco traces the series of changes in nuclear testing that morphed from aboveground explosive tests to underground testing to the current regime of what is called "Science-Based Stockpile Stewardship." Each step in this transition has led researchers away from the immediate experience of the bomb as a weapon and toward an aesthetic experience of the bomb in and for itself. As he explains,

> The post–Cold War experimental program known as "Science-Based Stockpile Stewardship" (1995–2010), which relies on an increasingly virtual bomb, systematically confuses bodies and machines in such a way as to transform the experience of nuclear science from a military reality to one of potentially infinite technoaesthetic pleasure. The structural achievement of post-Cold War nuclear science in Los Alamos, I ultimately argue, is to have reinvented the bomb at precisely the moment when the US nuclear project and the laboratory's future seemed most uncertain as an unending technonational project that is simultaneously fragile, essential, and beautiful.[11]

---

10. National Academy of Engineering and National Research Council, *Assuring the US Department of Defense*.

11. Masco, "Nuclear Technoaesthetics," 350.

The experience of the bomb as a mathematical simulation takes precedence over any abstract knowledge of the bomb as a destructive military object or as a tool of policy. As Masco writes, "A sensory engagement with the bomb produces not fear of the explosion but, rather, an increasing concern about the viability of the machine as an embodied aesthetic form."[12]

Within such a regime, the problem of recruiting scientists to participate in nuclear weapons projects becomes a matter of marketing the technoaesthetic experience itself. As the memories of Manhattan Project–era urgency and Cold War national existential crisis fade into history, another means of recruitment must be found:

> The more immediate question, however, is not how do you train the bodies once you have them in the program, but how do you get bodies into the program in the first place? After all, without an active nuclear weapons design project, it is difficult to sell a career in nuclear weapons physics–gerontology to new PhDs, who are now more familiar with post–Cold War security scandals at Los Alamos than with the pleasures of conducting nuclear weapons science.[13]

Given these challenges, the answer seems to be to market the experience itself, rather than merely rely on an appeal to national service in the face of an active or potential war. In such a context, the laboratory itself becomes less a place that exists purely for the purpose of research and more a tool for marketing and recruitment:

> One of the immediate goals of the SBSS [Science-Based Stockpile Stewardship] program is, therefore, to build a state-of-the-art infrastructure of experimental laboratories at Los Alamos and Lawrence Livermore National Laboratories that will be enticing to a new generation of scientists and counter the banality of yearly surveillance reports with cutting-edge science. If the Cold War nuclear project was devoted to producing new generations of bombs, the post–Cold War project is to produce a new generation of nuclear weapons scientists capable of tending to those bombs.[14]

As the last stop on the aforementioned pipeline of human resources, research facilities like Los Alamos are dependent on the constant pressure of

---

12. Masco, "Nuclear Technoaesthetics," 360.
13. Masco, "Nuclear Technoaesthetics," 363–64.
14. Masco, "Nuclear Technoaesthetics," 364.

a combined effort of education and marketing that posits weapons research as a career that is both exciting and fulfilling.

In passages that bear quoting at length, Masco continues by describing the depths to which contemporary weapons science is configured as a technoaesthetic spectacle. He writes,

> The weapons laboratory of the early 21st century will ultimately allow weapons scientists to walk inside a virtual hydrogen bomb and experience the most extremely destructive force imaginable through physical senses that are not vaporized by the assault of the explosion but, rather, are tuned to the aesthetic properties of the simulation. The promise of SBSS is, thus, not only to perfect and indefinitely maintain nuclear weapons technologies through nonnuclear testing but also to resolve the multigenerational technoaesthetic confusion of bodies and machines in Los Alamos by creating a conceptual space in which weapons scientists and weapons of mass destruction can comfortably coexist at the very moment of detonation. The bomb's new body is increasingly that of the weapons scientists themselves, as the intellectual pleasure of nuclear weapons science and a tactile sensory experience of the exploding bomb are being merged through a massively engineered technoaesthetic spectacle in virtual reality. The intimacy of this conceptual project—the desire to physically interact with a thermonuclear explosion in all its nanosecond and atomic detail—eliminates fear of the exploding bomb altogether in favor of a phantasmagoria.[15]

This triumph of the aesthetic, Masco argues, goes hand in hand with the depoliticization of the atomic project. At federal laboratories like Los Alamos, the "pleasures of nuclear weapons science are being reinvented" through "new experimental facilities that promise to free nuclear science from the politics of the bomb."[16] This process is not merely a matter of academic speculation. It is also reflected in internal communications produced by scientists for scientists:

> Weapons science [is] no longer a temporary political solution to the global crisis but an aesthetic project capable of existing finally on its own terms. To this end, the bomb as aesthetic project is already a highly developed discourse in the laboratory; consider, for example, how two successful implosion studies

---

15. Masco, "Nuclear Technoaesthetics," 366.
16. Masco, "Nuclear Technoaesthetics," 367.

were recently described in the Los Alamos laboratory's publication *Dateline: Los Alamos*:

"Two explosions rock two mesas at Los Alamos. Separated by a couple of chilly fall days and 10 miles, both experiments capture images of exploding objects very much like the primaries of nuclear weapons, absent the nuclear materials that produce criticality.

"Both are milestones in Los Alamos' efforts to focus the most sophisticated technology available onto its mission of maintaining the safety and reliability of an aging nuclear stockpile. And both experiments were looking for symmetry. Symmetry is beauty. Psychologists have found that the human eye judges a person attractive when it perceives symmetry in facial features. Los Alamos scientists and engineers also think symmetry is beautiful. Because without symmetry, nuclear weapons don't work."[17]

In this, the depoliticized spectacle of weapons research, the appeal of the experiment to the scientists themselves takes priority over other considerations. Moreover, the aesthetic value of the experiment is such that it potentiates confusion between the beauty of an explosion and the beauty of the human face. In the case of the bomb, it "works" (without further elaboration of what that entails) because it is beautiful, and not vice versa.

Thinking Like an Engineer

The aforementioned detachment from both the political and the human is intensified by the habits of thought that are common to the technical professions. In particular, my own profession of engineering has been noted as possessing a *habitus* that makes engagement with the moral aspects of the work particularly challenging. Writing in a study of engineering ethics, Michael Davis lists five "imperatives of engineering" that were first described by engineer and historian Eugene Ferguson. The last two of those values that mark those who, in Davis' words, "think like an engineer" are particularly worth noting. The fourth imperative, Davis writes, is "a tendency to disregard human scale, preferring the very large or the very small."[18] As he explains,

> The problem, I think, is not so much that engineers disregard human scale as that they are seldom needed for things on a

17. Masco, "Nuclear Technoaesthetics," 367.
18. Davis, *Thinking Like an Engineer*, 14.

human scale. Generally, asking engineers to work on a human scale is like asking lawyers to prepare a partnership agreement for two children operating a lemonade stand. They can do it, but either they will do what anyone else could do or they will do something out of all proportion to the job.[19]

Whether it is a matter of choice or of professional circumstances, however, this detachment from the human scale becomes part of the educational and professional habitus within which technology, including military technology, is designed and built.

The last of Ferguson's imperatives, "putting technical brilliance ahead of human need," bears further examination. Davis argues that this is "a failing inconsistent with one of engineering's fundamental values." Tracing the history of engineering as a profession from the Enlightenment through the nineteenth century, Davis argues that engineering is, "by definition, an instrument of material progress." As he writes,

> Engineering remains an undertaking committed to human progress. So, for example, the most widely adopted code of engineering ethics in the United States begins: '[Engineers uphold and advance the integrity, honor, and dignity of the engineering profession by] using their knowledge and skill for the enhancement of human welfare.[20]

And yet it may be precisely this grounding in a narrative of development and progress that, far from humanizing it, actually contributes to the *dehumanizing* aspects of engineering as a profession. Within this narrative of human progress writ large, the individual human scale that Davis emphasizes is subsumed and even eclipsed. Instead, the lives of individual human beings on both a physical and temporal scale become the scaffolding on which a necessary stage in the world-historical process is erected.

As I first noted in an essay in the *Journal of Moral Theology*, this problem of detachment is compounded by the cursory attention given to ethical formation in both engineering education and professional practice.[21] Moreover, the predominant form of education in "engineering ethics" is tied to an profoundly individualizing—even isolating—discourse of autonomous decision-making within the context of canned case studies to be analyzed from a detached and abstract theoretical perspective. One

---

19. Davis, *Thinking Like an Engineer*, 14.

20. Davis, *Thinking Like an Engineer*, 15.

21. Portions of sections 3 and 4 previously appeared in an edited form in Slade, "Unmanned," *Journal of Moral Theology* 4 (2015) 111–30.

popular ethics textbook quite blithely instructs the student to "choose their personal engineering ethics threshold," to methodically evaluate their crises of conscience by ticking boxes on an "Ethics Dilemma Scorecard," and then to "determine a suitable course of action once this threshold is reached."[22]

At the same time, this approach to moral formation has been repeatedly tried and found wanting. Writing in a meta-analysis of forty-two engineering ethics courses, civil engineering professor and engineering education researcher David Haws has found almost all of them to be inadequate to the task, and he finds most engineering faculty ambivalent at best toward the project of teaching future engineers to incorporate ethical commitments into their work.

> Most of us, as engineers, feel that the computational aspects of engineering . . . are the most important topics for our students to learn. We feel that . . . ethics should be taught in other departments (or in the home, or other "institutions of faith"). We feel that as engineers we should concentrate on developing a good product and then let the rest of the world worry about how, where and when that product is used. . . . This, of course, is the problem. And by the time we realize that this is an ethical problem (like the weapon designers of Los Alamos), it's usually too late.[23]

Haws argues that this predicament is related to the nature of the students that become engineers and not the habituation entailed by their nurture. As he writes, "Engineering attracts convergent thinkers who tend to become oblivious" to the "wider ramifications of their work."[24] While Haws may be at least partially correct in positing that engineering attracts students who approach problem-solving from what they believe to be an objective, decontextualized standpoint, that hypothesis does not account for the entire predicament of "thinking like an engineer." Both engineering education and the work of design itself contribute to a sense of abstract detachment from the particularity of existence. Engineering design, as a system-building activity, already presupposes a progression "from function to form," through a "process of synthesis" that "emanates from Hegel's philosophy," in the words of one design textbook.[25] Meanwhile, the iconic narratives of aerospace and defense engineering in particular—inevitable progress, national necessity, and the assumptions of international competition in weapons development

---

22. Baura, *Engineering Ethics*, xviii, 194.
23. Haws, "Ethics Instruction," 223.
24. Haws, "Ethics Instruction," 223.
25. Chakrabarti, *Engineering Design Synthesis*, 9.

that has been dubbed the "offensive-defensive" dialectic—function to place both the work of engineering and those who carry out that work as participants in a necessary world-historical process.[26] The trajectory of world history demands ever more complicated weaponry, so the argument goes, and thus those weapons must necessarily be produced. Otherwise, a nation might fall behind in the temporal sense or even outside of history altogether.

An Inconvenient Appendage

As Julia Watkin argues in her commentary on Kierkegaard's *Concluding Unscientific Postscript*, however, a thinker within such a system loses contact with ethics—and with oneself as well. She writes,

> Loss of contact with ethics occurs firstly through the thinker's make-believe standpoint in which he or she takes some fantastical God's-eye position outside the universe, that is, outside existence. Since objective thinking, in that it concerns description of the world, has no relation to the individual thinker's personal life, daily life becomes an inconvenient appendage to the great work of System-building (*CUP*, 1:119, 122–23). Secondly, there is a loss of ethics in the Hegelian-style System because it contains ethics and morality as a necessary process. Yet in a necessary process there can be no freedom and hence no ethics.[27]

Some practicing professionals have become disillusioned with both the aforementioned idealization of progress and the failure of the technological disciplines to form their students to act ethically. As early as the 1970s, Samuel Florman, a civil engineer with experience in the construction industry, traced out a technological declension narrative in his book *The Existential Pleasures of Engineering*, and laid much of the blame for the profession's "dark night of the spirit" firmly at the feet of the education process.

> Part of the problem is surely the stultifying influence of engineering schools. In too many of these institutions, the least bit of imagination, social concern, or cultural interest is snuffed out under a crushing load of purely technical subjects. This

---

26. Cassidy, *Counterinsurgency*, 46.
27. Watkin, "Boom!," 101.

situation appears to be improving, although a whole generation of engineers has already been disfigured.[28]

Florman, of course, was writing in an era when the process of teaching itself seemed to be the greatest impediment to moral conduct in students and engineers alike. Forty years later, engineering education may have covered itself with a veneer of social concern, through the addition of student chapters of groups such as Engineers Without Borders or through the incorporation of study abroad or service-learning programs into the curriculum. And yet the problem at the heart of technical education as a process remains the same, perhaps even intensified by current emphases on universities as utilitarian means to employment and financial stability, rather than of the education of persons. The STEM-ification of everything, in which technical education becomes an omnipresent means to an economic end, has exacerbated the problems that already existed within the discipline.

How might it be possible to break through this scholastic disposition, which, in the words of Pierre Bourdieu, sets a "distance from directly perceived reality" as the "precondition for most symbolic constructions," and which posits an aesthetic universalism that makes possible "the disinterested play of sensibility" and the "pure exercise of the faculty of feeling"?[29] Bourdieu argues that the problem of this perspective lies in its reliance on "a point of view on which no point of view can be taken," in which bodies are "reduced to a pure gaze, and therefore indifferent and interchangeable."[30] It constructs a frame "through which one sees" but "which is not seen."[31] And as such, it prevents the exercise of practical, rather than merely theoretical reason—the reason that "enables one to act as one 'should' without positing a Kantian 'should,' a rule of conduct."[32] He suggests that the answer to the paradox of determinism and freedom within such scholastic universes is the practical knowledge that comes from knowing oneself as determined rather than determining, as comprehended rather than comprehending, as wretched rather than great. This, of course, leads us as Christians squarely into the realm of theology.[33]

For his part, Florman proposed a solution through his reading of Goethe's *Faust*, who, "jaded with every conceivable worldly experience,"

---

28. Florman, *Existential Pleasures*, 92.
29. Bourdieu, *Pascalian Meditations*, 17, 73.
30. Bourdieu, *Pascalian Meditations*, 22.
31. Bourdieu, *Pascalian Meditations*, 22.
32. Bourdieu, *Pascalian Meditations*, 139.
33. Bourdieu, *Pascalian Meditations*, 131.

found "in a land-reclamation project" the "contentment that had eluded him all his life."[34]

> Faust's soul was saved, not because he reclaimed land, but because, in Goethe's words, "whoever aspiring, struggles on, for him there is salvation." In this sense—in the knowledge that we are engaged in the struggle to improve the lot of Everyman— we can still share Goethe's enthusiasm, and a taste of Faust's salvation.[35]

Florman's narrative of salvation hinges on embracing the concreteness of existence by "turning away from abstract religion and philosophy and returning to a less intellectualized brick-and-mortar existence" in which we "arrive closer to God through leading a normal life" and "enjoying the blessings of bourgeois society."[36] But this is a particularity that still lies within a trajectory of human progress, and it is still in thrall to a poetic idealization of the work of a heroic individual. It is a call to work out one's salvation, but crucially it neglects the fear and trembling that must accompany such work.

Søren Kierkegaard too engages with Faust through his pseudonym Johannes de Silentio, but what emerges is a cautionary tale more than a model to be emulated. This Faust is "too ideal a figure to go around in bedroom slippers," a "doubter" who "wants to save the universal" by "being hidden and by remaining silent."[37] Yet even this Faust may be saved, "if the doubter can become the single individual who as the single individual stands in an absolute relation to the absolute," if his "doubt" is turned into "guilt."[38] As Louise Carroll Keeley has suggested, this pivotal move is narrated through another story, that of Tobias and Sarah from the book of Tobit, and it is one that hinges on reception rather than heroic action.[39]

> If a poet read this story and were to use it, I wager a hundred to one that he would make everything center on the young Tobias. . . . Tobias behaves gallantly and resolutely and chivalrously, but any man who does not have the courage for that . . . has not even grasped the little mystery that it is better to give than to receive and has no intimation of the great mystery that it is far more difficult to receive than to give.[40]

34. Florman, *Existential Pleasures*, 145.
35. Florman, *Existential Pleasures*, 145.
36. Florman, *Existential Pleasures*, 148.
37. Kierkegaard, *Fear and Trembling*, 107, 110.
38. Kierkegaard, *Fear and Trembling*, 111.
39. Keeley, "Parables of Problem III," 127–54.
40. Keeley, "Parables of Problem III," 102.

The hero is not Tobias but Sarah, who receives the loving work of another in a parable that Kierkegaard uses as an analogy for the work of Christ:

> Sarah is the heroic character. She is the one I want to approach as I have never approached any girl or been tempted in thought to approach anyone of whom I have read. For what love for God it takes to be willing to let oneself be healed when from the very beginning one in all innocence has been botched, from the very beginning has been a damaged specimen of a human being! What ethical maturity to take upon oneself the responsibility of letting the loved one do something so hazardous! What faith in God that she would not in the very next moment hate the man to whom she owed everything![41]

If, as J. Robert Oppenheimer said in the wake of the Manhattan Project, the builders of military technology "have known sin," it stands as an indictment of an inability to grasp the reality and the totality of sin beforehand. And yet this seems to be a mistake we as engineers are bent on repeating.

---

41. Kierkegaard, *Fear and Trembling*, 104.

Part Four

RESISTING THE BUSINESS OF WAR

9

Communal Responses to the Business of War

JUSTIN BRONSON BARRINGER

Introduction

It seems that most popular and scholarly discussions about war focus on the violence done by militaries and on the appropriateness of governments putting these militaries into battle, but fewer discussions include the social and economic conditions that might instigate or necessitate war in the first place. As other essays in this volume have made clear, the business of war is just that—a business. And that business ought to be considered through the same lenses through which we assess the moral and ethical aspects of other businesses. However, warmaking is also a unique sort of business because of the way it relies on destruction of lives and property; social infrastructures and economic systems; morality and decency. Thus, for Christians this ought to raise questions about how the church can offer a response to both the economic, violent, and moral aspects of war, preferably at the same time. What might be appropriate and distinctly Christian responses to the business of war?

A few biblical texts come to mind with regard to this volume's focus on business and war. Each biblical text showcases a community with practices and ways of being in the world that relate to the business of war in opposing ways. The first is exemplified in Sodom, about which Ezekiel wrote, "'Now this was the sin of your sister Sodom: She and her daughters were arrogant, overfed and unconcerned; they did not help the poor and needy" (16:49). The second and third are a pair that together provide an alternative to the arrogance, apathy, greed, and gluttony of Sodom. Acts chapters 2 and 4 delineate four practices in which the earliest Christians participated together: simplicity, community, charity, and spirituality. These first Christians shared everything in common and even sold extra possessions for the good of the group and its mission, thus embodying a form of simplicity that values others over excess possessions. In this way, along with their shared meals and common purse, they practiced community. Their community not only shared money and possessions in common, but they made sure that everyone's needs were met, thus practicing charity. And finally, they prayed, shared in Eucharist, preached, and performed miracles, all constituent parts of the practice of Christian spirituality. In this essay, I will argue that the Acts practices offer an antidote to the malady known as the military-industrial complex (MIC), which deadens us to the cry of the poor like those content to do so in Sodom.

In this essay, I argue for specific practices that seek to both serve as prophetic witness and practical social strategy, shaping disciples to refuse, as much as possible, to participate in the systems—economic, political, and philosophical—that perpetuate war and its requisite moral deformation, oppression, and isolation. In what follows, I examine the work and witness of Andrew Bacevich, Bayard Rustin, James William McClendon, the Berrigan brothers, and others with attention to what seems to me to be deep resonance in their work with the practices from the Acts texts above. I hope to show that these practices—simplicity, community, charity, spirituality—are deeply relevant for Christians who seek to resist, subvert, or provide prophetic critiques of the MIC.

Daniel Berrigan sets up the complex interconnectedness of the problem of neoliberal capitalist business and war and the grounds for the practices that form a Christian response to this death-dealing duo when he writes,

> Suppose the implications of the Death game stink in one's nostrils, with all their assorted smells and whiffs of duplicity, of political corruption, or promises broken, and life destroyed, and property misused, and racism encouraged, the poor benignly neglected, and the rich seated unassailably in places of power. And religion in the midst of this game ambiguous in its own

voice, and the spiritual goods of the people diminished beyond recognition.

Supposing all this to be true, what is the tactic of the believer? ... Quite simply, I think, reading the New Testament, one says NO. Quite simply, one puts his life where the Gospel tells him it should be, if indeed the Gospel has something to say at all. One submits in a very true way to Death, in order to destroy the power of Death from within.

There are, of course, as many ways of doing this ... But as the Savior reminds us, with a certain vigor, based upon a certain unkillable vision of his own, our reaction had better be something—something of this sort.[1]

This powerful poetic description of problem and response leads to questions about what the "something of this sort" might look like in the face of the business of war in particular. To begin suggesting what such a "something" might be, I turn to Bayard Rustin, activist and mentor of Martin Luther King Jr., who asserts, "For eight years I have believed war to be impractical and a denial of our Hebrew-Christian tradition. The social teachings of Jesus are: (1) respect for personality; (2) service to the 'summum bonum'; (3) overcoming evil with good; and (4) the brotherhood of man,"[2] and who further claims that each of those principles is broken by Christian participation in war and capitulation to current unjust economic arrangements. It was this sort of thinking that caused Rustin to set his life against war and often make declarations like the following, which he said during the beginning of World War II: "I came to the firm and immovable conviction that war was wrong and opposed directly to the Christian ideal."[3] Rustin's summation of Jesus' social teaching and his suggestion that the business of war violates that teaching provides the basis for my argument that the four aforementioned practices are both a faithful and potentially effective response offered by Christians to the economics and violence of war. I will attempt to show the connection of respect for personality to the practice of simplicity, service as the *summum bonum* to the practice charity, overcoming evil with good to the practice of spirituality, and the brotherhood of man (that is, the siblinghood of humanity) with the practice of community.

It may be too simple to state it as such, but the economic/social problem that undergirds American warmaking the most could be summed up in one word—consumption. Philip Berrigan recognizes this unfortunate

---

1. Daniel Berrigan, cited in Stringfellow and Towne, *Suspect Tenderness*, 6.
2. Long, *I Must Resist*, 10.
3. D'Emilio, *Lost Prophet*, 72.

truth, noting the two-way stream of consumption, writing, "Indeed, few Americans understand how both the capitalistic and Soviet technocracies make people as mass-produced as assembly-line productions, with about as few options. In effect, people begin to resemble the products they consume: The system digests them, they digest its products."[4] Others in this volume have already demonstrated how the neoliberal, global economic system demands warmaking, but it is also worth suggesting that it desensitizes people to its supposed necessity by producing people that are little more than consumers, whose hearts and minds are replaced by digestive tracts that care more about more than about what that more is costing others. Distinctly Christian practices remind us of our unique yet shared identity in Christ. We do not need to be slaves to consumption, anonymous to the rest of the world, willfully ignorant of the way our choices perpetuate injustice, and lulled into hopeless spiritual ennui as we capitulate to the system and abdicate our responsibilities to an only ostensibly trustworthy establishment. Simplicity frees us from consumption, community from anonymity, charity (in its more classical meaning) from willful ignorance, and spirituality from hopelessness—or, more precisely put, it is friendship with Jesus, demonstrated in obedient praxis, that frees us from all these death-dealing powers.

Andrew Bacevich suggests that Americans in particular dress up war by pointing to a supposed tradition of being a liberating force in the world.

> Many Americans find such sentiments compelling. Yet to credit the United States with possessing a "liberating tradition" is equivalent to saying that Hollywood has a "a tradition of artistic excellence." The movie business is just that—a business. Its purpose is to make money. If once in a while a studio produces a film of aesthetic value, that may be cause for celebration, but profit, not revealing truth and beauty, defines the purpose of the enterprise. Something of the same can be said of the enterprise launched on July 4, 1776. . . . Their purpose was not to save mankind. It was to ensure that people like themselves enjoyed unencumbered access to the Jeffersonian trinity."[5]

That Jeffersonian trinity—*life, liberty, and the pursuit of happiness*—has grown to mean freedom to consume, or perhaps it always meant that at least for those to whom such a luxury was available. Now, however, what was once a rare luxury has become the norm for many Americans, which, with whatever good that has afforded the masses in this country, has exacerbated

---

4. Berrigan, *Prison Journals*, 23.
5. Bacevich, *Limits of Power*, 18–19.

the arrogance, apathy, and gluttony Ezekiel condemned, perhaps making America the new Sodom and certainly the epicenter of warmaking as an economic necessity. Bacevich points to Reinhold Niebuhr:

> Niebuhr once wrote disapprovingly of Americans, their "culture soft and vulgar, equating joy with happiness and happiness with comfort." Were he alive today, Niebuhr might amend that judgment, with Americans increasingly equating comfort with self-indulgence.
>
> The collective capacity of our domestic political economy to satisfy those appetites has not kept pace with demand. As a result, sustaining our pursuit of life, liberty, and happiness at home requires increasingly that Americans look beyond our borders. Whether the issue at hand be oil, credit, or the availability of cheap consumer goods, we expect the world to accommodate the American way of life.
>
> The resulting sense of entitlement has great implications for foreign policy. Simply put, as the American appetite for freedom has grown, so too has our penchant for empire."[6]

In other words, "for Americans, [William Appleman Williams] observed, 'abundance [is] freedom, and freedom [is] abundance.'"[7]

Christians ought to know better and to live better. We believe that freedom is slavery to Christ and that slavery to Christ is actually friendship with Christ, life and life abundant. But how do we make the case that freedom is in consuming Christ's body and blood rather than consuming goods paid for with countless other lives? McClendon argues that the virtue and practice of presence is fundamental to Christian embodiment of such an ethic because it is aligned with, flowing from, the presence of God with us as the basis for lives of simplicity, community, charity, and spirituality. He writes, "We remember that God's presence with us is one of the great gifts of the gospel, associated with the incarnation of the Word, the giving of the Spirit, and the return of the Lord; we recall that in Christian history his presence is celebrated at every eucharistic meal, invoked at every baptism, and claimed anew at every gathering of disciples."[8] That being the case, Christians live in such a way that rather than focusing on our own consumption, we instead focus on making our very selves, not just some excess resources, available for others, a way of living inconsonant with the notion of the plentitude of goods and the leisure to consume them

---

6. Bacevich, *Limits of Power*, 9.
7. Bacevich, *Limits of Power*, 23.
8. McClendon, *Ethics*, 106.

unendingly as freedom. This way of living is costly, yet in it, abundance has no end because it does not depend on models of economic scarcity but on the everlasting graciousness of God, which guarantees that we hunger and thirst no more. One might rightly ask what such a life of presence looks like. McClendon writes, "Presence is being one's self for someone else; it is refusing the temptation to withdraw mentally and emotionally; but it is also on occasion putting our own body's weight and shape alongside the neighbor, the friend, the lover in need."[9] This, perhaps more than any other act, testifies to the truth of Christian convictions and our hope for a world in which relationships of presence such as friendship are the order of the day instead of neoliberal capitalism and the scourge of war, both of which keep people apart, alienating one from another and creating jealousy, enmity, and estrangement.

We are to live in such a way that the ends we seek for the world are embodied now in the life of the church. If our ends are a just society where warmaking is no more and where economic justice prevails, then we are implored by the Christian faith to use means befitting those ends, but we cannot, must not, settle for simply less war or less rabid consumption, because we are called beyond that to the ministry of reconciliation, of presence with others, of friendship with those who are now our enemies or economic competition. This sort of world would be one where community, simplicity, charity, and spirituality were more common than radical individualism, self-indulgence, greed, and shallow religion, and therefore ought to be the sort of society Christians embody now.

Simplicity: Respect for Personality

In the immediate aftermath of 9/11, President Bush's response was to encourage the American people to go shopping, to buy, to spend—to consume. Soon after, of course, he declared that the US would "shock and awe" as the military invaded Iraq. The two are not unrelated. The MIC trades on such greed and violence, often under the guises of liberty and safety. In short, the message, at least implicitly, is that Americans' right to convenient consumerism is more important than the lives of Iraqi people. The multifaceted connection between greed and violence was evident both in the terrorist attacks of 9/11 and in the American response. It was, after all, the centers of commerce and the military that were hit by those airliners. Recognition of the connection between greed and violence is very old. In fact, church fathers like Chrysostom and Basil essentially called greed itself violence.

9. McClendon, *Ethics*, 106.

Chrysostom wrote, for instance, "You should think the same way about those who are rich and greedy. They are a kind of robbers lying in wait on the roads, stealing from passers-by, and burying others' goods in their own houses as if in caves and holes."[10] Basil even takes it a step further in his homily "In Time of Famine and Drought," saying, "For whoever has the ability to remedy the suffering of others, but chooses rather to withhold aid out of selfish motives, may properly be judged the equivalent of a murderer."[11] It is often the case that in the name of remedying the suffering of others, the MIC swings into action around the globe, but what if, in fact, it was for more selfish reasons that its major players typically bang the drums of war?

Bacevich seems to think that these less altruistic motives drive the American economy and its warmaking, as he notes the confusion of freedom with consumerism, the simple meeting of needs with the drive for having it all and then some. For example, he writes, "If one were to choose a single word to characterize [American] identity, it would have to be *more*. For the majority of contemporary Americans, the essence of life, liberty, and the pursuit of happiness centers on a relentless personal quest to acquire, to consume, to indulge, and to shed whatever constraints might interfere with those endeavors."[12] Christians, however, are to be a people defined by less (Phil 2). We ought to be on a relentless quest to give, to create, to show restraint, and to throw off whatever hinders these good works (Heb 12:1). Each of these requires both a desire for and persistent pursuit of simplicity.

Simplicity, as I am using the word here, is intended to be about both disentanglement from an abundance of material goods and an undivided will. The witness of the Berrigans is particularly compelling on both these points. Daniel and Philip lived their lives willing that the world be a peaceful and just place, and to that end they embraced the freedom of letting go of excess possessions and the desire to please others. A friend of Daniel's wrote, "Daniel Berrigan was a saintly man. . . . He was tremendously difficult to deal with, very uncompromising. Saintliness does not bespeak of politesse. It makes life both difficult and simple. When you follow your own moral compass, you're not pushed and pulled by everyday pressures of life. . . . You don't have the same complexity in your decisions."[13] Daniel's simplicity is poignantly depicted in an episode that took place after he was arrested and tried for one of his many acts of civil disobedience. "When he walked out of the courtroom, Dan, grinning, pulled out a toothbrush from

10. John Chrysostom, *On Wealth and Poverty*, 36.
11. Basil of Caesarea, "In Time of Famine and Drought," 85
12. Bacevich, *Limits of Power*, 16.
13. Polner and O'Grady, *Disarmed and Dangerous*, 8.

his shirt pocket, telling reporters he had come ready for 'anything, including jail.'"[14] Who knew that dental hygiene could serve as Christian witness? Dan Berrigan argued that it was precisely this sort of simplicity that was itself a real threat to violent and unjust powers. "We, who are without weapons or riches or a stake in this world, are become a danger to the masters of the kingdom of death."[15]

Bayard Rustin, in many ways, felt likewise, although he did have an appreciation for the "finer things" that is not so evident in the lives of the Berrigans. Though he was raised in a poor family and never graduated college, Rustin had a sophisticated taste in everything from food to music. However, Rustin's life is a testament to the fact that he was more concerned about causes than consumption and elevated people over prestige. Rustin, by necessity or choice, ended up as primarily a background figure of the civil rights movement and mid-century antiwar efforts. Yet it was he who most clearly articulated the theological and practical foundations on which these movements were erected. He taught Martin Luther King Jr. nonviolent civil disobedience, organized the famous March for Jobs and Freedom in Washington, DC, and gave direction to the protests against the war in Vietnam. It is widely agreed upon that Rustin was the brains of these movements, yet he stepped aside, or more precisely, allowed himself to be pushed to the background, to let folks like King shine.

As a Black gay pacifist during a time of high racial tension, a contentious war, and the Stonewall riots, Rustin had a lot to be angry about, but rather than let that anger lead to hate, Rustin chose to follow the way of Jesus, which demands respect for personality. Respect for personality is made possible by simplicity because one's vision is not blurred by multiplicity or consumer-driven greed and gluttony, and therefore one more clearly sees the personhood of the other. In fact, it is an act of simplicity itself because it is the choice to treat others with dignity regardless of circumstance. In this way, Rustin exemplified Christian simplicity.

It is not the case, however, that most Christians living in America embrace these forms of simplicity embodied by Rustin and the Berrigans. Indeed, American Christians seem to look more American than Christian. And as Bacevich reminds us, "Americans [have come] to count on an ever-larger economic pie to anesthetize the unruly and ameliorate tensions related to class, race, religion, and ethnicity. Money [has become] the preferred lubricant for keeping social and political friction within tolerable limits. Americans, Reinhold Niebuhr once observed, 'seek a solution for

---

14. Polner and O'Grady, *Disarmed and Dangerous*, 347.
15. Stringfellow and Towne, *Suspect Tenderness*, 9.

practically every problem of life in quantitative terms,' certain that more is better."[16] We want not only more, but more choices—more varieties of more—which complicates our lives, clouds our moral vision, inhibits our spiritual growth, and separates us from each other. Christians ought to know better. After all, Jesus spoke repeatedly about the dangers of such a view. It is this illusory "more" that keeps folks from entering the kingdom (Matt 19:24).

The situation American Christians must confront is further complicated by the fact that it is precisely our demand for more that both perpetuates war and destroys healthy economic systems. Bacevich writes, "Here is the central paradox of our time: While the defense of American freedom seems to demand that US troops fight in places like Iraq and Afghanistan, the exercise of that freedom at home undermines the nation's capacity to fight. A grand bazaar provides an inadequate basis upon which to erect a vast empire."[17] The church, however, has no need to build an empire because we are to be satisfied with the simplicity of God's kingdom, willing only to please the One whose salvation is our joy. We believe in a community of communities making up the family of God rather than an empire competing to make consumption a cause for which we are willing to kill.

Community: Brotherhood of Man

There is perhaps an irony that simplicity seems increasingly less easy to achieve. If we are not careful, we may view the endeavor as a private and personal one. However, the best engine for simple living is community. Community takes investment. Like a Jackson Pollack painting, it is simultaneously remarkably simple and messy. While people seem to long for it, many of us have subjugated our need for community to our desire for more. Again, Bacevich offers insight on this point: "As individuals, Americans never cease to expect more. As members of a community, especially as members of a national community, they choose to contribute less."[18] This is true in the American church as well. Thus, we need a reversal, precisely the sort of reversal that Jesus inaugurated in his ministry, where we are willing to contribute more to our communities and expect less as individuals.

Here again, we approach a paradox because this mentality does not deprive individuals but it enriches and supports them, even as it is often

16. Bacevich, *Limits of Power*, 23.
17. Bacevich, *Limits of Power*, 11.
18. Bacevich, *Limits of Power*, 10.

strenuous and demanding. Daniel Berrigan once again serves as an example of this truth; as his friend Don Moore wrote,

> Dan helps us to confront the demands that community life should be making upon each one of us. . . . He will not let us keep private our disappointments or problems or discouragements. It is a failure of community, in Dan's mind, if someone is shouldering a burden alone. . . . If someone is reluctant to speak out, perhaps the community is at fault. Perhaps the community has not manifested to one of its own a loving openness and acceptance. This demands that the community, or better, that each member of the community carefully nourishes with the others a spirit of concern, friendship, trust, and sense of presence.[19]

Yet Moore continues, "It is almost a matter of routine now within the community that each Jesuit's problems and predicaments are, to the extent that he wishes it, the community's problems and predicaments. This is as it should be; we are not alone, and we are all, in St. Paul's terms, ministers of reconciliation."[20]

It is precisely ministers of reconciliation that a world consumed by consumption and driven by the business of war needs urgently. As Daniel Berrigan alluded to, Christian community teaches us about conflict resolution, the redemptive power of inconvenience for the sake of another, and especially that we are not our own. It teaches us to draw close to God, the One who resolves conflict by giving himself, the One who from the time of Creation to the time of the Eschaton continues to volunteer to be inconvenienced for the sake of humanity and has even given himself up to us as One who, though self-sufficient and necessary, made himself dependent in the incarnation and expendable on the cross. Jesus is not his own; he belongs to the Father and the Spirit. The Father belongs to the Son and Spirit, and the Spirit likewise belongs to the Father and the Son. This is what the community of the Trinity teaches us.

In line with this core Christian doctrine, Bayard Rustin's vision of community flowed from his belief that the teachings of Jesus pointed to a brotherhood of man. Biographer Jervis Anderson wrote that "Bayard seemed to envelop people with his sense of the oneness of humanity."[21] This belief compelled Rustin to work with virtually anyone who offered to share in his struggle against oppression. Furthermore, Rustin wrote that "segregation, separation, according to Jesus, is the basis of continual violence. . . . That which separates

---

19. Moore, "Life in Community," 141.
20. Moore, "Life in Community," 142.
21. Anderson, *Bayard Rustin*, 5.

man from his brother is evil and must be resisted."²² Often it is our hoarding of seemingly scarce goods that keeps us apart, and thus whenever we share those goods or sacrifice our supposed allotment for the sake of others, we undermine violence. For Rustin, it was bringing people together that was perhaps the greatest threat to the war machine that sought—and still seeks—to keep people apart. This is something that the military-industrial complex relies on as its puppeteers seek to maintain economic divisions so as to have a limitless stream of soldiers flowing in from the ongoing economic draft, on the one hand, and an ever-growing constituency of well-educated, well-paid contractors, weapons designers, engineers, and public relations experts, on the other. Unfortunately, even supposed political liberals are complicit in this enterprise, as their various ideas of government social engineering often bolster economic systems that lead people to rely on political and military structures to make ends meet. Rustin saw this as he argued that it was poor (Black) folks, even as a result of the best intentions of liberal White elites, that were drawn into the most dangerous fighting positions in any given war. Furthermore, even though Rustin was adamantly opposed to war, he saw segregation in the military as problematic. It perpetuated injustice on a number of levels, in the US and abroad.[23]

Jesus too was confronted by the temptation to sacrifice community for the sake of expediency, or prestige, or comfort. The clearest example of this is, of course, Jesus' encounter with Satan (recorded in all of the Synoptic Gospels), who offered Jesus each of these, but at the cost of sacrificing his community with Father and Spirit, along with the community of the coming peaceable kingdom that Jesus made possible on the cross. Scripture has other examples as well, including the time recorded in John 6 when the crowd tried to make Jesus king by force after he had miraculously fed thousands, but Jesus, we are told, withdrew to be by himself. It might seem odd to point to a passage in which Jesus withdrew from a crowd to be alone in a discussion about community, but I want to suggest that Jesus knew that a community built merely on feeding people was a false community and that the power dynamics of such a relationship would prevent the full flourishing of the members of this crowd.

This understanding becomes evident the next day, after Jesus literally walked on water to get back to his disciples, when Jesus told the crowd that full stomachs do not provide sufficient basis for forming a community of disciples. Rather, such a community must be built on spiritual nourishment as well. Jesus offered himself as spiritual nourishment, changing the power

22. Long, *I Must Resist*, 12.
23. Long, *I Must Resist*, 110–26.

dynamic by making it clear that he was not merely interested in giving stuff to people but rather would not settle for less than giving the fullness of himself to them. Upon realizing that receiving such a gift, the gift of God's friendship, would also entail the demands of a deeper relationship than merely that of provider and consumer, many people deserted him. This, however, clarified who was up to the task of practicing community and who only wanted to be fed. In all this, we see that Jesus rejected a system set up on the basis of earthly power, which seems to be related here to satanic power, and authority that settled for making consumption—even perhaps overconsumption (as the story tells us that everyone ate their fill)—the raison d'etre of human existence. Satan wants us to settle for bread from a stone, but Jesus tells us that the only bread sufficient for life eternal is the bread of his flesh, the bread of communion shared with God and all those who have been called to eat the body broken for us.

It seems, then, that Jesus is both sustained by the community, namely with the Father and Spirit, but also to some degree with his disciples, while also making it possible for others to join this community, one that negates the separations caused by wealth inequity, race, artificial borders of nation-states, and patriotic allegiances. His time with Father and Spirit in eternity and his disciples on earth made possible Jesus' sacrifice on the cross even when he felt abandoned by everyone. In this way, community is vital for followers of Christ as well because it prepares Christians for the lonely times that will likely result from opposition to economic injustice and war.

Rustin knew well, in his own life and the lives of others, the pain of being ostracized and abused because of outspokenness about economic injustice and militarism, among other issues, but Rustin also knew the value of the respect for personality, that is, the care for unique individuals as such, and thus, as Michael Long notes, "Unlike some Radicals who focused merely on systems—the military-industrial complex, capitalism, and racism, for example—Rustin often made heartfelt appeals on behalf of individuals in dire straits."[24] In a letter to President Kennedy from 1962, Rustin recounts the story of an elderly man who had long been a conscientious objector since before World War I and who had quit paying taxes after the atomic bomb was dropped on Hiroshima because "he could not conscientiously pay for weapons of destruction any longer."[25] As a result, this man, Max Sandin, had his social security payment and his union pension garnished, leaving him destitute. While Rustin acknowledged that he, unlike the Berrigans, believed in the principle that "conscientious objectors should be willing, when [they]

---

24. Long, *I Must Resist*, 251.
25. Long, *I Must Resist*, 252.

resist the state, to accept the penalties that the state imposes," he argues that this case has "extenuating circumstances . . . because of [Sandin's] sincerity and his age and his health."[26] The appeal here is not made on the basis of a commitment to ideas of justice and nonviolence but a commitment to a person, one whose decisions of conscience had proven to be costly. Rustin, along with the community at the Peace Action Center, where Sandin was staying at the time since he had no income, demonstrated the sustaining power of fidelity in the face of hardship brought on by one's rejection of the business of war. Our loneliness, the loneliness caused by violence and greed and consumerism, is most powerfully assuaged by belonging to a community committed to sustaining each of its members, to full human flourishing, and to continually drawing the connections between economics and war so that injustices may be resisted together.

Furthermore, Christians need community because opposition to injustice and war must be taught. For instance, it was from his Quaker predecessors that Bayard Rustin learned the social teachings of Jesus and their particular frame of understanding them to demand nonviolent action. Rustin, in turn, along with his friend Glenn Smiley, taught these lessons to Martin Luther King Jr. during the Montgomery bus boycott. According to Anderson, at the beginning of the boycott, King kept guns and had armed guards, but Rustin talked King into giving those up and embracing nonviolence fully. Rustin said to King, "If in the heat and flow of battle a leader's house is bombed and he shoots back, then that is an encouragement to his followers to pick up guns. If, on the other hand, he has no guns around him, and his followers know it, then they will rise to the nonviolent occasion."[27] Similarly, and no doubt historically connected, Rustin was making essentially the same arguments against World War II that King would later level against the war in Vietnam, and likewise Rustin, even before King's ascendency, had named the connection that King would call the "triple evils" of racism, militarism, and materialism. In short, King was surrounded by a community, of which Rustin was a key member, that taught him about faithfully naming and opposing these evils.

As Christians look to the witness of Jesus and previous generations of the faithful, they learn to be a marker for future generations of goodness rather than evil. Bacevich writes, "History will not judge kindly a people who find nothing amiss in the prospect of endless armed conflict so long as they themselves are spared the effects. Nor will it view with favor an electorate that delivers political power into the hands of leaders unable

26. Long, *I Must Resist*, 252.
27. Anderson, *Bayard Rustin*, 188.

to envision any alternative to perpetual war."[28] Yet this is where we find ourselves, and the Christian church in America and elsewhere must decide without delay to live otherwise, to refuse to support unjust war and to protest political powers hell-bent on keeping the war machine moving along, leaving destruction in its wake. The church ought to be leading the way as a people who do indeed find something amiss with endless armed conflicts and who recognize the proper human telos that enables us to envision another way of life and the Spirit that empowers us to do so.

Rather than settle for perpetual armed conflict and the unjust economic systems that demand more blood so long as it is someone else's, Christians envision another world, and we live as if it is already here *because we know it is* and that it is coming. Jesus tells the apostles that he gives them his peace and leaves it with them (John 14:27). It is in our participation in the Eucharist that our actions most resemble and conform to Christ's nonviolent form of life. Followers of Christ give so that others may have peace and abundance rather than take so that we may indulge.

Charity: Service as the Summum Bonum

In my first youth ministry position, the youth group was made up almost entirely of students from low-income families. Some of them wanted to go to college but felt it was out of their reach financially. So, some went into the military, hoping that they could get an education during or after their military stint. Rustin drew attention to this reality several decades ago:

> And even during this horrible Vietnam war, many Negro young men who would have no alternative but to stand on street corners . . . are convinced that by joining the armed forces they can learn a trade, earn a salary, and be in a position to enter the job market on their return. . . . All this means that thousands of Negroes, in order to rehabilitate themselves, are forced to take a stand beyond morality and exploit the opportunities presented to them by their country's military involvement. I myself can afford the luxury of drawing those moral lines, but it is more difficult to suggest to people who are hungry, jobless, or living in slums that they turn their backs on opportunities that promise them a measure of economic betterment. . . . If this attitude on the part of thousands of Negroes horrifies the peace movement, then perhaps the peace movement might well conclude that it

---

28. Bacevich, *Limits of Power*, 13.

must give a large part of its energy to the struggle to secure the social and economic uplift of the Negro community.[29]

This quote represents the crux of my argument. If we are to be against war, we are to be against the business of war, that is, we must oppose and undermine all the ways that war becomes financially attractive to various socioeconomic groups. It is not enough simply to argue that war is wrong or that people should not participate in unjust wars; it is the church's responsibility to see to it that those whose hunger and poverty limit their choices, and prevent them from considering the morality of war, are provided enough economic stability that they are at least able to weigh the various moral claims and make the decision themselves rather than having it made for them by their abjection. Likewise, it is the Christian call to put ourselves, as much as possible, into their experience of hunger and suffering, and so better understand their predicament and offer a more convincing witness.

Rustin played a significant role in shaping Martin Luther King Jr.'s understanding of the triple evils. For instance, Rustin suggests that economic and other social issues kept many African-American folks from joining the peace movement of his day. Yet he also writes, "It may well be that the solution to one problem has implications for the solution of another."[30] This suggests that meeting economic needs, through a variety of charity and justice activities, is one way to grow the peace movement and prevent the military-industrial complex from so successfully recruiting people because the poor, when their economic needs are met, will be perhaps less inclined to capitulate to the war machine, since they will have more freedom to do otherwise; and the rich, when their time and money is devoted to causes of peace and justice, rather than ensuring their own success by either actively or passively supporting the violent status quo, will consider the moral implications of a job over a lucrative salary.[31]

It is evident in the lives of the Berrigans and Rustin that a deep spirituality—the Berrigans' from their Catholic commitments, Rustin's from his Quaker roots—guided and sustained their continued actions for community and against injustice, as well as the times of incarceration they often faced for those actions. As it was for the Berrigans and Rustin along with their compatriots, so it is for all followers of Christ: to sustain a healthy, loving, Christian community requires a robust and ever-developing practice of Christian spirituality. It is in fact Christian spirituality, which I am broadly defining as

---

29. Rustin, *Two Crosses*, 149–50.
30. Rustin, *Two Crosses*, 148.
31. For example, see Kara Slade's essay in this volume.

intentional and disciplined openness and obedience to the Holy Spirit, that undergirds and informs the other aforementioned practices.

Spirituality: Overcoming Evil with Good

Bacevich claims, along with Niebuhr, that it is hubris and sanctimony that keep the American military-industrial, empire-seeking, shopping-and-spending machine going, at least for now. The response, as I see it, is to produce a spirituality in people that encourages humility and sincerity. If we are to follow Jesus' command to overcome evil with good, then we ought to have some understanding of what constitutes good, and we ought to have at least some of that good present in our own lives before we can rightly expect it of others. Dan Berrigan suggests that "it is in the Word of God one finds the resources to keep going in such times as these."[32]

The Berrigans, McClendon, and Rustin all agree that there is an order to the way goodness spreads. It must begin in individuals and communities, especially the church community, then move outward to society. As this process relates to war, Rustin writes, "The truth is that war is wrong. It is then our duty to make war impossible, first in us, then in society."[33] Rustin had in mind a spirituality that first shaped him so that he could play a part in shaping the social order. He, like McClendon, was interested in the church's witness, especially the consistency, or lack thereof, between the church's preaching and its actions. Rustin was quick to call out incongruities, saying, for instance, that segregation in the church continued to crucify Christ.[34] For Rustin, it was paramount that Christian spirituality form the church to be a body that first demonstrated goodness within so that it could faithfully call those outside the church to repentance as well.

To cultivate such a spirituality that shapes individuals and communities to eliminate warring in their own hearts, then to bear witness to the reality of God's shalom in the world, Christians must be disciplined. We see this in the Plowshares movement, for example, whose members Dan Berrigan described as "spiritually disciplined and well-prepared people who can do these things and who can take the heat."[35] And no doubt those who oppose warmaking powers, whether they be governments, economic systems, or hedonistic philosophies, will face some heat as they seek to enact a different sort of community, one that seeks to shape all of society to be more peaceful and just.

---

32. Quoted in Stringfellow and Towne, *Suspect Tenderness*, 5.
33. Long, *I Must Resist*, 2.
34. Long, *I Must Resist*, 179.
35. Quoted in Polner and O'Grady, *Disarmed and Dangerous*, 350.

Of course, the Christian telos goes beyond simply shaping society; it centers on the shalom brought about by friendship with YHWH. If we are to show the way, to teach warmaking powers and ordinary citizens about their responsibilities, then we must have a clear sense of what God is doing in the world. Then we can begin to see how both the church and state fit into fulfilling the *missio Dei*. According to McClendon, "For Christians, questions about lasting peace can never be separated from eschatology. . . . Our eschatology and our peacemaking are two sides of a single coin." And by including eschatology in discussions about peacemaking, Christians can rightly critique "pacifists who [believe] in 'the brotherhood of man,' [and thus think] that world peace [is] just around the corner."[36] Notably, for Rustin, the idea of the brotherhood of man did not lead to the naïve pacifism of many advocates of the Social Gospel, but instead it led to a lifelong commitment to working for peace and justice even if they were not soon coming. Even World War II, which notably turned Reinhold Niebuhr from his earlier pacifism, did not deter Rustin, who, although given a religious exemption for conscientious objection, "chose imprisonment over the protections to which he was entitled as a religious conscientious objector."[37]

Anderson goes on to quote Rustin's response to the summons from the draft board for his physical examination in preparation to send him to a civilian work camp: "I cannot voluntarily submit to an order stemming from the selective service act. War is wrong. Conscription is a concomitant of modern war. . . . Conscription for war is inconsistent with freedom of conscience which is not merely the right to believe but to act on the degree of truth one receives, to follow a vocation which is God-inspired and God-directed. . . . Though joyfully following the will of God, I regret that I must break the law of the State. I am prepared for whatever may follow."[38] On the other side of this time in prison, Rustin continued to speak and act as a pacifist, speaking and working against every one of America's wars during his lifetime. In short, Rustin exemplifies not the naïve pacifist of Niebuhr's famous critique but one who recognizes God's work in the world and who joins in that work, no matter the cost or the length of the journey to peaceful resolution. A commitment to the siblinghood of humanity need not entail naiveté but rather demands working faithfully to bear witness to the way God is bringing about that reality. We see such work, of course, in the early church, even with all its problems, as the first Christians discerned together God's work among them and in the wider world.

36. McClendon, *Ethics*, 318.
37. Anderson, *Bayard Rustin*, 98.
38. Anderson, *Bayard Rustin*, 98.

Conclusion: Acts 2 Community

Bacevich recounts a speech by Jimmy Carter that, despite its unpopularity then and now, rings truer today than when it was first given, in July 1979. "In a nation that was proud of hard work, strong families, close-knit communities, and our faith in God," Carter said, "too many of us now tend to worship self-indulgence and consumption. Human identity is no longer defined by what one does, but by what one owns. But we've discovered that owning things and consuming things does not satisfy our longing for meaning. We've learned that piling up material goods cannot fill the emptiness of lives which have no confidence or purpose."[39] Bacevich expounds, "In other words, the spreading American crisis of confidence was an outward manifestation of an underlying crisis of values."[40]

If this is the case, then it is the Christian church that is best positioned to lead the movement of reversing the crisis. It is followers of Christ whose collective story and moral formation equip them with the tools needed to respond and lead others in the right direction. The above practices seek to strike at the root causes of the problem rather than settling for treating symptoms and merely changing policies in hopes that a change of heart will follow. Even as recent wars have lost popular support, few have decried the underlying causes and presuppositions necessary to make the venture possible and seemingly necessary in the first place. How many today are speaking up against greed as attendant to violence? Very few, it seems. Thus, we the church must point to those causes, the sins that are most acutely dominating American consciousness and lifestyles, and we must practice a different way of life. This way of life is outlined at the end of Acts 2:

> They devoted themselves to the apostles' teaching and to fellowship, to the breaking of bread and to prayer. Everyone was filled with awe at the many wonders and signs performed by the apostles. All the believers were together and had everything in common. They sold property and possessions to give to anyone who had need. Every day they continued to meet together in the temple courts. They broke bread in their homes and ate together with glad and sincere hearts, praising God and enjoying the favor of all the people. And the Lord added to their number daily those who were being saved. (2:42–47)

---

39. Quoted in Bacevich, *Limits of Power*, 33.

40. Bacevich, *Limits of Power*, 33.

10

Building Peace in a Violent Nation
A Kingian Response to the Interconnected Violence of Racism, Materialism, and Militarism

JAMES MCCARTY

Introduction

In March 2008, seventeen-year-old Jamiel Shaw Jr. was murdered in Los Angeles, where he lived with his father in an underserved neighborhood. Jamiel was killed by two gang members for walking in the wrong neighborhood with a red backpack, though he was not a member of a rival gang—the murder was a case of mistaken identity. At the time, Jamiel's mother, Army Sgt. Anita Shaw, was serving her second tour in Iraq. Sgt. Shaw, an African-American woman who had served in the California Army National Guard for about ten years, enlisted in the army full-time after a long and unfruitful search for employment. Before enlisting she received four hundred dollars a month in public assistance as well as two hundred dollars in food stamps to meet the needs of her family.[1]

---

1. Esquivel, "Returning Home."

In talking about the murder of her son, Sgt. Shaw described the gang members as "terrorists."[2] She compared the streets of Los Angeles to her assignment in the Middle East. "The only thing is we don't have sand and dirt flying all around . . . but we have the bullets," she said.[3] She continued, "I don't know if I can say this with me being in the military, but we need to be cleaning up the streets of the United States instead of cleaning up Iraq."[4]

Just over forty years earlier, Martin Luther King Jr. publicly denounced the Vietnam War when he delivered a speech entitled "A Time to Break Silence" or "Beyond Vietnam." In this speech, delivered at Riverside Church in New York City, King linked United States military violence overseas to the violence occurring in urban ghettos in the US, particularly in Chicago. He declared that his advocacy for nonviolent social action could no longer be directed primarily toward social activists working for domestic civil rights. If he was to propose a coherent understanding of nonviolence, he must also advocate for nonviolence abroad and denounce the violence of the US government.

King's day-to-day work at the time included teaching mostly Black youth in Chicago's primarily Black urban neighborhoods to practice nonviolent civil disobedience in order to bring about social change. In the midst of this work, these young people insightfully asked King about the extreme violence used by the American government in Vietnam to bring about social change there. It made little sense in the minds of those Chicago youth to be nonviolent when engaging their own government when it was so clear that the American government understood violence as the best way to create the social change it desired in Vietnam. When King realized this he decided that, as he put it, "I could never again raise my voice against the violence of the oppressed in the ghettos without having first spoken clearly to the greatest purveyor of violence in the world today—my own government."[5] King understood that we are formed into our virtues and vices, in part, by the societies we live in. If one's society is violent, it is difficult, if not nonsensical, to be nonviolent when engaging that society. Nonviolence would never be wholly compelling to a people formed in a state that was in a constant posture of violence.

In this essay, I will draw on King's public resistance to the Vietnam War to propose a path forward for us today in a world not dissimilar to the one King inhabited. In particular, I will draw on King's analysis and critique

2. Finnstrom et al., "Football Star."
3. Esquivel, "Returning Home."
4. Esquivel, "Returning Home."
5. King, "Time to Break Silence," in *Testament of Hope*, 233.

of the three interconnected evils of racism, materialism, and militarism that existed during his life. Toward the end of his life King argued that one could not separate American racism from its warmaking and its economic inequality; to cure any of these evils one must have a remedy for all three. This insight sits at the heart of King's work toward the end of his life and informed his analysis of the injustices that continued to exist in American society after the passage of federal civil rights legislation.

I will apply this analysis to our present context to demonstrate its relevance in our time and to recommend the kinds of actions that can work to dismantle contemporary violence at exactly those places where the three evils intersect. In doing so, I will demonstrate that American violence still grows from the fertile evils of racism, materialism, and militarism. I also suggest practical ways to respond that help build a kind of just peace that is dependent upon resisting and dismantling these interconnected evils.

I will do this in three parts. First, I will provide a survey of some of the most pervasive forms of violence in contemporary American society. These include racialized mass incarceration, the continuing experience of racialized hate crimes, and the phenomenon of mass shootings. Second, I will walk through King's own use of this analysis in resisting the Vietnam War and apply a similar analysis to the contemporary "War on Terror." This analysis will demonstrate that the United States is uniquely violent and that its violence is rooted in the triple evils. Third, I will propose actions and interventions intended to address American violence at the intersections of these evils on three levels: the personal, the political, and the communal. Such an approach to social action, I argue, is what is required to build a just peace in a nation plagued by the violence particular to the United States. In making these three moves, I intend to demonstrate that action that responds to one of the triple evils as isolated from the others will be ineffectual. It is only those actions that address racism, materialism, and militarism at those places where they most obviously intersect and overlap that have any real chance of dismantling our violence and building a just peace.

Violence in the United States Today

We are now living more than fifty years after King delivered "A Time to Break Silence"—a speech given exactly one year before he was assassinated—and the United States is in the midst of a seemingly never-ending "War on Terror" that has lasted nearly twenty years and moved through Afghanistan, Iraq, Syria, and several other nations. In addition, we are now in the era of the Movement for Black Lives (sometimes referred to as the

Black Lives Matter Movement). The Movement for Black Lives is primarily a nationwide response to the direct violence of the killing of dozens of unarmed Black people by police in recent years and the indirect violence of the mass incarceration of Black and Brown people in the US since the start of the "War on Drugs."[6] The Movement also seeks to end the militarization of American police departments.[7] This militarization has included local police departments across the nation cumulatively receiving more than four billion dollars' worth of military-grade equipment that has been used to police many poor, primarily Black and Brown, communities.[8] This equipment has included grenade launchers fitted for tear gas canisters and armored trucks resistant to mines one might encounter in a war zone. Images of nonviolent and/or unarmed protesters affiliated with the Movement facing down these weapons have been documented in multiple cities across the US.

Beyond the debilitating persistence of these structural forms of racism, recent years have seen an increase in hate crimes and an emboldened White supremacist movement in American society. In 2012, a White supremacist and former member of the military shot and killed six people gathering at a Sikh temple in Wisconsin.[9] In 2015, Emanuel African Methodist Episcopal Church in Charleston, South Carolina, was the site of a mass shooting. Nine Black Americans were killed by White supremacist Dylann Roof while they were studying the Bible. Roof explicitly claimed that the goal of the massacre was to start a race war in the US.[10] In 2017, White supremacists marched in Charlottesville, Virginia, chanting racist statements including, "Jews will not replace us!" They were met by counter-protesters, one of whom was killed while protesting.[11] And in 2018, a man with a history of making anti-Semitic comments on social media shot eighteen and killed eleven members of the Tree of Life Synagogue in Pittsburgh, Pennsylvania, while shouting, "All Jews must die."[12] And these are just the most high-profile examples of White supremacist ideas leading to acts of violence. It is becoming increasingly clear that the effects of structural racism and the politics of White

---

6. Movement for Black Lives, "Platform."

7. For a brief and accessible account of the militarization of policing by a Christian ethicist and former law enforcement officer, see Winright, "Militarized Policing," 10–12.

8. Movement for Black Lives, "End the War."

9. For a series of contemporary news stories covering the event, see Peralta, "Sikh Temple Shooting."

10. For a timeline of events related to this event, see https://www.nbcnews.com/storyline/charleston-church-shooting.

11. Heim, "Recounting a Day of Rage."

12. KDKA, "11 Dead, Several Others Shot."

supremacy are as much a part of American public life today as at any time during the twentieth century.

Violence in American society is not relegated to explicitly racist violence either. We are living through the era of regular mass shootings across the United States. Since the horror of the mass shooting at Columbine High School in 1999, the number, size, and location of mass shootings in the United States has grown. Most recently, the largest mass shootings in recent US history occurred in Orlando, Florida, and Las Vegas, Nevada. In 2016, forty-nine primarily gay Latinx people were killed and more than fifty others injured at a gay night club by Omar Mateen.[13] In 2017, Stephen Paddock killed fifty-eight and injured more than five hundred at a concert on the Las Vegas Strip.[14] These examples are exceptional only in the number of people shot. There were 427 mass shootings in the US in 2017, wounding 2,000 and killing 590.[15]

In addition to the prevalence of mass shootings in the US, in 2018 the country experienced its tenth straight year as the only country in the Americas to carry out executions, and between 2006 and 2015 the United States was among the top five executioners in the world.[16] The US has both the largest number of people incarcerated and the highest incarceration rate in the world. Approximately half of the world's incarcerated people can be found in the US, China, and Russia.[17] The US does not merely incarcerate more people than any other country in the world then, but it does so at rates that dwarf the rates in most other countries. We are by many measures—from our incarceration rate, to the persistence of the use of the death penalty, to the never-ending stream of mass shootings in the country—one of the most violent nations in the world.

This exceptional characteristic of American life is not new. As King remarked, the United States is the greatest purveyor of violence in the world. And then, after years of being a victim of violence and being hounded by the FBI, King was assassinated exactly one year after denouncing the war

---

13. For a timeline of news reports related to this event, see https://www.nytimes.com/news-event/2016-orlando-shooting.

14. For a number of news reports related to this event, see https://www.cbsnews.com/feature/las-vegas-shooting/.

15. The Office for Victims of Crime, a component of the Office for Justice Programs, US Department of Justice, defines a mass shooting as an event in which four people have been killed by firearms.

16. See the website of Amnesty International: https://www.amnesty.org/en/latest/news/2019/04/death-penalty-facts-and-figures-2018/.

17. *BBC News*, "World Prison Populations," available at http://news.bbc.co.uk/2/shared/spl/hi/uk/06/prisons/html/nn2page1.stm.

in Vietnam while in Memphis to support striking sanitation workers seeking just wages and working conditions. In addition to his work with the Memphis march, he was in the midst of planning a national Poor People's Campaign that would lobby for an Economic Bill of Rights that included, among other initiatives, the idea of a national guaranteed income. King died a violent death standing at the center of what he called America's "triple evils": racism, militarism, and materialism (a combination of the effects of classism and capitalism).

"A Time to Break Silence" on America's Triple Evils

King's sermon "A Time to Break Silence" marked a pivotal transition in his public career. In many ways, it is the signal event in his transition from focusing on civil rights in the US to human rights around the world. It very publicly marked his entrance into global debates about the ethics of war and the role of the US on the global stage. It was the most important public example of King linking the oppression of Black people in America to the oppression of Black and Brown people around the world in a kind of postcolonial critique. And it marked King's explicit linking of US military spending to its own social welfare system. Finally, it marked the national "launch" of his work explicitly naming America's triple evils of "racism, extreme materialism, and militarism." This moral and political analysis framed the public ministry of King's last year of life.

In "A Time to Break Silence," King questioned America's intentions for entering the war, critiqued America's presence in Vietnam, and spoke on behalf of poor Vietnamese civilians who were suffering as a result of the war. In addition to these criticisms, he linked the plight of the poor in America with America's commitment of material resources to the war and linked the violence in America's ghettos to America's violence in Vietnam. For King, the Vietnam War was an expression of America's misplaced priorities and an attack on the poor both within its own borders and around the world.

After the sermon's introduction King quickly articulated the reasons he opposed American involvement in the Vietnam War. The first reason King gave was that he saw "the war as an enemy of the poor."[18] King believed that the war in Vietnam was taking resources, especially money and time, away from those who needed it most. In King's view, Lyndon Johnson's War on Poverty was replaced with the war in Vietnam. The second criticism King leveled against American intervention in Vietnam was that it was the poor who were fighting—and dying—for the benefit of the rich. For

---

18. King, "Time to Break Silence," in *Testament of Hope*, 233.

King, this "cruel manipulation of the poor" was morally reprehensible.[19] In King's eyes, it was an abuse to send those who benefited least from America's capitalism to fight the poor in another country in order to prevent another political-economic system from taking root there. The third reason King publicly opposed the Vietnam War was to reverse his own hypocrisy of calling on the oppressed in the US to nonviolent resistance of their government without calling on that government to do the same. King's fourth reason for speaking against the war was simply and ambitiously "to save the soul of America."[20] "If America's soul becomes totally poisoned," he declared, "part of the autopsy must read Vietnam."[21] For King, the war was a symptom of something much deeper that threatened the spiritual health of the nation. As he said after four little Black girls were killed in a Birmingham church bombing relatively soon after the 1963 March on Washington, his dream for the US was turning into a nightmare. According to King, the triple evils of racism, materialism, and militarism were poisoning the soul of America.

King concluded the sermon by declaring that America "must undergo a radical revolution of values."[22] This revolution required a "shift from [being] a 'thing-oriented' society to a 'person-oriented' society."[23] This revolution of values would restructure the economic system to be more fair and equitable because "an edifice which produces beggars needs restructuring." A revolution of values would reject war and pursue nonviolent alternatives to international conflict. A values revolution would restructure its federal budget to create a more just society that meets the needs of its most vulnerable citizens rather than pursue military action around the world. "A nation that continues year after year to spend more money on military defense than on programs of social uplift is approaching spiritual death," he said.[24]

King's diagnosis that America's militarism is connected to its racism and its materialism (i.e., poverty, inequality, and hyper-consumerism) is still relevant today. Indeed, many of King's criticisms of the Vietnam War are applicable to the current "War on Terror." The United States still spends more on the military than on programs of social uplift. We still send our poor to fight our wars. We still teach our youth that violence is the way to achieve social change. Sadly, our situation is not very different from King's context; indeed, it may be worse. Many of us recognize what King knew in

19. King, "Time to Break Silence," in *Testament of Hope*, 233.
20. King, "Time to Break Silence," in *Testament of Hope*, 233.
21. King, "Time to Break Silence," in *Testament of Hope*, 233.
22. King, "Time to Break Silence," in *Testament of Hope*, 240.
23. King, "Time to Break Silence," in *Testament of Hope*, 240.
24. King, "Time to Break Silence," in *Testament of Hope*, 240–41.

1967: that our social support system is insufficient—or that our economic system needs to be restructured—and that we are wrongly engaged in military action around the world.

However, we often seem to miss King's point that these evils are interconnected. In part, each individual evil exists because the others exist. It is no coincidence that Jamiel Shaw was killed in the streets of Los Angeles while his mother risked being killed in Iraq. Racialized urban poverty and violence is directly related to America's racism, materialism, and militarism, both overseas and in the privatized prison system. Just as executive leaders of corporations with government contracts to make military equipment, their employees, and their stockholders make money by making weapons and selling them to the US government, foreign governments, or to domestic police departments, private corporations are making money by building prisons and filling them to their full capacity. In both cases, it is Black and Brown people who receive the brunt of their violence. In addition, America's militarism, foreign and domestic, is directly related to the ability of inner-city gangs to obtain high-powered weapons designed to kill at an efficient rate. As it was with the Shaws, so it is with many poor families of color living in urban areas. If our foreign policy is ever racist or militaristic or materialistic, it is safe to assume that our domestic policy will be as well.

How to Build a Just Peace in a Violent Nation

This analysis of the interconnected and trenchant evils of racism, materialism, and militarism in American society can be overwhelming and disheartening. How should one respond to such a pervasive, complex, and deeply rooted problem at the core of our life together? How does one not despair at the enormity of the violence we face in the United States? What would it take to revolutionize our values to such a degree that we would move from a thing-oriented society to a people-oriented society? What Herculean effort is required to restructure our social order in such a way that it would cease to create beggars here and abroad? It would seem the interconnected and mutually supportive evils of racism, materialism, and militarism reinforce each other to such a degree that they can never be overcome.

However, we know that previous manifestations of these interlocking patterns have been defeated in the past. Chattel slavery is a relic even if its legacies continue to impact us today. Jim Crow laws are dead even if their progeny continue to exist. Immigration policies that exclude people of

Asian descent have been reversed. And if we look around the globe, we see countless acts of resistance and successful revolutions of values.

That which makes building a just peace in such a violent nation (and world) seem so daunting also makes radical change possible. Because racism, materialism, and militarism are so deeply and necessarily intertwined in the American experiment, to chip away at one necessarily weakens the foundations of the others. Those who fight racism undercut the logic that seeks to justify racialized inequality and the hasty, ill-advised use of violence to resolve conflicts. Those who protest for peace by advocating for nuclear disarmament or in opposition to particular wars, for example, remind us that there are values more important than profit-making and that our loyalties can transcend tribe or race. And those who experiment with more cooperative economic systems remind us that competition is not the only way to achieve prosperity and, therefore, that racial divisions and violent conflict are not the only ways to secure our basic rights and needs. There are myriad ways, then, to build peace in a nation that is violent in the ways that the United States is. Peacebuilding can occur at all levels of society, but in this conclusion, I will focus on three specifically: the individual, the political, and the communal.

At the individual level, one can resist the mundane and daily ways that the triple evils impose themselves on our lives. For example, people with a 401(k) or similar retirement plan can apply "moral filters" to their investment portfolios to make sure the portfolio is not profiting from companies that produce weapons. Such weapons fuel our wars, militarize police, and supply the black-market arms trade. Or, since we now know that climate change is disproportionately impacting people in the global south and has contributed to ethnic conflicts like the decades-long Sudanese civil war(s), people can divest from fossil fuel companies that are driving this particular effect of global capitalism that has contributed to global racial inequality and violence.

One of the lasting legacies of slavery in the US, an evil system based in both racism and materialism, is the trenchant racial segregation that still defines so many of our lives and makes it so easy for us to ignore the racialized injustice and violence many communities of color experience at the hands of an increasingly militarized police force. White people can desegregate their lives and communities by living in neighborhoods where they are the racial minority and by being active citizens who work to secure justice for their neighbors. People, especially White people, can become members of a religious community composed primarily of people of another race. And as members of that community, they can spend time learning from their differently-raced neighbors in such a way as to be better allies in their pursuit of racial justice.[25]

Finally, individuals can volunteer at their nearest prison in ways that match their skills and the needs of those imprisoned. In bearing witness to the locus of so much of our violence and acting to subvert the violent and racist logic that separates us and enables us as a society to keep people in cages for years and decades, we can build solidarity across racial and class lines. This can be an act of opposition to the racism and materialism that dehumanize particular humans by elevating the "rights" of property over the rights and needs of the incarcerated. This kind of action can be a step toward restoration and relationship rather than merciless retribution. And bearing witness in this way can add a nonviolent presence into an inherently violent system. These small acts of subversion will not dismantle the triple evils on their own, but each act can help dismantle the evils in our own lives and can chip away at the ideological foundations upon which these systems have been built over centuries.

At the political level, one can participate in any action or movement that explicitly recognizes the link between at least two of the three evils King helped us to see. For example, The Innocence Project works to exonerate people sentenced to life in prison or capital punishment based on advances in DNA technology. We know that poor people are almost exclusively those sentenced to death and that Black people receive harsher sentences than White people for similar crimes. In the twenty-five years that The Innocence Project has been in existence, it has helped exonerate more than two hundred wrongly convicted individuals. By working to reverse unjust convictions that disproportionately affect poor people and people of color, The Innocence Project reverses some of the effects of racism and classism. And by reducing the number of people executed by the state they very tangibly make it so that our society commits less violence than it would have without their intervention.[26]

---

25. There is a danger, of course, in such action; namely, the danger of White people overtaking spaces created and sustained by and for people of color. Gentrification—the transformation of a neighborhood from being a primarily minoritized community to one that is predominantly occupied by people from dominant social identities (seen especially when Black communities become whiter through demographic shifts and economic investment from White-owned companies)—is just one example of such a danger. This danger reminds well-meaning White people that an anti-racist life is not composed of any one action or decision but is a lifelong project of justice and repentance that may require ongoing work in light of the ways White supremacist systems can be perpetuated even through benign or well-meaning actions performed by people racialized as White.

26. See https://www.innocenceproject.org/about/.

The Movement for Black Lives is another contemporary movement working to attack the triple evils at their roots. It works to demilitarize and deprivatize the police, abolish capital punishment, end the use of money bail and other financial burdens that increase the negative impacts of poor people's interactions with law enforcement, and other such practices that explicitly attack racism, classism, and state violence at its various intersections. It is tempting for a variety of pragmatic reasons to focus one's explicitly political efforts on more specific interventions or proposed policies. However, exposing the connections between state violence and racism, for example, not only has the possibility of remedying unjust laws but of exposing the interconnections of the triple evils in a way that resists one unjust law being replaced with another that further entrenches some other aspect of the triple evils and their intersections.

Third, there is another contemporary political movement that explicitly looks at the intersections of racism, materialism, and militarism. Repairers of the Breach is a nonpartisan, nonprofit organization seeking to organize a moral revival and movement.[27] Repairers was founded by the Rev. Dr. William J. Barber II and explicitly understands itself to be participating in a twenty-first-century revival of the Poor People's Campaign that King was planning when he was assassinated.[28] The movement explicitly seeks a "moral revival" not dissimilar to King's "revolution of values" that intends to revolutionize our economic and political structures in such a way as to be less racist, materialist, and militarist. In addition, Repairers has added a focus on combating climate change as a contemporary manifestation of the injustice these triple evils have wrought.

As I write this essay, in the United States in early 2019, these are three examples of political movements and/or organizations working to dismantle our violent economic and political structure, which continues to produce beggars at the intersections of racism, materialism, and militarism. In another time or place, the movements and specifics will likely be different. However, the legacies of these three postindustrial and globalized phenomena are evils that humans will be working to dismantle for the foreseeable future. The political lesson of King is not about any specific political movement or cause but about the intersections of the triple evils and how these shape the world in which we live.

Finally, at the communal level we can build peace by building communities that reject the triple evils and the moral logics that undergird them.

27. See the section "Our History" at https://www.breachrepairers.org/about.

28. A major partner in this revival is the Kairos Center for Religions, Rights, and Social Justice, which is led by the Rev. Dr. Liz Theoharis. More information can be found at their website, https://kairoscenter.org/.

And we can build communities that espouse person-centeredness over thing-centeredness. We can build communities that choose nonviolence as the norm of conflict transformation rather than violence. We can build communities of cooperation rather than communities of competition.

One example from my own context may prove helpful as a concluding example. King County (the county which houses the city of Seattle, Washington) is presently running a pilot program intended to reduce the number of youth incarcerated by the county. The county has piloted the use of peacemaking circles, a practice of the global restorative justice movement, in the juvenile detention system. Peacemaking circles are a particular restorative justice practice that has emerged out of the traditions of the Tagish T'lingit First Nation people; my first teachers in circle practice were Saroeum Phoung (who learned from Tagish T'lingit elders) and Shasta Cano-Martin (a leader of the Lummi Nation). Like other circle processes, the peacemaking circle as practiced in Seattle emphasizes the equality of everyone who participates, the importance of community as the setting of moral meaning and action, the social and life contexts of victims and offenders in instances of crime, and the ongoing nature of justice, reparation, and reconciliation.[29]

A typical peacemaking circle process as practiced in the pilot program is begun after an instance of a felony crime charge against a juvenile. Typically, these charges are centered on some act of actual or threatened violence. If the prosecutor, judge, defendant, victim, and their families agree to participate, a circle process will begin. "Sitting in circle," as practitioners refer to the practice, includes countless hours of norm creation, storytelling, and communal discernment. Typically, the victim and their family, the alleged and their family, and the wider community will participate in a variety of circles to learn what happened during the alleged crime, the context surrounding that incident, the life contexts of the offender and victim, and the harms done to everyone involved. In addition, community members commit to supporting the victim, offender, and their families and to remain connected to all who were directly involved for an extended period of time. Finally, a circle process concludes only after all who are directly involved come to an agreement about the path forward.

Peacemaking circles seek alternative modes of "making right" the harms caused by crime by forming community-created means of reparation to victims and the community; by encouraging offenders to take responsibility and to make ongoing reparation to the victim and the community; and by

---

29. See King County Zero Youth Detention, "Sharing of Peace" and "Peacemaking Circle Pilot."

fostering community support to help victims find healing and to promote greater participation in how crime is addressed. These processes, when successful, reduce the number of youth incarcerated (especially youth of color), reduce the stigma of a felony conviction (and therefore increase the chances that offenders do not start a cycle of incarceration and poverty), and bring a sense of pride and relationship to communities that otherwise may have been further divided by an instance of violent crime.[30]

In each of these ways, peacemaking circles are "person-centered" and institutionalize values that promote racial justice, nonviolence, and human dignity. They are a practice of community-building that takes an instance of crime as an opportunity to build more just community structures rather than to divide communities by segregating certain members in prison.

Conclusion

Martin Luther King Jr. argued that if the United States of America was ever going to be a just nation it would have to have a revolution of values that would undercut the structures of racism, materialism, and militarism. For King, this meant making explicit the political and moral links between the Vietnam War and the often racialized violence in America's cities. It meant linking the repression of human rights around the world to the denial of civil rights to Black Americans in the US. And it meant marching with striking garbage collectors while putting together a national political movement to radically restructure the American economic system. It would be impossible to revolutionize American values, King believed, if the economic and political structures that link racism, materialism, and militarism were not dismantled.

The particularities of the links between these triple evils have evolved over the last fifty years. Economic globalization, the continuing development of military technology, and the evolution of racial injustice mean that our context is not exactly the same as King's context. However, his key insight at the end of his life that racism, materialism, and militarism are interconnected and any effort to defeat one must include efforts to link them together is still true. To build peace in a nation as structurally violent as the United States, one cannot focus merely on one form of social engagement. One cannot isolate racism or economic inequality or the prevention of war if one desires to revolutionize the values that have built the structures that

---

30. On peacemaking circles and their use in response to youth crime, see the following volumes: Pranis, Stuart, and Wedge, *Peacemaking Circles*; Pranis, *The Little Book of Peacemaking*; and Boyes-Watson, *Peacemaking Circles and Urban Youth*.

have made our society one of the most violent in the world. Rather, one must work at those places in our social and political life where the intersections and interdependence of racism, materialism, and militarism are most evident. If we do that in our lives, our homes, our communities, and in our economic and political systems, we very well may revolutionize our entire society. And then we may know something like "the beloved community" or "the great world house." But we will only peek over the mountaintop and get a glimpse of such a sight if we can see clearly now that our violence is not merely gunshots and explosions. Rather, our violence is rooted deeply in the structures and values that form the fabric of our shared life. It has always been so, but history is not destiny. If we defeat the triple evils of racism, materialism, and militarism we can build a new society of human dignity, equity, and peace.

11

The Costs of *Jus Ante Bellum* and *Jus Post Bellum*

TOBIAS WINRIGHT and NATHANIEL HIBNER

Introduction

"All too often we go to more trouble and expense to demolish a town than would be needed to build a new one, and we fight wars with such extravagance, at such expense, and with such enthusiasm and diligence, that peace could have been preserved for a tenth of all that," wrote the Dutch Christian humanist Desiderius Erasmus (c. 1466–1536) of Rotterdam in his *Education of a Christian Prince* (1516).[1] Of course, as other chapters in the present volume on the "business" of war note, there are those who also seem to profit from such expenses. For most people, however, be they soldiers or civilians, there are costs, financial and otherwise. A half-millennium ago, Erasmus instructed the prince that if he were "truly Christian" he would "consider how honorable, how wholesome a thing is peace" and recognize "how calamitous as well as wicked a thing is war and how even the most just

---

1. Erasmus, *Education of a Christian Prince*, 107.

of wars brings with it a train of evils—if indeed any war can really be called just."[2]

These candid words surely resonate with our fellow contributors to this volume who are pacifists and nonviolent peacemakers. Yet "honest" just war thinkers and practitioners can—and should—acknowledge their truth.[3] Although perhaps no war "can really be called just," some few wars are regarded by just war theorists as morally "justified"[4] even if they are "imperfectly just."[5] As Virgil Michel, OSB, wrote in the years between the first two world wars, "even a legitimate war of self-defense must be considered a great evil (even if not a moral evil, or a sin), for it, too, will be fraught with all the horrible consequences that modern warfare entails."[6] Such an approach to just war theory—and there is more than one version of just war theory,[7] just as there are numerous types of pacifism[8]—also has as its goal, or *telos*, what Erasmus referred to as the "wholesome . . . thing," namely, peace. Hence, Rear Admiral Louis V. Iasiello, the twenty-third chief of US Navy chaplains, posits that "the ultimate goal of all just conflicts [is] the establishment of a just and lasting peace."[9] Indeed, recent scholarly work in the just war tradition has recovered this emphasis, anchoring the aim of a just peace in the principle of right, or just, intention.[10]

A part of this recovery has been recent imaginative efforts to extend the scope of just war theory to include—in addition to its two traditional categories of criteria, *jus ad bellum* (justice in embarking upon war) and *jus in bello* (just conduct during war)—two more categories: *jus ante bellum* (justice before to minimize the likelihood of war) and *jus post bellum* (justice in the wake of war to minimize the likelihood of its rekindling). The thread that links and is integrated throughout all four categories is, we

---

2. Erasmus, *Education of a Christian Prince*, 72.

3. We take seriously the call to be "honest" just war thinkers and practitioners in Yoder, *When War Is Unjust*.

4. Ramsey, *War and the Christian Conscience*, 15.

5. Allman and Winright, "Growing Edges," 173–91. The phrase was drawn from Langan, "Imperfectly Just War," 361–65.

6. Michel, *Christian in the World*, 183; the parenthetical clarification is his.

7. Winright, "Hawks and Doves," 32–35; Winright, "Two Rival Versions," 221–39. See also Palmer-Fernández, "Just War Moralities," 580–605.

8. Yoder, *Nevertheless*.

9. Iasiello, "Jus Post Bellum," 33, 37.

10. Baer and Capizzi, "Just-War Theory," 163–75. Capizzi develops this further in his monograph *Politics, Justice, and War*, 60–61.

believe, the right intent to achieve and sustain a just and lasting peace for all, not only for one's own but also for those who are named "enemy."[11]

As reckoned in this volume's other chapters, war itself is a "business" that has costs for many and financial returns for some. Indeed, both the *jus ad bellum* and *jus in bello* categories of just war theory include a criterion known as "proportionality," which requires an accounting of whether going to war and conducting it will result in more harm, damage, and costs than any good that might be achieved. In other words, proportionality entails weighing the goods and evils, the benefits and costs, the so-called blood and treasure of war. We think that concern for proportionality arises from that right intent of establishing and maintaining a just and lasting peace. Thus, it makes sense for considerations of proportionality to be a part of *jus ante bellum* and *jus post bellum* too.

As such, we believe a case can be made that working for a just peace in pre- and postwar settings is a fiscally responsible pursuit. In this chapter, we suggest that the practices of *jus ante bellum*, while costly, would be more than worth it to undertake because they usually prevent war—with all of its even greater costs, including the expenses of *jus post bellum*. At the same time, we suggest that *jus ante bellum*, which includes just peacemaking practices, may be better "business" than the "business of war." In addition, some of the costs of *jus post bellum* will be highlighted in what follows, since these perhaps have not factored sufficiently, if at all, until recently, into proportionality considerations. In their book *After the Smoke Clears: The Just War Tradition and Post War Justice*, with regard to the restorative phase of *jus post bellum*, the authors note,

> The restoration efforts outlined here are expensive and laborious. That is a good thing. Waging war is one of the most destructive and evil human activities. . . . By burdening those who engage in war . . . with security and policing, political reform, economic recovery, social rehabilitation, and environmental cleanup, the true cost of war would be revealed; perhaps the often feverish rush to war might be quelled. War is and ought to be expensive.[12]

The *jus post bellum* category increases the costs of going to war, but the benefits of the just peace that follows also need to be acknowledged, including that the likelihood of a reigniting of that war is reduced. In this way, the positive results of *jus post bellum* should be similar to those of *jus ante*

---

11. Allman and Winright, "Growing Edges," 180.
12. Allman and Winright, *After the Smoke Clears*, 172.

bellum. Both would be responsible, fiscally and morally, when considered from a just war perspective.

Just Peacemaking and *Jus Ante Bellum*

Erasmus advised the Christian prince, "Finally putting aside all emotion, let him apply just a little reason to the problem by counting up the true cost of the war and deciding whether the object he seeks to achieve by it is worth that much, even if he were certain of victory, which does not always favor even the best of causes. Weigh up the anxieties, expense, dangers, the long and difficult preparations."[13] The "true cost" includes the blood and treasure of war, but Erasmus added here "the long and difficult preparations" for war. Recruiting, training, and equipping military personnel all require a great deal of time, energy, and money. Rarely, if ever, are the preparations for war incorporated within just war reasoning about proportionality and *jus ad bellum*.

As the dean of contemporary just war theory Michael Walzer has noted, critics of just war accuse it of focusing on the time immediately prior to embarking on war and then on the conduct of war, without giving as much attention to wider questions, such as "imperial ambition and the global struggle for resources and power."[14] Although preparations for war aren't his direct concern here, his point about just war theorists' alleged myopic concentration on *jus ad bellum* and *jus in bello* criteria is relevant here. Religious ethicist John Kelsay referred to this as just war theory's lack of "historical thickness."[15] Similarly, Yoder wrote of just war theory's problematic "punctualism": "What is either right or wrong is that punctual decision, based upon the facts of the case at just that instant, and the just war tradition delivers the criteria for adjudicating that decision. This procedure undervalues the longitudinal dimensions of the conflict."[16] Accordingly, a number of scholars have called for more formal attention to the less-immediately-prior period before *jus ad bellum* considerations about whether embarking upon war would be justified. Some have named it *jus ante bellum*, justice with regard to the time before war is imminent or dangerously "clear and present."[17] As Maureen O'Connell puts it, *jus ante bellum* "is not a crisis-driven or reactionary approach to war and

13. Erasmus, *Education of a Christian Prince*, 72.
14. Walzer, *Arguing About War*, xi.
15. Kelsay, "Refine and Improve," 27.
16. Yoder, "Just War Tradition," 296.
17. Allman and Winright, "Growing Edges," 176–78.

peacemaking that demands swift calculations and forecasting... with little time for imagining alternative solutions to the way things are.... It is an ongoing, deliberate, and proactive approach to building relationships of peace."[18] O'Connell highlights the emerging field of faith-based diplomacy, which fosters a number of intentional dispositions and actions that promote peace and justice even in the absence of armed conflict, as a concrete example of *jus ante bellum*.[19] Such diplomacy can be especially effective with regard to when religion plays a part in igniting conflict. However, O'Connell does not devote explicit attention to how this practice impacts the "business" of war.

Jus ante bellum is also addressed by Roger Wertheimer, a philosopher who has served as the Distinguished Chair of Ethics at the US Naval Academy. He conceives of *jus ante bellum* primarily as *jus in disciplina bellica*, the ethics of educating for warfare.[20] His focus is professional military education at military academies and war colleges, preparing military personnel to perform "the deliberate infliction of the greatest evils on other persons," namely, injuring and killing them in war.[21] He emphasizes the goods, virtues, and character that pertain to a professional military and that should be inculcated among those who are preparing for military service. Again, he limits his treatment of *jus ante bellum* to preparing military personnel professionally and ethically for their duties. In a more recent essay, "*Jus Ante Bellum*: Principles of Prewar Conduct," Wertheimer provides more of a history of, or a review of the literature concerning, *jus ante bellum*, including hints of it in the work of Walzer and others.[22] He reiterates his focus on professionalism and education, so that *jus in disciplina bellica* is a principle or norm within the more general area of *jus ante bellum*. Although he does not discuss it, his proposal will obviously require money for instruction, training, practice, and implementation. We assume that this investment would likely save money in the long run.

As O'Connell notes, though, considerations about *jus ante bellum*, without using that term, initially fell under the purview of just peacemaking theory, which was developed during the 1990s with the leadership of Glen Stassen. In the introduction to *Just Peacemaking: The New Paradigm*

18. O'Connell, "Jus *Ante* Bellum," 20.

19. For an article that argues that the approach of faith-based diplomacy is flawed, given the excessive influence of both "military culture" and conservative evangelicals in chaplaincy and military leadership, see Marsden, "Faith-Based Diplomacy," 475–98. For a more recent, positive assessment of its potential, see Black, "Faith-Based diplomacy."

20. Wertheimer, *Empowering Our Military Conscience*, ix.

21. Wertheimer, *Empowering Our Military Conscience*, 134.

22. Wertheimer, "*Jus Ante Bellum*," 54–68.

for the Ethics of Peace and War, Stassen et al. write, "We now have three paradigms for the ethics of peace and war: pacifism, just war theory, and just peacemaking theory."[23] In their view, "just war theory alone gives us tunnel vision."[24] By concentrating only on when military action is morally justified, just war theory diverts attention away from preventive measures that might avert war. Just peacemaking, therefore, seeks to address the root causes of armed conflict.

Just peacemaking includes ten practices—rather than principles or criteria—that are ethically normative, empirically observable, and demonstrably effective for preventing wars. These ten practices are (1) supporting nonviolent direct action; (2) taking independent initiatives to reduce threats; (3) using cooperative conflict resolution; (4) acknowledging responsibility for conflict and injustice (and seeking repentance and forgiveness); (5) advancing democracy, human rights, and interdependence; (6) fostering just and sustainable economic development; (7) working with emerging cooperative forces in the international system; (8) strengthening the United Nations and other international efforts for cooperation and human rights; (9) reducing offensive weapons and the weapons trade; and (10) encouraging grassroots peacemaking groups and voluntary associations. Not only do these practices diminish the likelihood of war, but they are fiscally responsible. At least, this seems to be an assumption that surfaces in connection with a number of these practices. An axiom of Benjamin Franklin comes to mind: an ounce of prevention is worth a pound of cure.

So, in connection with working with emerging cooperative forces in the international system, Paul W. Schroeder observes that during the early twenty-first century, "a steep rise in the costs and dangers of major war as a tool of statecraft and a corresponding decline in the applicability and potential benefits of even a successful use of large-scale military force as a way of solving major problems" have resulted in a "decline in the utility of war" and, instead, the "rise of the trading state" in which "the priority is now placed . . . on success in trade and the economy."[25] In his chapter on strengthening the United Nations and international efforts for cooperation and human rights, Michael Joseph Smith similarly writes, "As the debate on the Iraq War has shown, the normative legitimacy of war, imperialism, and conquest has markedly declined. Thus, states now increasingly define even their security goals in terms of creating wealth and welfare in the

---

23. Stassen et al., introduction to *Just Peacemaking*, 1.
24. Stassen et al., introduction to *Just Peacemaking*, 2, original emphasis.
25. Schroeder, "Emerging Cooperative Forces," 159.

context of an interdependent global economy."[26] Of course, at the time we are writing (2018, a decade after the most recent edition of *Just Peacemaking* was published), these may no longer be such an either/or, at least for a nation such as the United States with its present president and presidential administration.

Likewise, in the chapter on supporting nonviolent direct action, John Cartwright and Susan Thistlethwaite defend boycotts, strikes, and sanctions as effective nonviolent methods that "can produce corrections of systemic injustice without the violence of war," especially by applying economic pressure on oppressive regimes.[27] Presumably, such methods cost less not only in blood but also in treasure. Likewise, in their chapter on reducing offensive weapons and the weapons trade, Barbara Green and Glen Stassen argue that an advantage of reducing offensive weapons is that it reduces also "the monetary cost of weapons build-ups," thereby also resulting in the reduction of the percentage of GNP that a nation spends on military weapons.[28] This link is similar to the Second Vatican Council's observation in its document *Gaudium et spes* (The Church in the Modern World): "While extravagant sums are being spent for the furnishing of ever new weapons, an adequate remedy cannot be provided for the multiple miseries afflicting the whole modern world. . . . The arms race is an utterly treacherous trap for humanity, and one which ensnares the poor to an intolerable degree."[29] The money spent on arms could be better spent on other problems, such as illiteracy and poverty. Military spending drains a nation's treasure, if not its blood.

In *Imperial Delusions: American Militarism and Endless War*, Carl Boggs makes the same observation: "While the Pentagon system functions as a stimulus to economic growth, such growth has been increasingly detrimental to the social infrastructure. The American developmental model favors the military sector and global priorities over a wide range of civilian programs and services. . . . It takes little imagination to perceive that enormous material, human, and technological resources have been devoted mainly to waste and destruction."[30] So too does Jeffrey D. Sachs state, "The single most important issue in allocating national resources is war versus peace, or as macroeconomists put it, 'guns versus butter.'"[31] Sachs notes,

26. Smith, "Strengthen the United Nations," 170.
27. Cartwright and Thistlethwaite, "Support Nonviolent Direct Action," 46.
28. Green and Stassen, "Reduce Offensive Weapons," 180.
29. Second Vatican Council, *Gaudium et spes*, 81.
30. Boggs, *Imperial Delusions*, 32.
31. Sachs, "The Fatal Expense of American Imperialism."

The scale of US military operations is remarkable. The US Department of Defense has (as of a 2010 inventory) 4,999 military facilities, of which 4,249 are in the United States; eighty-eight are in overseas US territories; and 662 are in thirty-six foreign countries and foreign territories, in all regions of the world. Not counted in this list are the secret facilities of the US intelligence agencies. The cost of running these military operations and the wars they support is extraordinary, around $900 billion per year, or five percent of US national income, when one adds the budgets of the Pentagon, the intelligence agencies, homeland security, nuclear weapons programs in the Department of Energy, and veterans' benefits. The $900 billion in annual spending is roughly one-quarter of all federal government outlays.[32]

Sachs emphasizes that the "perpetual war" which the US sees itself fighting, especially in the Middle East, has "massively diverted resources away from civilian needs toward the military, and helped to create mass budget deficits and the buildup of public debt." For his part, Boggs refers to our "war economy" that "depends on a convergence of factors: its own deeply embedded culture, bureaucratic leverage, political conservatism, the fetishism of technology, [and] a mass belief system saturated with national hubris."[33] The problem is both wide and deep. It is systemic, structural, and institutional. It is also cultural. Thus, there are no easy answers or solutions. Sachs recommends, "It's time to abandon the reveries, burdens, and self-deceptions of empire and to invest in sustainable development at home and in partnership with the rest of the world." Of course, this is easier said than done.

Green and Stassen recognize the existence of some obstacles too. One is the fact that the United States, Russia, China, and some other nations profit from weapons exports to other nations. Along with that, weapons manufacturers make a lot of money from the weapons trade, and they often contribute donations to politicians for their ongoing support. As Green and Stassen conclude, "Until the power of money to corrupt the decision-making process is curtailed, it will be hard to make the process peaceable."[34] Boggs, like Sachs, views the obstacle as even more behemothian: "The Pentagon system thrives on an entrenched corporate oligopoly in which myths of free-market capitalism and its fierce competition and risks are scarcely operative; sales are to governments alone, and profitability is usually ensured."[35] The

32. Sachs, "The Fatal Expense of American Imperialism."
33. Boggs, *Imperial Delusions*, 27.
34. Green and Stassen, "Reduce Offensive Weapons," 194.
35. Boggs, *Imperial Delusions*, 27.

"business" of war is powerful indeed. Somehow, just peacemaking practices need to become viewed as even "better business" by those who currently seek to profit from war.

Suppose we consider the US Peace Corps as an expression and instantiation of *jus ante bellum*. It is substantially cheaper than a military presence and seems to, in many cases, have positive and lasting effects that may even prevent war. Compared with the financial figures provided by Sachs above about the costs of present US military operations, the US Peace Corps fiscal year 2016 budget request asked for 410 million dollars. This would cover the nearly 220,000 volunteers in sixty-four countries worldwide and help to create the infrastructure needed to support a larger corps. The director, Carolyn Hessler-Radelet, argues that an increase in funding would further the mission of the organization. She describes the volunteers, stating, "By living and working at the local level, Peace Corps Volunteers are our country's best ambassadors, promoting a positive image of the United States and furthering the cause of peace throughout the world."[36] Or consider foreign aid provided by the US to other countries. In terms of direct aid, the United States has a proposed 34 billion dollars in foreign aid for fiscal year 2017. This money will provide assistance to programs in more than one hundred countries through over twenty government programs. The list of support includes "expanding free markets, combating extremism, ensuring stable democracies, and addressing the root causes of poverty, while simultaneously fostering global good will."[37] Of the total budget, 8.31 billion dollars will go directly towards peace and security.

Increasing support for the Peace Corps and increasing the budget for foreign aid obviously will increase the costs for each of these; however, doing so should decrease the costs from war. As for *jus ante bellum*, Wertheimer's surveys demonstrate that it remains a nascent category with differing understandings of what it includes and entails—in some cases, such as O'Connell's, it seems to overlap with and extend just peacemaking. As such, it will seek to minimize the likelihood of war and its costs in blood and treasure. *Jus ante bellum* thus could provide long-term financial benefit to the nation, although, of course, the military-industrial complex would lose out.

---

36. Peace Corps, "Congressional Budget Justication, Fiscal Year 2016," v.

37. See "What Is U.S. Government Foreign Assistance?," available at https://www.foreignassistance.gov.

Jus Post Bellum

Erasmus reminded the prince that, in waging war, he will be "compelled to expose young men to all kinds of peril and to make countless orphans, widows, and childless old people, and to reduce countless others to beggary and misery, often in a single hour."[38] These are costs or consequences of war that should not be neglected when considering the *jus ad bellum* category of proportionality: the evils resulting from war should not outweigh the very evils that one is seeking to stop in the first place. Children and the elderly are also noncombatants and, according to the *jus in bello* criterion of discrimination, they should not be intentionally and directly targeted or harmed. But even if they are "collateral damage"—that is, their harm is foreseen but unintended—such harm still should not be disproportionate to the good objective sought by a specific military action. As noted at the outset of this essay, the costs of war in blood and treasure are high. These include the deaths and injuries of military personnel but also the harms inflicted upon their families, friends, and others in their society. Furthermore, there is the destruction of homes and infrastructure (roads, bridges, power plants, electrical grids, schools, etc.), the pollution from the actual smoke of war and contamination of soil and water from bombs and other ordnance, and so many other effects of war that are often are not calculated, even by just war theorists, when determining whether to embark upon war or not, or considering how, once undertaken, it should be conducted.

The development of the category of *jus post bellum*, in part, attempts to address what happens after the shooting stops, and it seeks to address effects of war such as these and more. In so doing, it is anchored in the principle of right intent, which seeks to establish and bolster what's needed for a just and lasting peace. Although the seeds of *jus post bellum* have been present in the thought of various just war theorists for centuries, as an explicit category it has gained more attention and gotten more traction only in recent decades.[39] While there appears to be a consensus that *jus post bellum* ought to be a part of just war theory, whether as an additional category or as integrated within *jus ad bellum* and *jus in bello*, a variety of principles, practices, or priorities have been proposed. The book *After the Smoke Clears* suggests four *jus post bellum* criteria, with the first being the just cause principle and the following three being phases: (1) the reconciliation phase, (2) the punishment phase,

---

38. Erasmus, *Education of a Christian Prince*, 72.

39. In addition to Allman and Winright, *After the Smoke Clears*, others who give serious attention to *jus post bellum* include (these are not exhaustive): Bellamy, "The Responsibilities of Victory"; Orend, "A Just War Theory Perspective"; Orend, "*Jus Post Bellum*"; Bass, "*Jus Post Bellum*"; Schuck, "When the Shooting Stops."

and (3) the restoration phase.[40] The reconciliation phase includes, for example, truth commissions; the punishment phase includes, among other things, compensation; and the restoration phase includes environmental cleanup. These *jus post bellum* expectations add to the financial costs of war too, and they ought to give governing authorities additional pause when contemplating war. A brief highlighting of a few of these *jus post bellum* expectations should suffice to show what we have in mind in this regard.

Truth commissions are a component of the reconciliation phase. Apologies, amnesties, and other acts are also included in this phase. For the sake of this present essay, the cost of truth commissions is noteworthy. The other components of the reconciliation phase are probably comparable in this regard. According to a United Nations report, *Rule-of-Law Tools for Post-Conflict States: Truth Commissions*, "A major challenge faced by virtually all truth commissions is raising sufficient funds to carry out their work. The budget of a truth commission is typically over five million US dollars and can easily total twelve million or more."[41] Of course, the more money that is spent, the better the health of the post-conflict nation's economy and, we suspect, the quality of the truth commission.[42]

The punishment phase includes compensation, reparations, and war crimes trials. These can include restitution, for instance, for families of loved ones wrongfully killed in a drone strike. Indeed, the US has had to pay for deaths and other damages to families in Afghanistan. Between 2003 and 2013, thousands of compensation payments were made by the US in its long-running combat operations there, with some "condolence payments" given for innocents killed or injured, while others were given for a broad range of damages: a child's bicycle run over, an onion field crushed, twenty-one sheep killed in rocket fire.[43] According to the US Army, 5,766 claims marked for Afghanistan were filed between February 2003 and August 2011, of which 1,671 were paid, for a total of about 3.1 million dollars.[44] This is just a sliver of the costs associated with this phase of *jus post bellum*, and they should factor into the equation of proportionality, too.

The restoration phase includes such things as security and policing, political reform, economic restoration, social rehabilitation, and ecological cleanup. With regard to the last, some munitions are being called

---

40. The second half of Allman and Winright's *After the Smoke Clears* covers the four *jus post bellum* criteria, principles, or phases.

41. Office of the United Nations High Commissioner for Human Rights, *Rule-of-Law Tools*.

42. Olsen, Payne, and Reiter, "At What Cost?," 165–84.

43. Currier, "Our Condolences."

44. Currier, "Our Condolences."

weapons of long-term destruction (WLTDs) along the lines of weapons of mass destruction (WMDs). Two examples are cluster munitions and ammunition containing depleted uranium.[45] These cause casualties years after war supposedly stops, and they negatively impact other components of restoration, including economic restoration. Like landmines, cluster munitions are now under a UN ban, although a number of nations, including the US, have not signed on to it.[46] They are bomblets that cover as much of a footprint as two football fields, and many of them do not explode upon impact. Even decades later, unexploded cluster bomblets can be deadly to children, farmers, and fishermen. How many remember when the US dropped cluster munitions over Laos in connection with the Vietnam War? There are still casualties from the leftover cluster bomblets in that country. Thus, the US continues to pay millions of dollars to help clean them out of there.[47] As for depleted uranium, in Iraq, the cost has been at least 30 million US dollars for the toxic cleanup.[48] If the US and a handful of other nations are going to continue to use weapons such as cluster munitions or ammunition containing depleted uranium, then the long-term costs in blood and treasure should be taken into account by just war theorists.

Finally, in recent years attention has been given to what has been termed "moral injury."[49] Initially addressed by psychologist Jonathan Shay in his 1995 book, *Achilles in Vietnam: Combat Trauma and the Undoing of Character*, and more recently studied by philosopher Nancy Sherman in her *Afterwar: Healing the Moral Wounds of Our Soldiers*, moral injury is a debilitating sense of shame and guilt that military personnel experience because of actions they have done or observed in war.[50] Having participated in war, some warriors feel moral guilt even if they think their involvement and their conduct were justified. The symptoms of moral injury may resemble those of PTSD, but these two conditions are not synonymous. There is a high cost in blood, as suicide rates are higher among combat veterans with moral injury.[51] There is also a high cost in treasure due to moral injury. Dr. Lewis Jeffery Lee, a retired US Navy SEAL who now is Mental Health Chaplain

---

45. Allman and Winright, *After the Smoke Clears*, 165–72.

46. Winright, "Morality of Cluster Bombing," 11–12.

47. Blakesmore, "Why the US Is Pledging Millions."

48. Edwards, "Iraq's Depleted Uranium Clean-Up." See also Allman, "Postwar Justice," 9–13.

49. Winright and Jeschke, "Combat and Confession," 169–87.

50. Shay, *Achilles in Vietnam*; Sherman, *Afterwar*. See also Brock and Lettini, *Soul Repair*; Graham, *Moral Injury*; Jensen and Childs, *Moral Warriors*; Meagher and Pryer, *War and Moral Injury*; Shay, "Moral Injury," 182–91.

51. Bryan et al., "Moral Injury, Suicidal Ideation," 154–60.

for the VA (Veterans Affairs) San Diego Health System, has written extensively about moral injury, and in particular its costs, challenges, and treatments. Again, the figures and estimates he provides include financial costs, resource expenditures, and much more—which he suggests "contribute to the moral-ethical costs of war."[52]

These are just a few of the practices that are enumerated within *jus post bellum* phases, indicating the "true costs" of war and its aftermath. Like just peacemaking and *jus ante bellum* practices, addressing *jus post bellum* concerns mitigates the likelihood of the reigniting of conflict as well as even more costs in treasure and in blood over the long term. Just-war theorists should take these costs into account when trying to determine proportionality and the "business" of war.

Ending with Erasmus

We began with Erasmus, and we shall now end with him. In *The Education of a Christian Prince*, Erasmus warned about the terrible costs of war. Five years later, in *The Complaint of Peace*, a personified Peace observes, concerning the incarnation of Jesus Christ, "What induced the Son of God to come down from heaven to earth, but a gracious desire to reconcile the world to his Father? to cement the hearts of men by mutual and indissoluble love? . . . For my sake, then, he was sent on this gracious embassy; it was my business which he condescended to transact."[53] Turning to the Christian ruler again, Erasmus has Peace instruct him "to contemplate the model of him who is your sovereign; observe how he entered upon his reign, how he conducted it, how he departed from this world, and learn to reign from his example."[54] In this way, the governing authority "will find that the very first object of your heart should be to preserve your country in a state of peace." For Erasmus, the "business" of Peace is what the Lord Jesus Christ has "transacted" and prioritizes diplomacy ("this gracious embassy").

Any "business" of war—and, in particular, of *just* war—should be directed by the "business" of peace and, as such, ultimately toward a truly just and lasting peace. That is the right intent of just war. Recent efforts by scholars and practitioners to broaden the scope of just war theory to encompass *jus ante bellum* and *jus post bellum* is due, in part, to a renewed emphasis on that ethical end. As these dimensions or facets of just war reasoning continue to gain traction, it will be necessary also to take into

52. Lee, *Moral Injury Reconciliation*, 63.
53. Erasmus, *Complaint of Peace*, 18.
54. Erasmus, *Complaint of Peace*, 19.

account their accompanying costs in both blood and treasure. Doing so will hopefully put in place more obstacles to justifying war but also may create opportunities that pay off in their making and sustaining of a just peace. For, as we have seen, the "business" of peace is essential to just war's right intent, and that should prove to be cheaper, more cost effective, and perhaps ultimately more "profitable" than the "business" of war.

12

Masquerade
Public Policy and the Military-Industrial Complex

STAN GOFF

No one can serve two masters. Either you will hate the one and love the other, or you will be devoted to the one and despise the other. You cannot serve both God and money.

—MATTHEW 6:24 (NIV)

Power relations are culturally constructed, but masquerade—to the powerful and powerless alike—as inevitable and natural. To reveal their arbitrary foundation is thus an epistemologically arduous task.

—ALF HORNBORG, *THE POWER OF THE MACHINE*

PART FOUR: RESISTING THE BUSINESS OF WAR

Introduction

In 1960, President Eisenhower coined the term "military-industrial complex" (MIC) to refer to the symbiotic and metastatic growth of the war-integrated military and industrial establishments. The MIC, however, is a not a fixed establishment per se. It is a meshwork of power relations with a semiformal interlocking directorate which has, since Eisenhower's Cassandra-like warning,[1] grown into something more akin to a military-industrial-financial-digital-media complex in today's political ecology.

The first purpose of this essay is to shed light on the particulars of this dynamic complexity with an eye to its implications for church and public policy. Most accounts of the MIC are decontextualized by artificial academic disciplinary boundaries and overly simplistic models of understanding social phenomena; but the MIC is embedded in historic economic, political, sociological, psychological, and ecological contexts. The United States is not a hermetically sealed political entity but the chief financial and military power in a late capitalist *world* system. Readers will see how this dynamic presents *American* Christians with a moral conundrum inasmuch as we are all embedded in the MIC, whether we like it or not. It also presents us with a political conundrum because the eventual abolition of the MIC will require us to sacrifice some of those things we associate with our "standard of living."

The second purpose of this essay applies to questions of policy but only after establishing context by first addressing the "core-periphery dynamic" and unequal exchange, accumulation regimes and crises, the role of money in progressive "enclosures," the role of the state, the emergence of military Keynesianism and the subsequent emergence of financialization, militarism as a gender dynamic, and domestic economic ramifications.

Cores, Peripheries, Unequal Exchange

I am composing this treatment on a computer. Computers, as just one example, have become irreplaceable in the current US and world economy. Computers are made from several essential and *imported* materials—cobalt from the Democratic Republic of Congo, iron from Brazil, palladium from Botswana, gold from Costa Rica, copper from Chile, selenium from the Philippines, zinc from Peru, silver and antimony from Mexico, chromium, manganese, and platinum from South Africa, and aluminum, arsenic,

---

1. Cassandra (or Kassandra): in mythology, the daughter of King Priam and Queen Hecuba of Troy, who was cursed to make true prophecies that no one believed.

barium, cadmium, lead, and mercury from China.² These "strategic" materials are essential now for every core nation's governance and management systems, in maintaining our energy and transportation grids, in education, and in high-technology weapons systems.

American power *assures* the reliable inflow of these and other key materials through *financial hegemony* combined with *military power*, working hand in hand, ensuring importation but at *unequal exchange rates*.³ Exchange inequality itself can be superficially shown in the correspondence between two statistical tables: annual per capita gross national income (GNI) and annual per capita energy consumption.⁴

Country	2018 per capita GNI (US dollars)	Most recent year per capita energy consumption (kg of oil equivalent)
Botswana	7,750	1,301
Brazil	9,140	1,496
Chile	14,670	2,006
China	9,479	2,237
Congo, Dem. Rep.	490	389
Costa Rica	11,510	1,023
Mexico	9,180	1,537
Peru	6,530	790
Philippines	3,830	474
South Africa	5,720	2,695
United States	62,850	6,804

Reference: World Bank⁵

2. Rockwood, "Earth's Most Precious Metals."

3. Liberal economics denies that "unequal exchange" exists. It supports this claim in two ways. First, it reduces all exchanges to money exchange, referring to anything outside that transaction as "external." Second, it narrows the window of observation to the exchange itself by two "private individuals"—without any history leading to the exchange—which is ideological cover for the first. In other words, the denial of unequal exchange is the exclusion of all "comparative advantage" going into an exchange. Determined either thermodynamically (net use of materials and energy) or by measuring which party leaves the most hours of labor at the exchange, unequal exchange is demonstrable.

4. Ecologically, as this shows, capitalism actually rewards those who environmentally "consume" the most.

5. For 2018 per capita GNI see https://data.worldbank.org/indicator/ny.gnp.pcap.cd. For energy consumption see https://data.worldbank.org/indicator/EG.USE.PCAP.KG.OE.

These statistics provide corresponding *economic* and *ecological* glimpses of the inequality of exchange built into "globalization."[6] American militarism and its psychic, ideological, and economic correlates cannot be grasped apart from the dynamics of a *world* system—a system which itself is already regulated by *international* policy over which the United States exercises predominant control through (1) military power and disposition, (2) exclusive veto power within the International Monetary Fund, (3) the designated international currency, (4) enforced peripheral dependency, and (5) debt and debt leverage.

Unequal exchange results in living standard disparities[7] and facilitates the import of useful materials and the export of its consequent environmental and social destruction. For example, the poisonous moonscape and cruel working conditions of a South African gold mine are not visible to me as someone living in the United States while I write on this computer.

The core-periphery dynamic describes modern imperial relations organized into multinational blocs. Core nations are those we refer to as "developed." The peripheral nations and/or internal peripheries[8] are always referred to as un-*developed* or under-*developed*. The study of flows—money, materials, people and talents, energy, etc.—reveals not a developmental race from past to modern but a parasitic system of unequal exchange.[9] The core imports *order* from and exports *disorder* to the financially and/or militarily subjugated periphery. This system of unequal exchange between core nations and peripheral ones constitutes then a modern imperial tributary economy.[10]

This dynamic is not new but is the fundamental dynamic of empires. The Roman Empire itself was substantially built up (and later degraded) in a similar process and on a smaller scale. The popular support for the regime were always the Roman citizens *in Rome*, but the provision of a "standard of living" to ensure social quiescence at home was secured militarily and financially abroad. And the ecological causes and effects were profoundly

---

6. A black box category that is generally represented by monetary input-output models with actual processes concealed inside the "box."

7. Invariably based on access to industrial goods.

8. African America is arguably an internal periphery of the United States.

9. Meaning that this is not a competitive relationship, with peripheries falling behind in the race to Development, but a parasitic relationship wherein the core survives on various extractions from the periphery and uses the periphery as a dump for developmental wastes and destructions. Characterizing inequality temporally, as separated actors positioned differently along the "march to progress," conceals the spatial reality of a parasitic relation, within which the cores gain at the expense of peripheries.

10. When vassals pay *tribute* to masters.

instrumental in Rome's eventual dissolution. Demand for grain and timber deforested a good deal of the Mediterranean, from what is now Italy through Syria and into North Africa. Deforestation led to erosion, which closed key ports with silt; and when the empire's ceaseless expansion to provide for Rome led to its political destabilization, follow-on pastoral populations grazed the now deforested land into complete deserts.[11]

Now we see this core-periphery dynamic writ very large, destabilizing the entire world's climate, stripping off the topsoil, looting the fisheries, acidifying the oceans, poisoning and drying out the major freshwater aquifers, accelerating deforestation, and wiping out species at the highest rate since the Cretaceous-Paleocene extinction.[12] Absent this core-periphery dynamic—which requires the MIC—the American "standard of living" would be impossible. To describe our embeddedness in this dynamic, we need to describe its drivers.

Accumulation—Regimes and Crises

Woe to those who join house to house, who add field to field, until there is no more room, and you are made to dwell alone in the midst of the land.

—Isaiah 5:8 (ESV)

I find that in the course of what we now call the second millennium it grew out of the Church and became, in my opinion, not a post-Christian reality, but a perverted Christian reality.

—Ivan Illich, *The Rivers North of the Future*

---

11. Ponting, *Green History*, 76–7.

12. Moore, "Rise and Fall of Cheap Nature." It is difficult, given how familiar language reinforces an episteme, to express this in non-Cartesian terms; but this is not a function of Humans having an impact on Nature, or even of Capitalism having an impact on Nature. The aggregated and emerging *totality* of relations between all things, human and not, actually constitute an ecology, of which we are a part. Late capitalism does not "impact" ecology (like a subject doing something to an object), it *is* an ecology. Jason W. Moore: "To register the bloody history of this Human/Nature binary is a moral protest. It is also an analytical protest. For capitalism does not thrive on violence and inequality alone. It is a prodigiously creative and productive system too—at least until recently. The symbolic, material, and bodily violence of this audacious separation—Humanity and Nature—performed a special kind of 'work' for the modern world. Backed by imperial power and capitalist rationality, it mobilized the unpaid work and energy of humans—especially women, especially the enslaved—in service to transforming landscapes with a singular purpose: the endless accumulation of capital." From the Abstract.

The global order of which we are each a small part is a *regime*—not in the sense of a command structure but a *systematic social arrangement* centered on some main objective. Today's global regime is a regime centered on *accumulation*. That is not to say that every person within that system joined field to field, but that the motives of those who occupy the citadels of power are driven more than anything else by the desire to accumulate, because accumulation—of *money* in modern times—is power. The MIC is nested *within* this accumulation regime, not alongside it.

> Any account of accumulation will need to consider (1) the social institutions that regulate exchange, (2) the symbolic systems that ultimately define exchange values and exchange rates, and (3) the thermodynamic and other physical circumstances that allow us to determine the direction of net flows of energy and materials.[13]

We have already seen an example of material flows and an oblique picture of exchange rates in the data above. These materials are moved from more peripheral nations to the core nation of the United States (speaking as an American) *physically*; they use *energy* and machines to carry them as well as energy for the electronic and/or industrial systems used to organize and transform them. The overwhelming majority of that energy comes from fossil hydrocarbons—coal, oil, and gas—a *thermodynamic* condition. Moore points out that accumulation depends on "cheap nature," which includes cheap energy, cheap natural resources, cheap food, and cheap labor.[14] Once any of these "four cheaps" becomes no-longer-cheap, accumulation (the rate of profit) is imperiled and the state steps in. Remember my computer with all the parts from afar? Our social system would summarily collapse if computers suddenly and magically disappeared; and without cheap imported goods, the United States economy would crash.[15] In a scenario

---

13. Hornborg, *Power of the Machine*, 67.

14. Moore, "Rise and Fall of Cheap Nature." Labor here, while not generally thought of as Nature, is naturalized (defined into objectified Nature), e.g., "human resources" and "labor markets."

15. Amadeo, "US Imports and Exports." Circa 2016, the US exported $2.2 trillion and imported $2.7 trillion. That is a half-trillion-dollar trade deficit (which we'll describe again further down). Our big exports are, not coincidentally, also military products, like aircraft, pharmaceuticals, chemicals, and telecommunications. These are indirectly subsidized through defense contracts. But the real "vulnerability," for those who see a threat in foreign dependency, is that half of all imports into the United States are consumer goods, from shoes to phones, which we import for sale at prices that could not be supported by the cost of labor inside the United States. The Walmart customer—himself perhaps on a tight budget—gets an unseen boost from the Indonesian factory worker who can add value to commodities at a rate of five dollars a day. This, as we will see, constitutes *unequal exchange*.

even closer to the bone, what would happen if by magic or catastrophe supplies of fossil hydrocarbons ended?[16] These are matters that cannot be left to themselves, and the dominant fraction of society is quite aware of that.[17]

Given that the current accumulation regime, to which all other aspects of modern society must adapt, must assure these flows of materials—including the coal, oil, and gas that make their inter-regional and international movement possible—this is a key responsibility of the modern nation-state. The armed forces are ultimately responsible for this assurance, themselves constituting the most expensive institution in human history. The United States Navy maintains eleven carrier strike groups with supporting expeditionary and battleship strike groups, prowling the planet's sea lanes at a cost of approximately 156 billion dollars a year, primarily to ensure that one of those thermodynamic resources—oil—is not disrupted. Interestingly, the United States military itself is the single biggest institutional consumer of oil in the world—around ten million barrels a year.[18] In other words, the Department of Defense (DOD) is burning up the very resource it is most relied upon to protect in order to ensure uninterrupted accumulation.[19] Money is essential to this accumulation. We cannot fully appreciate the policy implications of the MIC—as an organ of a state committed to an accumulation regime—without an excursus into "the secret life of money" itself.[20]

Ecology of Mammon

When everyone is dependent upon money for survival, money becomes an entitlement for the holders. It entitles me to a resource or even to the labor of others. Money-exchange is a "private" choice, that is, it is "invisible" to the law ("public"). Money is entitlement to some *thing-for-sale*,[21] but that *thing* is an immanent amalgamation of appropriated resources, knowledge, and work. And when someone pays you for your work on a job, you are not just receiving this modern survival necessity—money—exchanged for specific tasks. You are paid for timed obedience. Rent-a-slave.[22] *Power is the ability to demand obedience.* The customer is always right.

16. Without oil, grocery stores would be bare in a matter of days, not weeks.
17. Moore, "Nature/Society."
18. Union of Concerned Scientists, "The US Military and Oil."
19. A contradiction they must simultaneously face and ignore.
20. Ched Myers, foreword to Goff, *Mammon's Ecology*, x.
21. Heretofore referred to as commodities.
22. A construction worker will be told to do this or that on the job, but it might be different from hour to hour. But he or she will be paid the same per hour regardless of what he or she is told to do. What this worker is selling, for a designated time, is *obedience*.

Enclosures

Historically, people who could live with little or no money have been loath to do mindless, dangerous, donkey work for strangers. They had to be disciplined. Money wasn't always a necessity; and making money into a survival necessity was not an unguided process of social evolution. As Karl Polanyi showed in *The Great Transformation*, our universal dependence on money was the intentional outcome of uniformly unpopular "enclosure" policies.[23]

Discussions of policy (and money) nowadays seldom bring up the history of *enclosure*. Not simply the "Inclosure Acts" implemented in Great Britain between the seventeenth and twentieth centuries—which gave us a *name* for this phenomenon. Enclosure is constituted by all measures, legal and extra-legal, that strategically aim to separate people who had achieved local subsistence from their land. In Great Britain, there was a twofold incentive for enclosure: the land was coveted for the mass production of wool, and the factory owners needed those uprooted and hungry bodies in the city slums to toil in their "satanic mills."

European accumulation, prior to enclosure, was principally a matter of direct and local expropriation combined with military plunder, like the feudal lord receiving expropriated goods as *shares*.[24] A peasant family grew enough food, fuel, and fodder for itself, and it gave a tributary surplus share to the manorial lord. That might be a share of butter or livestock or wheat or even artisanal production. But it was *not money*. Prior to dependence on money as a general measure of value, production and consumption were *co-located*. A peasant woman did not *buy* eggs at a distant market. She collected eggs from her own chicken coop. Ivan Illich noted, "The last five hundred years of warfare . . . has been waged by the modern State against all forms of Subsistence."[25] The transformation of people, places, and things into commodities is the core practice of capitalism. Privatization is commodification is enclosure. The commons, when necessary, will be liquidated to maintain the cheap flows required to ensure profit.

Industrializing Atlantic states needed people to sweat in the new factories. They needed large swaths of land to produce foreign exchange commodities—like wool in Great Britain. The state forced peasants off the land and into the factories, granting the land as *private* property to large-scale operators, whereupon the former peasants came to depend on

---

23. Polanyi, *Great Transformation*, 187–200.

24. In exchange for military protection.

25. Illich, "Vernacular Values." Subsistence is a threat precisely because it allows people to live with varying degrees of independence from the money-nexus. People who subsist are loathe to obey masters whose hold on them is the scarcity of money.

money for survival. Enclosure continues today, using policy as its weapon.[26] Modern-day enclosure is called "development" in peripheral nations and "privatization" in core and peripheral nations.

With generalized dependence on money, accumulation becomes possible on a heretofore unthinkable scale. This is a progressive process of *abstraction* because specie money (gold) becomes impracticable, then bank notes replace them that are *exchangeable for gold*, then bank notes come to stand alone as fiat currency (money with no specie backing). These successive abstractions *accelerate the velocity of exchange*, dissolving the bonds of community and ecology that interfere with exchange velocity. "Globalization" would not have been possible without a base-currency that trumps all others, namely, the American dollar—now traded internationally (as purely abstract value) on computers.

General-purpose money becomes not a carrier of value in itself (like gold) but a *sign* of pure exchange—a "nothing in itself."[27] Money accomplishes these things by making things that are different, alike. As Hornborg puts it, "Viewed from outer space, money is an ecosemiotic phenomenon that has very tangible effects on ecosystems and the biosphere as a whole. If it were not for general-purpose money, nobody would be able to trade tracts of rain forest for Coca-Cola."[28]

Money strips actual things, whether goods or services, of their *qualities* (use-values) and reduces them—as commodities—to a single symbol of quantity, or "price." It might be five dollars or it might be five hundred dollars, but it is measured only in dollars, like a piano that plays only one note. If a mahogany forest is not first converted into the language of money, it cannot be exchanged for bottled sugar water. Without those dollars as pure symbols of value that reduce actual material to a price, Dell and Apple and Hewlett-Packard could not purchase cobalt from the Democratic Republic of Congo or selenium from the Philippines. We don't *barter* Michigan apples for Peruvian zinc. Pure quantity (price) usurps quality (the actual thing paid for) by *decontextualization*.

This "generalized interchangeability" dissolves the differences between goods by reducing them to price, and it dissolves the bonds of community to such a degree that human beings themselves are transformed into commodities. With successive enclosures and its consequent specialization and

---

26. Regressive tax structures, intellectual property laws, "takings" legislation, eminent domain (for projects like stadia), "trade" rules, zoning, and transfer of decision-making authority from "public" to "private" actors.
27. Hornborg, *Power of the Machine*, 167.
28. Hornborg, *Power of the Machine*, 170.

deskilling, people come to depend absolutely on money-mediated relations, that is, "jobs."²⁹

The State—Military Keynesianism and Debtor Imperialism

You mean to tell me that the success of my program and my reelection hinges on the Federal Reserve and a bunch of fucking bond traders?³⁰

—PRESIDENT BILL CLINTON, 1992, TO HIS ECONOMIC ADVISORS (WHO NODDED THEIR ASSENT)

A peasant, a hunter-gatherer, a pastoral nomad—as has been shown by history—will resist labor-for-money until s/he is left with no other choice. This is why enclosures were necessary to *create* monetary dependency and for the "industrial" of the military-industrial complex to be possible.

The political expression of the moneyed class is the *nation-state*, a system wherein loyalty to a person with protean territory has been replaced by loyalty to a geographic polity with protean government. The nation-state and capitalism are symbiotic.³¹ The nation-state is organized for two

---

29. Exchanges of obedience for money. As to dissolving community, how many readers' family members have been spread across the country or the world to pursue a living?

30. Woodward, *Agenda*, 73.

31. Even the state socialisms of the twentieth century were "developed" industrially through capitalist relations of production and massive imports from other capitalist centers. Today's "communist" China is arguably the most successful capitalist state of the past two and a half decades. "It is difficult for me to read the Soviet project as a fundamental rupture. The great industrialization drive of the 1930s relied—*massively*—on the importation of fixed capital, which by 1931 constituted ninety percent of Soviet imports. The Soviets were so desperate to obtain hard currency that 'the state was prepared to export anything and everything, from gold, oil and furs to the pictures in the Hermitage Museum' (Kagarlitsky 2007, 272–73). If the Soviet project resembles other modes of production, it is surely the tributary, not socialist, mode of production, through which the state directly extracts the surplus. Nor did the Soviets turn inwards after 1945. Soviet trade with OECD countries (in constant dollars) increased 8.9 percent annually between 1950 and 1970, rising to 17.9 percent a year in the following decade—a trend accompanied by sharply deteriorating terms of trade and rising debt across the Soviet-led zone. Need we recall that the 1980s debt crisis was detonated not by Mexico but by Poland in 1981?" Moore, "Anthropocene," footnote 3.

things: sustained accumulation and war. These, we shall see, are not separate activities.

The social relations that arise with generalized money-dependency are governed by profit; but markets become saturated, and so new markets must be sought out or invented. If demand falters, there is *demand production*—advertising, fads, and fashions—as well as further commodification of the commons.[32] This cancerlike dynamic is called "growth" by economists; and it is now widely considered the single diagnostic indicator of economic health. This also accounts for the constant *expansion* into new geographic regions and/or previously protected markets.

Market-society rips an uprooted "individual" from the non-market bonds that embed her locally and casts her adrift in desperate search of this critical, intentionally scarce, nothing-in-itself money.

How does this look to us now? One inexact but useful term for what we do now is "military Keynesianism," or using military spending to maintain or boost "growth." In our own case, this is not direct cause and effect but a substitution model. The United States runs a trade deficit. It imports more in money-value than it exports. In any *abstracted* economic model, a country that imports more than it exports is losing wealth . . . and jobs. But that is not altogether true, as we can see. The United States runs the world's biggest trade deficit and *biggest national debt*, and yet sits astride the global economy as the uber-Leviathan.

The Department of Defense (DOD) serves the United States as a surrogate export market. People do have jobs, making things to sell, to an entity that exists somewhat apart, almost like the foreign nation of DOD. In 2015, the annual trade deficit was around 600 billion dollars.[33] That's more than half a trillion dollars. Excluding the covert military spending through the Department of Energy, the Central Intelligence Agency, and other non-DOD agencies, the Department of Defense (formerly the War Department) spends approximately 630 billion dollars (2015). The US is also the second largest exporter of weapons in the world, so production *for* the DOD underwrites the foreign profits of weapons manufacturers. And given the unstable political ecology of the world at large, it is likely that these weapons abroad

32. Mies and Bennholdt-Thomsen, *Subsistence Perspective*, 20. "The simultaneous forceful conquering, acquisition and destruction of 'non-capitalistic economies'—the traditional subsistence economies—is not only the bloody pre-history of capitalism, of the 'original accumulation,' as Marx supposed, but is still today the basic precondition for the ongoing accumulation of capital, what generally is called 'economic growth'" (ibid., 10).

33. Manufacturers Alliance for Productivity and Innovation (MAPI), "Report on U.S. Trade in Manufactures," available at https://mapifoundation.org/economic/2016/8/15/report-on-us-trade-in-manufactures.

will one day be used in wars our leaders will find irresistible. And they will be obliged to develop counter-measure weapons to the ones they have exported. So it becomes self-perpetuating. How do we get away with this?

The United States, through its dominant position in the international institutions of financial governance and the domination of international markets by the American dollar, compels the rest of the world *to finance our military expenditures* through "dollar hegemony."[34] The US prints dollars and everyone else has to sell things abroad to get dollars.[35] The value accruing to the United States in this process more than compensates for the cost of US wars and the expenses of maintaining the most inefficient and expensive military in history. The biggest of those payout schemes is achieved paradoxically by the world-historical magnitude of the US debt.

"If you owe the bank $100 that's your problem. If you owe the bank $100 million, that's the bank's problem."[36] Since the abandonment of fixed currency exchange rates, weaker currencies are vulnerable to currency speculation—betting on the exchange rates of foreign currencies. In the 1990s, this practice wrecked several Asian economies and almost toppled the whole international financial system.[37] Central banks around the world now stash as many US dollars as possible in their reserves as a hedge against currency raids. These dollar reserves, however, mean that every central bank now has a powerful stake in supporting the value of the US dollar, even at the expense of their own economies. If the dollar—for whatever reason—suddenly lost half its value, then half the purchasing power residing in a foreign central bank holding dollars would be wiped out.

Central banks must invest these dollars somewhere to hold down exchange rates; and the only market large enough to absorb them is the US Treasury, which takes them in as loans through something called Treasury bills (bonds). In other words, the United States Treasury, for example, owes China's central bank 1.2 trillion US dollars.[38] The United States, as of 2015, owes the rest of the world around 4.1 trillion US dollars.[39] This might seem to be a problem, owing a debt that all your creditors know you are incapable of repaying; but in this case, it means the foreign central banks cannot sell

---

34. Liu, "Dollar Hegemony."

35. Local farmers, for example, are pushed off the land by enclosure to make way for large-scale export agricultural products (like bananas or coffee) to get the needed dollars. Thus the term "banana republic."

36. J. Paul Getty, an apocryphal quote—readers surely understand it.

37. Gowan, *Global Gamble*, Part 2.

38. Amadeo, "US Debt to China."

39. Total debt is 14.8 trillion dollars (2017), according to the Council on Foreign Relations. McBride and Chatzky, "The National Debt Dilemma."

off their dollar-assets without selling *down* the value of their own central bank reserves. Paradoxically, the US can now control the international economy as its principal debtor: "debtor imperialism."

> Strange as it may seem and irrational as it would be in a more logical system of world diplomacy, the dollar glut is what finances America's global military build-up. It forces foreign central banks to bear the costs of America's expanding military empire, effectively taxation without representation. Keeping international reserves in dollars means recycling their dollar inflows to buy US Treasury bills, debt issued largely to finance the military.[40]

In other words, the rest of the world finances our military. The US can print money with abandon without risking inflationary devaluation because no one wants to risk the nightmare of a run on the dollar. The US then effectively exports inflation, allowing the US government to spend profligately *through the DOD.*

> Most central banks today hold down their exchange rates by recycling their dollar inflows to buy US Treasury IOUs. This recycling enables the United States to finance its overseas military spending and also its domestic budget deficit (largely military in character) since the 1950s. So Europe and Asia have used their foreign exchange earnings to finance a unipolar US buildup of military bases to surround them.[41]

We often engage in slogan-mongering like, "Money for schools (or hospitals or puppies) and not for war," as if this is a zero-sum game with one pot of money that never changes value, which we can divvy up like cookies at a day care center. This perennial "guns or butter" notion is a failure to appreciate the nature of money not as a fixed quantity but as a special kind of sign operating in relation to a shifting network of other social and ecological phenomena—one in which that sign's value read as purchasing power is contingent on those relations. If you change the relation, you risk changing (and losing) the value of the sign.

The purchasing power of a unit of money doesn't emerge unscathed after disruptions in political ecology; and it is not automatically redistributed. In a very real sense—albeit one that cannot be described on a bumper sticker or a Facebook meme—the *value* of the US dollar is predicated on an

---

40. Hudson, "Military Spending," para. 3.
41. Hudson, "Dollar Hegemony and China," para. 12.

international regime,[42] itself rooted unstably in a core-periphery dynamic. The purchasing power of that money is not being *transferred* from domestic schools and hospitals, but from the treasuries of "allies" and "trading partners" around the world.[43]

Absent these relations, the dollar could very well lose its value, whereupon it would be insufficient for war *or* schools. If we want to diminish the significance of the MIC and the war culture/economy in which it is embedded, the ecology itself has to be re-formed,[44] with fear and trembling, but changed nonetheless . . . and this must be the objective of policy.

Domestic Ramification

The DOD spends around 17 percent of the total US budget. In 2015, as noted above, DOD expenditures were in the vicinity of 630 billion US dollars. Many people think most of the military spending goes to overpriced weapons systems or sweetheart deals for supplies or, now, for hiring mercenaries. It is true, we do spend a lot of money on high-tech weapons systems, and many of those systems overrun costs in production and fail to work as advertised. They are also all made almost exclusively of nonstandard parts, so when a tank needs a hex nut, it's not one you can get at Ace or Lowe's for fifty cents; it will cost four hundred dollars from an exclusive supplier. And we've all heard about contractors selling the DOD 7,000-dollar coffee pots. When you swim around that kind of money, the pilot fish will latch on. But that hardly accounts for more than half a trillion dollars. Ninety-three percent of all the fuel used by the US government is used by the military. The DOD uses around 30,000 gigawatt hours of electricity each year—roughly the quantity used by Denmark. The DOD consumes 4.6 billion gallons of gas every year, or 12.4 million gallons per day. Who gets paid?

Let's think now about smaller, local contractors. Around fifty thousand troops are stationed in my old haunt, Fort Bragg. If the post is prepared to feed even twenty thousand of them each day, breakfast eggs at two per person per morning means someone sells Fort Bragg—one post—forty thousand eggs a day. Some enterprise, then, depends on the military in part or in whole for its income, and that means there are x number of jobs

42. Gowan, *Global Gamble*. Gowan calls this the "Dollar–Wall Street Regime."

43. The purpose of starving schools and hospitals is to privatize, to enclose them for profit-taking.

44. There will be risks, but the choices we make now may be analogous to jumping out of the car while it's moving or staying inside while it plunges over a cliff. There is no painless way forward.

in place to ensure the steady flow of eggs to hungry paratroopers. Other companies supply the things egg mills require. Other companies supply them, and so on. The DOD financial "benefit" ramifies.

The Department of Defense budget, as this is written, is the equivalent of 9.5 million "average US consumers," or almost 3 percent, in an economy that averaged 3.22 percent growth between 1947 and 2017. This generalization does not account for the concentration of military spending in areas that depend on defense industries or large urban centers that depend, as retail economies, on military installations. The town of Fayetteville, North Carolina, adjacent to Fort Bragg, has almost 205,000 people within the city limits. Fayetteville has fifty thousand troops, another twenty thousand civilian employees, and all these earners' families. They spend the money that gets injected by DOD. Without it, Fayetteville would experience retail Armageddon. The "money for schools" in Fayetteville comes from property taxes that are paid into the community through the DOD. Where is the either/or?

Fort Bragg is a FORSCOM base (major army ground units). There are thirteen more FORSCOM posts in the United States: in Georgia, Kentucky, Louisiana, Texas, Nebraska, Colorado, California, Alaska, Hawaii, and Washington State. This is just the army; I haven't included the air force, marines, navy, and coast guard. In one guise or another, we now have almost 1.4 million people in uniform. Two of my children joined, one while working at McDonald's, the other while working at Walmart. The day they joined, they started receiving the equivalent of almost 20,000 dollars a year, plus a housing allowance, a food allowance, and free healthcare for themselves and their families. Within six years, they could receive—*before* extra pays ("jump" pay, overseas pay, proficiency pay, combat pay, local cost-of-living allowances)—more than 45,000 dollars a year. Armed services members can retire after twenty active years at 50 percent of their base pay, which, if they achieve an E-9 pay grade,[45] is now about 2,600 dollars a month for the rest of their lives—at age 38 or 39, with not one day of college education. A Virginia candidate for Congress will have a very difficult time saying, "Money for *x* and not for war," when 14 percent of the struggling state's total budget is precisely money-for-war. There are 4,742 DOD-operated sites and offices throughout the United States. The DOD pumps 8.4 billion dollars into the District of Columbia; 6.5 billion into Fort Hood, Texas; 6.4 billion into San Diego; 5.8 billion into Oshkosh, Wisconsin; 5.7 billion into Huntsville, Alabama; 5.3 billion into Arlington, Virginia; 4.9 billion into

---

45. Highest enlisted pay grade.

Tucson, Arizona; 4.7 billion into Fayetteville, North Carolina; 4.6 billion into St. Louis, Missouri; and 4.4 billion into Louisville, Kentucky.[46]

Top contractor Lockheed-Martin employs 110,000 people. How many families, then, depend on Lockheed-Martin for their livelihood? Add to that Boeing, Raytheon, Northrop-Grumman, United Technologies, L3 Communications, Huntington Ingalls, Honeywell, Textron, General Electric, AECOM, Booz Allen Hamilton, Leidos, Bechtel, Orbital ATK, SAIC, Exelis, CACI International, Harris, Hewlett-Packard, Rockwell Collins, CSC, Oshkosh, General Atomics, Aerojet Rocketdyne, Dyncorp, Engility, Fluor, Accenture, ManTech, PAE, Moog, AAR Corp, Alion Science and Technology, Curtiss-Wright, Ball Aerospace & Technologies, Wyle, and Battelle—and this is just a partial list of top US companies involved in aerospace and defense.[47] If you live in the US, it is likely that you personally know someone who works directly or indirectly for one of these companies. And here is where we come back to that notion of simply redirecting funds, because there is no magic wand any one person or even legislative body can wave to change this absent the risk of disorganizing an entire national economy that is interfused with war spending from the grandest to the most granular scale.

For Christians who experience this as a *moral* dilemma, what policies can reduce our complicity? If indeed politics is "the art of the possible," there may be one major stumbling block to enacting said policies: the psychic economy of war.

The (Masculinized) Psychic Economy

What frustrates us is twofold. First, the MIC seems invulnerable, a juggernaut beneath the wheels of which people are continually crushed. Second, the more we discover about it, the more we recognize our inescapable complicity. If policy can be wielded to change it, breaking that seeming invulnerability and inevitability must be the goal of such policy. If this is possible, how is it possible? I want to file the latter question until we answer the "if." Let's begin on a terrain where Christians' footprints can occasionally be found: the soul. "For whoever wishes to save his life will lose it; but whoever loses his life for My sake will find it" (Matt 16:25 NASB). The Greek for "life" is *psuché* (ψυχή) or, in today's English, *psyche*. It is interchangeable in other parts of the New Testament with *soul* or *person*. When we speak of personhood, as Christians, we are talking about the soul. The soul is not insubstantial. It is

---

46. Brancato et al., "Defense Contract Spending."
47. Choi, "Biggest Defense Contractors."

embodied. Bodies are sexed, and sexed bodies are regulated by *gender*.[48] The psychic economy of war is twofold: it is the effect of market society on how we know, our dominant epistemology, and it is rooted even more deeply in gender.

One key feature of the collective American psyche that has endured since the American Civil War is the apotheosis of the nation, what Robert Bellah called our civil religion.[49] This love of the nation is more than ideological because it is *felt* by actual persons to be sacred and so inoculated against critical intervention. It is a distinctly militaristic kind of emotional attachment that is displayed in our favorite stories of military leaders, soldiers, and war, and therefore it is closely identified with our "national masculinity." And *that* is identified with men's personal masculinity, the power of which cannot be overestimated in politics and in the history of knowledge.

Hegemonic American masculinity is defined by conquest, by "agonistic values," the idea that we are most perfected in battle, real and sublimated. War is the stage where we can *perform* masculinity. Masculinity is constructed by conquest. Maria Mies shows how, in modernity, this maps onto Man conquering Nature.

> The destruction of nature as a living organism—and the rise of modern science and technology, together with the rise of male scientists as the new high priests—had its close parallel in the violent attack on women during the witch hunt which raged through Europe for some centuries. . . . [Carolyn] Merchant does not extend her analysis to the relation of the New Men to their colonies. Yet an understanding of this relation is absolutely necessary because we cannot understand the modern developments, including our present problems, unless we include all those who were *"defined into nature"* . . . Mother Earth, Women and Colonies.[50]

Man conquers nature. Women, colonies, and ecosystems then are "defined into nature," set outside the strategic edifice of male subjectivity. *Subject* acts on *object*. In *The Death of Nature*, Carolyn Merchant shows how this "objectification" for conquest corresponds to what she calls nature's "death," the de-animation of nature through the fifteenth- and sixteenth-century alchemist Agrippa, who wanted to elevate man alongside God in his dominion

---

48. Here meaning the cultural norms imposed as a system of male power over women and sexual minorities.

49. Bellah, "Civil Religion in America."

50. Mies, *Patriarchy and Accumulation*, 75, italics added.

over nature (echoes of Genesis), yet who himself still bitterly opposed mining and other rapacious extractions from nature. Merchant says that Bacon "stood Agrippa on his head," by agreeing with the apotheosis of man over nature but insisting that the material world be aggressively *conquered and subdued*—all in those gendered terms that compared the quest for knowledge to the interrogation and torture of witches.[51]

Women, colonies, and even enemies being "defined into nature" is the moral prequel to conquest. The psychic economy of the military-industrial complex then is a "masculine" psyche, *masculinity* here generally defined as those *cultural* constructions and expectations associated with males and conquest.[52] The gendered-ness of the psychic economy corresponds to the *competitive, agonal* exchange economies of the military-economic condominium.

> So the man whose identity is formed by . . . agonistic values . . . is a profound threat to others, and in a world torn apart by violence of every kind, it is still true that men are predominantly if not exclusively responsible for that violence. . . . In recent years, studies of masculinity have begun to address the problem of male violence, but we have yet to reach a stage when church leaders, politicians and policy-makers fully acknowledge its destructive significance.[53]

No remedial and redemptive task is more necessary as prequel to advocating for peace—and for policies aimed at promoting peace—than denaturalizing and thereby unmasking the association between violence and masculinity. No task will be more intellectually arduous, because this association is one into which we have been indoctrinated almost from birth; and so many men and women alike have internalized this construction of gender to such a degree that challenges to it feel like threats to our very identities. Christians, however, do have one special resource in the redemptive

---

51. Goff, *Borderline*, 143–44.

52. Women largely accept dominant constructions of masculinity too in a militarized culture because every consciousness is to some extent colonized in male-dominant society by the presumptions of male power in language and practice. There are those who want to rescue masculinity by inventing a subset called "toxic masculinity," but the separation into masculine and feminine spheres is, in itself, already constructive of gender as a division of power. In this author's view, *all* masculinity carries the potential to be "toxic" (an interesting sort of chemical metaphor), that is, dangerous to women; and the potential danger inheres in the so-called "complementarity" of masculinity-femininity.

53. Beattie, *New Catholic Feminism*, 232.

mission to shatter this association—and that is the exemplary life of Jesus of Nazareth.

Policy and Politics

We are in a state of structural sin, structures that interject themselves between our moral and practical reason. That may be why we are so often keen to accept the prevailing national myths and ideological justifications of capital and state as comforting rationalizations.

Whether one is channeling Derrida or Wittgenstein or Lacan, the power of language over the character of the mind is undeniable. Hegemonic discourse shapes our psychic *oikos*. That is precisely why our *defamiliarization* is prerequisite to developing an authentic critique of the MIC.

"To confront modernity," says Hornborg, "through public discourse is, paradoxically, to be absorbed by it."[54] Now that we have traveled up several key tributaries of the MIC, we are perhaps sufficiently defamiliarized to discuss public policy. The first policy prescription is to strengthen all laws that protect women. Every advance against martial masculinity is tied up with the continuing feminist project of emancipating women and all gender and sexual minorities.

As one who feels strongly that there is a perversion of the gospels growing out of the Constantinian impulse—joining church to power—I have to remind myself, as someone who also pays fairly close attention to the goings-on of the world, that Christians ought not to use policy to enforce "Christian morality." More subtly still, we need to be mindful whether or not those policies we support are likely to require violence—even against our "enemies"—in policy execution.[55] Given what we have surveyed in these few preceding pages, what kinds of policies might we look to that will lessen the chance for war and violence generally and allow us to tactically retreat from those ways in which we are made structurally complicit in the MIC? And in what kinds of practices might Christians engage to resist the MIC and foster nonviolent resistance in others?

Christians—if we are to act as a community—need to consider ways to carefully and systematically begin disentangling ourselves and our children from our utter dependency on money. This will take experimentation and practice, and it will be nourished by many small failures, but we have to try

---

54. Hornborg, *Power of the Machine*, 228.

55. In elections, we can have 51 percent lording it over 49 percent, which is no more than a sublimated form of warfare. No matter where you hide, the world finds you. No matter where you hide, God finds you.

reskill ourselves and others for coming seasons. It is money-dependency more than any other single factor that locks us into the current system. Reducing this dependency will initially (perhaps paradoxically) require massive institutional (state) support.

Christians are not alone in the recognition that money-dependency secures our complicity. This is the central insight of the relocalization movement—a movement to transfer dependency on monetized inputs from afar, to local community-produced interdependency.[56] Churches are uniquely positioned—as the regular meeting places of large numbers of people who live near each other—to become incubators for the reskilling required to begin the long journey to a relocalized future.[57] Relocalization includes several initiatives: (1) local, decentralized, and sustainable food production, (2) dramatic energy conservation, (3) an across-the-board reuse ethic, (4) reskilling (all crafts, food production, food preservation, building and tinkering, salvage, sewing, soap-making, etc.), (5) barter agreements, (6) labor sharing, and (7) stronger intergenerational cooperation, to name a few.

The shorthand for this nascent movement is "resilience," that is, intentional attempts at greater local independence from far-flung and ever more vulnerable supply grids, in order to increase resilience in the face of those shocks that will come with financial disorder, climate change, energy shortages, political neglect, and various capricious "natural" catastrophes.

Some people believe resilience-transition to be achievable through volunteerism; but the depth and scope of our *self-organized*[58] dependency means it can only be peacefully and realistically achieved with a long, deep draught of political will—with the assistance of a transition-mobilized state. This presupposes some sort of social democratic movement winning some form of political power that substantially overlaps in its goals with those of transition, because the initial emergency measures that will be essential

---

56. But which also sometimes has a black hole in its intellection where "the state" should be.

57. For reasons too lengthy to discuss here, many people believe, as I do, that humanity is going to be returned to relocalized existence soon enough, one way or another. The question is whether that happens after a total crash or a well-executed crash landing. Easier options have already slipped away.

58. Haken, "Self-Organization," para. 1. "Self-organization is the spontaneous often seemingly purposeful formation of spatial, temporal, spatiotemporal structures or functions in systems composed of few or many components." The connective tissue between these many components is relationship. Social change cannot be achieved by decrees. One way or another, it will be achieved in many small, barely visible stages because existing relationships resist change, and the mass of relationships will return relatively stable societies to their approximate defaults. These relationships cannot be measured, but they can be provisionally mapped.

for a peaceful transition are decidedly "social democratic," even "socialist," policies. This social democratic pole is on the rise as this is written, with the various initiatives following the 2016 presidential campaign of Bernie Sanders and as the only effective opposition to the corresponding rise of right-wing reaction (nativist, racist, masculinist). So we have to take elections seriously.

We are in crisis now. To use a medical analogy, before we can operate on the patient, we have to stabilize the patient. If we are aiming to offset the future disassembly of the war industries, two national programs must be established as soon as politically possible: a single-payer healthcare system for every person who shows up at the doctor's office and a massive public works jobs program that focuses on ameliorating our worst environmental problems (beginning in the poorest regions of the country) and transforming (redesigning, not simply rebuilding) public infrastructure. This is a "guaranteed employment" strategy, on the one hand, and on the other the elimination of the most dangerous financial risks for families—the cost of infirmity. In addition to public works jobs, a guaranteed minimum income for all is a first step toward removing the siren call of "jobs" that leads to reliance on multinational corporate military contractors (and the rich in general). These measures, enacted as a kind of neo-New Deal—as triage, not an end state—would substantially strengthen the majority against the depredations of the one percent, giving a more popular democracy a chance to take hold in lieu of continued (and potentially violent) crisis-reaction cycles.

We must address policy at every scale. At the local level, there are inevitably policies that need to be changed. Many municipalities, for example, prohibit laying hens or honeybees. Many neighborhoods—through restrictive covenants—prohibit clotheslines and vegetable gardens. Many local governments can be prevailed upon, with nagging effort, to put high-yielding perennial food plants in the commons. Schools can host gardens that are used for food as well as pedagogy. The state of California recently passed a law that superseded restrictive covenants of various kinds and granted every homeowner the right to grow food on her or his land. Likewise, municipalities have nullified restrictive covenants against clotheslines because they cut carbon emissions.

Returning to the wider political stage, there are several policies and actions that relate not only to the direct issue of war and the preparation for war but also to the specific economic context within which today's MIC is embedded. Free trade agreements come immediately to mind. These agreements are not only designed to lower the wage floor for all mass production workers, evade stringent environmental oversight, and dodge taxes; they are designed to allow American corporate behemoths to colonize the most profitable sectors within foreign economies. This is one of the main ways that US dollars flood foreign economies, whereupon foreign central banks are obliged to subsidize US military profligacy. Opposition to free trade agreements is substantial and growing, and Christians need to be there.[59] In tandem with opposition to neoliberal trade deals, Jubilee movements for debt forgiveness are essential. Overwhelming and unpayable debt are the leverage that US-dominated supranational organizations like the World Trade Organization and the International Monetary Fund use to force foreign domestic markets to open themselves to "investment" by the aforementioned behemoths.

Quixotic as it may now seem, we can also argue for the withdrawal of all US military forces from abroad. All of them. Across-the-water alliances with popular movements to eject US military bases is another area where active churches can make a difference. This applies not only to unpopular bases in places like Okinawa, but *implicitly* calls for the dissolution of *explicitly* military organizations like the North Atlantic Treaty Organization.

We can call for an end to corporate subsidies in the United States, beginning with "agricultural subsidies" that enrich transnational corporations, promoting meat production over vegetable production, pumping unhealthy processed foods into our diets, and destroying foreign livelihoods by agricultural "dumping." Without an end to these subsidies, local enterprises that are essential for relocalization—especially small farms—cannot survive in today's marketplace.

Public utilities must be returned to direct government control and no longer operated in order to maximize profit. In that vein, all credit institutions need to be nationalized as *public utilities* and placed under public control. Had this been the case in the past, there never would have been a series of crises related to "financial bubbles" that forced the public to bail out corporations that were (and still are) "too big to fail."[60] This is the very basis of the financial system within which the current MIC maliciously nests.

The potential for change in some yet unstated policy proposals is still unknown, but with an orientation to *abundance* instead of *scarcity*, toward *cooperation* instead of *competition* and *peace* instead of *war*, we will be better able to discern the real possibilities of future policy proposals. None of this happens, however, without repentance. Without a great spiritual "turning

---

59. Be warned, right-wing reactionaries also oppose these agreements, but not for the same reasons.

60. By the time this is published, there may have been another crash.

around" from strength to vulnerability, from center to margin, from power to love. This is where it begins.

> Peace I leave with you; My peace I give to you; not as the world gives do I give to you. Do not let your heart be troubled, nor let it be fearful.
>
> —John 14:27 (NASB)

Bibliography

Acheson, Ray, et al. "Assuring Destruction Forever: 2017 Edition." Women's International League for Peace and Freedom, April 2017. https://www.peace-institute.com/wp-content/uploads/2017/07/assuring-destruction-forever-20171.pdf.
Adeney, Miriam. *God's Foreign Policy: Practical Ways to Help the World's Poor*. Grand Rapids: Eerdmans, 1984.
Ahmed, Nafeez. "The Age of Climate Warfare Is Here. The Military-Industrial Complex Is Ready. Are You?" *The Guardian*, May 31, 2014. https://www.theguardian.com/environment/earth-insight/2014/may/30/climate-change-war-conflict-military-industrial-complex-syria-egypt-uprising.
Ahn, Moon-seok. "Mikukeun oe sadbaechireul seodurneunga?" [Why does the US hasten to deploy THAAD?]. *Inmoolkwa sasang [Figure and Thought]* 229 (2017) 82–83.
AIAA.org. "When Did You Know? Share Your Story." https://www.aiaa.org/ShareYourStory/. [As of December 2017, this webpage is no longer available on the AIAA site.]
Aizenman, Joshua, and Reuven Glick. "Military Expenditure, Threats, and Growth." *Journal of International Trade and Economic Development* 15 (2006) 129–55.
Alarcón, Rosalinda Hernández. *Problemática de la tierra reclama soluciones efectivas*. Guatemala City: Inforpress Centroamericana, 2000.
Alexander, Michelle. *The New Jim Crow: Mass Incarceration in the Age of Colorblindness*. New York: New Press, 2010.
Allman, Mark J. "Postwar Justice." *America* 193 (October 17, 2005) 9–13.
Allman, Mark J., and Tobias L. Winright. *After the Smoke Clears: The Just War Tradition and Post War Justice*. Maryknoll, NY: Orbis, 2010.
———. "Growing Edges of Just War Theory: Jus Ante Bellum, Jus Post Bellum, and Imperfect Justice." *Journal of the Society of Christian Ethics* 32 (2012) 173–91.
Almeida, Paul. *Waves of Protest: Popular Struggle in El Salvador, 1925–2005*. Minneapolis: University of Minnesota Press, 2008.
Alpert, Arnie. "The Continuing Cost of War." American Friends Service Committee, June 1, 2018. https://www.afsc.org/blogs/news-and-commentary/continuing-cost-war.
Amadeo, Kimberly. "US Debt to China: How Much Is It, Reasons Why, and What If China Sells." https://www.thebalance.com/u s debt-to-china-how-much-does-it-own-3306355.

———. "US Imports and Exports with Components and Statistics." https://www.thebalance.com/u-s-imports-and-exports-components-and-statistics-3306270.
Anderson, Jervis. *Bayard Rustin: Troubles I've Seen; a Biography*. New York: HarperCollins, 1997.
Andrés, Roberto Casas. *Dios pasó por El Salvador: La relevancia teológica de las tradiciones narrativas de los mártires Salvadoreños*. Bilbao: Desclée de Brouwer, 2009.
Appleby, R. Scott. *The Ambivalence of the Sacred: Religion, Violence, and Reconciliation*. Lanham, MD: Rowman & Littlefield, 2000.
Aquinas, Thomas. *Summa Theologica*. Translated by Fathers of the English Dominican Province. New York, 1947.
Asia News Monitor. "South Korea/United States: S. Korea Introduces $600 Million in Arms from US in 2010." October 1, 2011.
Associated Press in Raleigh, NC. "US Judge Approves Extradition of Salvadoran War Crimes Suspect to Spain." *The Guardian*, February 5, 2016. https://www.theguardian.com/world/2016/feb/05/el-salvador-war-crime-extradition-inocente-orlando-montano-morales-spain.
Augustine, Saint. *The City of God Against the Pagans*. Edited and translated by R. W. Dyson. New York: Cambridge University Press, 1998.
———. *On Christian Doctrine*. Translated by J. F. Shaw. Mineola, NY: Dover, 2009.
Avant, Deborah. "From Mercenary to Citizen Armies: Explaining Change in the Practice of War." *International Organization* 54 (2003) 41–72.
———. "The Implications of Marketized Security for IR Theory: The Democratic Peace, Late State Building, and the Nature and Frequency of Conflict." *Perspectives on Politics* 4 (2006) 507–28.
Avant, Deborah, and Lee Sigelman. "Private Security and Democracy: Lessons from the US in Iraq." *Security Studies* 19 (2010) 230–65.
Bacevich, Andrew J. "Blood for Oil." In *The New American Militarism: How Americans Are Seduced by War*, 175–204. Updated ed. Oxford: Oxford University Press, 2013.
———. *The Limits of Power: The End of American Exceptionalism*. New York: Metropolitan, 2008.
Baer, Helmut David, and Joseph E. Capizzi. "Just-War Theory and the Problem of International Politics: On the Central Role of Just Intention." *Journal of the Society of Christian Ethics* 26 (2006) 163–75.
Bainton, Roland H. *Christian Attitudes to War and Peace: A Historical Survey and Critical Re-evaluation*. 1960. Reprint, Eugene, OR: Wipf and Stock, 2008.
Baptist, Edward E. *The Half Has Never Been Told: Slavery and the Making of American Capitalism*. New York: Basic Books, 2014.
Barnet, Richard J. *Roots of War*. New York: Atheneum, 1972.
Barton, John. *Understanding Old Testament Ethics*. Louisville: Westminster John Knox, 2003.
Basil, of Caesarea, Saint. "In Time of Famine and Drought." In *On Social Justice*, translated by C. Paul Schroeder, 73–88. Crestwood, NY: St. Vladimir's Seminary Press, 2009.
Bass, Gary J. "Jus Post Bellum." *Philosophy and Public Affairs* 32 (2004) 384–412.
Bates, Eric. "What You Need to Know about Jesse Helms." *Mother Jones*, May/June 1995. https://www.motherjones.com/politics/1995/05/what-you-need-know-about-jesse-helms/.

Baura, Gail D. *Engineering Ethics: An Industrial Perspective*. Burlington, MA: Elsevier, 2006.

B. B. "Before You Vote." *HIS Magazine* 43 (October 1984) 4.

BBC Monitoring Asia Pacific. "US Military Sales to South Korea Estimated at 1.2bn Dollars in 2007." March 22, 2006, 1.

Beattie, Tina. *New Catholic Feminism*. New York: Routledge, 2006.

Beckert, Sven, and Christine Desan, eds. *American Capitalism: New Histories*. New York: Columbia University Press, 2018.

Beckert, Sven, and Seth Rockman, eds. *Slavery's Capitalism: A New History of American Economic Development*. Philadelphia: University of Pennsylvania Press, 2016.

Bellah, Robert N. "Civil Religion in America." http://www.robertbellah.com/articles_5.htm.

Bellamy, Alex J. "The Responsibilities of Victory: Jus Post Bellum and the Just War." *Review of International Studies* 34 (2008) 601–25.

Benites, Tulio. *Meditaciones de un católico ante la reforma agraria de Guatemala*. Guatemala: Ministerio de Educación Pública, 1952.

Benjamin, Barbara. "Immigrant Love: Embracing Our New Neighbors." *HIS Magazine* 42 (November 1981) 13.

———. *The Impossible Community: A Story of Hardship & Hope at Brooklyn College in New York*. Downers Grove: InterVarsity, 1978.

Bennett, Jody Ray. "Cheap Labor for Private Security." http://www.css.ethz.ch/en/services/digital-library/articles/article.html/98671/pdf.

Berrigan, Philip. *Prison Journals of a Priest Revolutionary*. New York: Holt, Rinehart & Winston, 1970.

Bethell, Leslie, and Ian Roxborough, eds. *Latin America between the Second World War and the Cold War: Crisis and Containment, 1944–1948*. New York: Cambridge University Press, 1997.

"Bibliography: People's Christian Coalition, November 1971." Box VII7, Folder "Peoples Christian Coalition Trinity," in Sojourners Collection, WCSC.

Bina, Mark W. "Private Military Contractor Liability and Accountability after Abu Ghraib." *The John Marshall Law Review* 38 (2005) 1237–63.

Black, Marigold. "Faith-Based Diplomacy in the New Strategic Order." *The Strategist*, October 10, 2018. https://www.aspistrategist.org.au/faith-based-diplomacy-in-the-new-strategic-order/.

Blakesmore, Erin. "Why the US Is Pledging Millions to Clean Up Bombs in Laos." *Smithsonian.com*, September 8, 2016. https://www.smithsonianmag.com/smartnews/why-us-pledging-millions-clean-bombs-laos-180960351/.

Boggs, Carl. *Imperial Delusions: American Militarism and Endless War*. Lanham, MD: Rowman & Littlefield, 2005.

Bonaventure, Saint. *The Life of St. Francis of Assisi*. Edited by Henry Edward Manning. Rockford, IL: Tan Classics, 1988.

Bonilla, Plutarco, et al. "A Letter of Tears to North American Christians." Folder "Discipleship Workshops," Evangelicals for Social Action Archives.

Bourdieu, Pierre. *Pascalian Meditations*. Translated by Richard Nice. Stanford: Stanford University Press, 1997.

Bowler, Kate. *Blessed: A History of the American Prosperity Gospel*. New York: Oxford University Press, 2013.

Boyes-Watson, Carolyn. *Peacemaking Circles and Urban Youth: Bringing Justice Home*. St. Paul: Living Justice, 2008.
Bradbury, John W. "Christianity and Democracy." *United Evangelical Action* 5 (December 1, 1944) 8.
Brancato, Kevin, et al. "Defense Contract Spending: A State-by-State Analysis." Bloomberg Government Study, November 2015. https://www.bbhub.io/bgov/sites/12/2015/10/BGOV_StatebyStateStudy.pdf.
Brands, Hal. *Latin America's Cold War*. Cambridge: Harvard University Press, 2010.
Bretherton, Luke. *Christianity and Contemporary Politics: The Conditions and Possibilities of Faithful Witness*. West Sussex, UK: Wiley-Blackwell, 2010.
Brock, Rita Nakashima, and Gabriella Lettini. *Soul Repair: Recovering from Moral Injury after War*. Boston: Beacon, 2013.
Brown, Peter. *Through the Eye of a Needle: Wealth, the Fall of Rome, and the Making of Christianity in the West, 350–550 AD*. Princeton: Princeton University Press, 2012.
Brubaker, Pamela K. "Neoliberalism and Economic Development (of Nations)." In *Globalization and Economic Justice: From Terrorism to Global Peace*, edited by Karikottuchira K. Kuriakose, 243–87. Piscataway, NJ: Gorgias, 2017.
Bryan, AnnaBelle O., et al. "Moral Injury, Suicidal Ideation, and Suicide Attempts in a Military Sample." *Traumatology* 20 (2014) 154–60.
Brzoska, Michael. "World Military Expenditures." In *Handbook of Defense Economics, Volume 1*, edited by Keith Hartley and Todd Sandler, 45–67. Amsterdam: Elsevier, 1995.
Buastavino, Clelia. "Letters to the Editor." *HIS Magazine* (March 1979) 2.
Buncombe, Andrew, and Patrick Cockburn. "Iraq's Death Squads: On the Brink of Civil War." *The Independent*, February 26, 2006. https://www.independent.co.uk/news/world/middle-east/iraqs-death-squads-on-the-brink-of-civil-war-6108236.html
Burns, Ken, and Lynn Novick, dirs. "*The War*: War Production." http://www.pbs.org/thewar/at_home_war_production.htm.
Burr, William, ed. "The Creation of SIOP-62: More Evidence on the Origins of Overkill." The National Security Archive, July 13, 2004. https://nsarchive2.gwu.edu/NSAEBB/NSAEBB130/.
Buxton, Nick. "The Elephant in Paris—the Military and Greenhouse Gas Emissions." *New Internationalist*, November 19, 2015. https://newint.org/blog/2015/11/19/the-military-and-greenhouse-gas-emissions/.
Buxton, Nick, and Ben Hayes, eds. *The Secure and the Dispossessed: How the Military and Corporations Are Shaping a Climate-Changed World*. London: Pluto, 2016.
———. "Ten Years On: Katrina, Militarisation, and Climate Change." openDemocracy, August 28, 2015. https://www.opendemocracy.net/nick-buxton-ben-hayes/ten-years-on-katrina-militarisation-and-climate-change.
Capizzi, Joseph E. *Politics, Justice, and War: Christian Governance and the Ethics of Warfare*. Oxford: Oxford University Press, 2015.
Carlson, Stanley W. "Angola: Caught in Between." *Vanguard*, March 1976, 6.
Carpenter, Joel. *Revive Us Again: The Reawakening of American Fundamentalism*. Oxford: Oxford University Press, 1997.
Cartwright, John, and Susan Thistlethwaite. "Support Nonviolent Direct Action." In *Just Peacemaking: The New Paradigm for the Ethics of Peace and War*, edited by Glen Stassen, 41–55. New ed. Cleveland: Pilgrim, 2008.

Cassidy, Robert M. *Counterinsurgency and the Global War on Terror.* Westport, CT: Praeger, 2006.
Chakrabarti, Amaresh, ed. *Engineering Design Synthesis: Understanding, Approaches, and Tools.* London: Springer, 2002.
Chasteen, John Charles. *Born in Blood and Fire: A Concise History of Latin America.* New York: Norton, 2001.
Childress, James. "Contemporary Pacifism: Its Major Types and Possible Contributions to Discourse about War." In *The American Search for Peace: Moral Reasoning, Religious Hope, and National Security,* edited by George Weigel and John P. Langan, 109–31. Washington, DC: Georgetown University Press, 1991.
Chilton, David. *Productive Christians in an Age of Guilt Manipulators: A Biblical Response to Ronald Sider.* Tyler, TX: Institute for Christian Economics, 1981.
Choi, David. "The Top 9 Biggest Defense Contractors in America." *Business Insider,* May 25, 2016. https://www.businessinsider.com/the-top-9-biggest-defense-contractors-in-america-2016-5.
Chomsky, Noam. "National Politics versus National Security." In *Sleepwalking to Armageddon: The Threat of Nuclear Annihilation,* edited by Helen Caldicott, 89–96. New York: New Press, 2017.
Christianity Today. "Patriots for Christ." March 2, 1962, 23.
Coats, Daniel R. "Statement for the Record: Worldwide Threat Assessment of the US Intelligence Community." February 13, 2018. https://www.dni.gov/index.php/newsroom/congressional-testimonies/item/1845-statement-for-the-record-worldwide-threat-assessment-of-the-us-intelligence-community.
Commission on Wartime Contracting in Iraq and Afghanistan. "At What Cost? Contingency Contracting in Iraq and Afghanistan." June 2009. http://www.wartimecontracting.gov/docs/CWC_Interim_Report_At_What_Cost_06-10-09.pdf.
———. "Transforming Wartime Contracting: Controlling Costs, Reducing Risks." August 2011. https://cybercemetery.unt.edu/archive/cwc/20110929213815/http://www.wartimecontracting.gov/docs/CWC_FinalReport-lowres.pdf.
Comprehensive Nuclear-Test-Ban Treaty Organization (CTBTO). "Manhattan Project." https://www.ctbto.org/nuclear-testing/history-of-nuclear-testing/manhattan-project/.
Conflict Armament Research. "Weapons of the Islamic State: A Three Year Investigation in Iraq and Syria." http://www.conflictarm.com/reports/weapons-of-the-islamic-state/.
Cowan, Benjamin A. *Securing Sex: Morality and Repression in the Making of Cold War Brazil.* Chapel Hill: University of North Carolina Press, 2016.
Crow, Loren D. "The Rhetoric of Psalm 44." *Zeitschrift für die alttestamentliche Wissenschaft* 104 (1992) 394–401.
Cullather, Nick. *Operation PBSUCCESS: The United States and Guatemala, 1952–1954.* Washington, DC: Center for the Study of Intelligence, Central Intelligence Agency, 1994.
———. *Secret History: The CIA's Classified Account of Its Operations in Guatemala, 1952–1954.* Stanford: Stanford University Press, 1999.
Cumings, Bruce. "Americans Once Carpet-Bombed North Korea. It's Time to Remember That Past." *The Guardian,* August 13, 2017. https://www.theguardian.

com/commentisfree/2017/aug/13/america-carpet-bombed-north-korea-remember-that-past.

Currier, Cora. "Our Condolences: How the US Paid for Death and Damage in Afghanistan." *The Intercept*, February 27, 2015. https://theintercept.com/2015/02/27/payments-civilians-afghanistan/.

Daggett, Stephen. "Costs of Major US Wars." June 29, 2010. https://fas.org/sgp/crs/natsec/RS22926.pdf.

Davis, Michael. *Thinking Like an Engineer: Studies in the Ethics of a Profession*. New York: Oxford University Press, 1998.

"Declaration of Punta del Este, 1961." In *Inter-American Relations: A Collection of Documents, Legislation, Descriptions of Inter-American Organizations, and Other Material Pertaining to Inter-American Affairs*, compiled by Barry Sklar and Virginia M. Hagen, 210–12. Washington, DC: US Government Printing Office, 1973.

Deere, Carmen Diana, and Magdalena de Lean León. *Mujer y tierra en Guatemala*. Serie Autores Invitados. Guatemala City: AVANCSO, 1999.

D'Emilio, John. *Lost Prophet: The Life and Times of Bayard Rustin*. Chicago: University of Chicago Press, 2003.

Dennis, Lane T. "The Counterculture." *The Other Side* 6 (November-December 1970) 15–37.

———. *A Reason for Hope*. Old Tappan, NJ: Revell, 1976.

Dickerson, Kelly, and Dave Mosher. "What's the Actual Difference between a Hydrogen Bomb and an Atomic Bomb? Fission vs. Fusion." *Business Insider*, February 4, 2017. https://www.sciencealert.com/what-are-the-actual-differences-between-a-hydrogen-and-an-atomic-bomb.

Dochuk, Darren. *From Bible Belt to Sunbelt: Plain-Folk Religion, Grassroots Politics, and the Rise of Evangelical Conservatism*. New York: Norton, 2010.

Dorrien, Gary. *Social Ethics in the Making: Interpreting an American Tradition*. West Sussex, UK: Wiley-Blackwell, 2009.

Dosal, Paul J. *Comandante Che: Guerrilla Soldier, Commander, and Strategist, 1956–1967*. University Park: Pennsylvania State University Press, 2003.

Dower, John W. *The Violent American Century: War and Terror since World War II*. Chicago: Haymarket, 2017.

Duke, James A., with Peggy-Ann K. Duke and Judith L. duCellier. *Duke's Handbook of Medicinal Plants of the Bible*. Boca Raton, FL: CRC, 2008.

Eckert, Amy. *Outsourcing War: The Just War Tradition in the Age of Military Privatization*. Ithaca: Cornell University Press, 2016.

Edwards, Rob. "Iraq's Depleted Uranium Clean-Up to Cost $30m as Contamination Spreads." *The Guardian*, March 6, 2013. https://www.theguardian.com/environment/2013/mar/06/iraq-depleted-uranium-clean-up-contamination-spreads.

Eichler, Maya. "Citizenship and the Contracting Out of Military Work: From National Conscription to Globalized Recruitment." *Citizenship Studies* 18 (2014) 600–614.

———, ed. *Gender and Private Security in Global Politics*. New York: Oxford University Press, 2015.

Eisenbrandt, Matt. *Assassination of a Saint: The Plot to Murder Óscar Romero and the Quest to Bring His Killers to Justice*. Oakland: University of California Press, 2017.

Eisenhower, Dwight D. "Transcript of President Dwight D. Eisenhower's Farewell Address (1961)." Transcribed by Dwight D. Eisenhower Presidential Library and Museum. President's Office, Washington, DC, January 17, 1961. https://www.ourdocuments.gov/doc.php?flash=false&doc=90&page=transcript.

Engelhardt, Tom. *Shadow Government: Surveillance, Secret Wars, and a Global Security State in a Single-Superpower World.* Chicago: Haymarket, 2014.

Enloe, Cynthia. *Globalization and Militarism: Feminists Make the Link.* New York: Rowman & Littlefield, 2007.

Erasmus, Desiderius. *The Complaint of Peace.* Translated from the *Querela pacis* (A.D. 1521). La Salle, IL: Open Court, 1974.

———. *The Education of a Christian Prince (1516).* In *Christian Peace and Nonviolence: A Documentary History,* edited by Michael G. Long, 71–74. Maryknoll, NY: Orbis, 2011.

Escobar Alas, José Luis. *Ustedes también darán testimonio, porque han estado conmigo desde el principio.* San Salvador: Grafika, 2017.

———. *Veo en la ciudad violencia y discordia.* San Salvador: Grafika, 1980.

Esquivel, Paloma. "Returning Home to a Tragedy." *Los Angeles Times,* March 9, 2008. http://articles.latimes.com/2008/mar/09/local/me-mother9.

Everett, James, ed. *The Implication of Third World Military Industrialization: Sowing the Serpents' Teeth.* Lexington, MA: Lexington, 1986.

Feder, Ernest. "Land Reform under the Alliance for Progress." *Journal of Farm Economics* 47 (1965) 652–68.

Feinstein, Andrew. *The Shadow World: Inside the Global Arms Trade.* New York: Picador, 2011.

Finnstrom, Kara, et al. "Football Star, 17, Slain Before He Could Answer Gang." March 13, 2008. http://www.cnn.com/2008/CRIME/03/10/gang.killing/index.html.

Florman, Samuel. *The Existential Pleasures of Engineering.* New York: St. Martin's, 1976.

Fong, Benjamin Y. "The Climate Crisis? It's Capitalism, Stupid!" *New York Times,* November 20, 2017. https://www.nytimes.com/2017/11/20/opinion/climate-capitalism-crisis.html.

Fox, R. Michael, ed. *Reverberations of the Exodus in Scripture.* Eugene, OR: Pickwick, 2014.

Francis, Pope. "In Flight Press Conference of His Holiness Pope Francis from Korea to Rome." August 18, 2014. https://www.ewtn.com/catholicism/library/in-flight-press-conference-from-korea-to-rome-13154.

Frankel, Anita. "Political Development in Guatemala, 1944–1954: The Impact of Foreign, Military, and Religious Elites." PhD diss., University of Connecticut, 1969.

Fraser, Nancy. "Is Capitalism Necessarily Racist?" *Politics/Letters* 15 (2019). http://quarterly.politicsslashletters.org/is-capitalism-necessarily-racist/.

Friedman, Thomas L. "A Manifesto for the Fast World." *The New York Times Magazine,* March 28, 1999. http://www.nytimes.com/1999/03/28/magazine/a-manifesto-for-the-fast-world.html.

Galeano, Eduardo. *Open Veins of Latin America: Five Centuries of the Pillage of a Continent.* 25th anniversary ed. New York: Monthly Review, 1997.

Galtung, Johan. "Peace, Negative and Positive." In *The Oxford International Encyclopedia of Peace,* edited by Nigel J. Young, 3:352–56. New York: Oxford University Press, 2010.

Garrett-Peltier, Heidi. "Job Opportunity Cost of War." Watson Institute for International and Public Affairs, Brown University, May 24, 2017. https://www.peri.umass.edu/publication/item/995-job-opportunity-cost-of-war.
Gettleman, Jeffrey. "Enraged Mob in Falluja Kills 4 American Contractors." *New York Times*, March 31, 2004. https://www.nytimes.com/2004/03/31/international/worldspecial/enraged-mob-in-falluja-kills-4-american.html.
Gill, Lesley. *The School of the Americas: Military Training and Political Violence in the Americas*. Durham: Duke University Press, 2004.
Glassman, Jim, and Young-Jin Choi. "The *Chaebol* and the US Military-Industrial Complex: Cold War Geopolitical Economy and South Korean Industrialization." *Environment and Planning A: Economy and Space* 46 (2014) 1160–80.
Gleijeses, Piero. "The Agrarian Reform of Jacobo Arbenz." *Journal of Latin American Studies* 21 (1989) 453–80.
———. *Conflicting Missions: Havana, Washington, and Africa, 1959–1976*. Chapel Hill: University of North Carolina Press, 2011.
———. *Shattered Hope: The Guatemalan Revolution and the United States, 1944–1954*. Princeton: Princeton University Press, 1992.
Gloege, Timothy E. W. *Guaranteed Pure: The Moody Bible Institute, Business, and the Making of Modern Evangelicalism*. Chapel Hill: University of North Carolina Press, 2015.
Godfrey, Richard, et al. "The Private Military Industry and Neoliberal Imperialism: Mapping the Terrain." *Organization* 21 (2014) 106–25.
Goff, Stan. *Borderline: Reflections on War, Sex, and Church*. Eugene, OR: Cascade, 2015.
———. *Mammon's Ecology: Metaphysics of the Empty Sign*. Eugene, OR: Cascade, 2018.
Goodchild, Philip. *Theology of Money*. Durham: Duke University Press, 2009.
Gowan, Peter. *The Global Gamble: Washington's Faustian Bid for World Dominance*. New York: Verso, 1999.
Graham, Larry. *Moral Injury: Restoring Wounded Souls*. Nashville: Abingdon, 2017.
Grandin, Greg. *Empire's Workshop: Latin America, the United States, and the Rise of the New Imperialism*. New York: Henry Holt, 2007.
Green, Barbara, and Glen Stassen. "Reduce Offensive Weapons and Weapons Trade." In *Just Peacemaking: The New Paradigm for the Ethics of Peace and War*, edited by Glen Stassen, 177–200. New ed. Cleveland: Pilgrim, 2008.
Greene, Graham. *The Quiet American*. New York: Penguin, 1955.
Gregory, Eric. *Politics and the Order of Love: An Augustinian Ethic of Democratic Citizenship*. Chicago: University of Chicago Press, 2008.
Grem, Darren. *The Blessings of Business: How Corporations Shaped Conservative Christianity*. Oxford: Oxford University Press, 2016.
Griffiths, Paul J., and George Weigel. "Just War: An Exchange." *First Things*, April 2002. https://www.firstthings.com/article/2002/04/just-war-an-exchange.
Guereña, Arantxa. "Unearthed: Land, Power and Inequality in Latin America." Oxfam International, November 2016. https://www-cdn.oxfam.org/s3fs-public/file_attachments/bp-land-power-inequality-latin-america-301116-en.pdf.
Gushee, David P., and Glen H. Stassen. *Kingdom Ethics: Following Jesus in Contemporary Context*. 2nd ed. Grand Rapids: Eerdmans, 2016.
Gutiérrez, Gustavo. *Las Casas: In Search of the Poor of Jesus Christ*. Maryknoll, NY: Orbis, 1993.

Hagedorn, Ann. *The Invisible Soldiers: How America Outsourced Our Security*. New York: Simon & Schuster, 2015.

Haken, Hermann. "Self-Organization." *Scholarpedia* 3(8):1401 (2008). http://www.scholarpedia.org/article/Self-organization.

Haltiwanger, John. "How Many Troops Does the US Have in Africa? Top Senators Didn't Know Military Was in Niger." *Newsweek*, October 23, 2017. http://www.newsweek.com/how-many-troops-does-us-have-africa-top-senators-didnt-know-military-was-niger-690937.

Hamm, Taik-Young. *Arming the Two Koreas: State, Capital, and Military Power*. New York: Routledge, 1999.

Hammond, Sarah. "'God's Business Men': Entrepreneurial Evangelicals in Depression and War." PhD diss., Yale University, 2010.

Hartung, William D. "Nuclear Politics." In *Sleepwalking to Armageddon: The Threat of Nuclear Annihilation*, edited by Helen Caldicott, 109–22. New York: New Press, 2017.

———. *Prophets of War: Lockheed Martin and the Making of the Military-Industrial Complex*. New York: Nation Books, 2012.

———. "Tomgram: William D. Hartung; 2018 Looks Like an Arms Bonanza." January 11, 2018. http://www.tomdispatch.com/blog/176372/.

Harvey, David. *The Enigma of Capital and the Crises of Capitalism*. Oxford: Oxford University Press, 2010.

———. *The New Imperialism*. Oxford: Oxford University Press, 2003.

———. *Seventeen Contradictions and the End of Capitalism*. Oxford: Oxford University Press, 2014.

Hatfield, Mark. "Mark Hatfield on World Hunger." *Right On* 6 (March 1975) 4.

Haws, David R. "Ethics Instruction in Engineering Education: A (Mini) Meta-Analysis." *Journal of Engineering Education* 90 (2001) 223–29.

Hays, Richard. *The Moral Vision of the New Testament: A Contemporary Introduction to New Testament Ethics*. San Fransisco: HarperSanFransisco, 1996.

Hefley, James C. *God Goes to High School*. Waco, TX: Word, 1970.

Heidebrecht, Paul. *God's Man in the Marketplace: The Story of Herbert J. Taylor*. Downers Grove: InterVarsity, 1990.

———. "Pragmatic Evangelical: Herbert Taylor, 1893–1978." *Methodist History* 26 (1988) 98–112.

Heim, Joe. "Recounting a Day of Rage, Hate, Violence and Death." *Washington Post*, August 14, 2017. https://www.washingtonpost.com/graphics/2017/local/charlottesville-timeline/?utm_term=.b4359e354cc1.

Heo, Uk. "The Political Economy of Defense Spending in South Korea." *Journal of Peace Research* 33 (1996) 483–90.

Hirschman, Albert O. *The Passions and the Interests: Political Arguments for Capitalism Before Its Triumph*. Princeton: Princeton University Press, 1977.

History.com Editors. "Korean War." http://www.history.com/topics/korean-war.

———. "The United States Presents the Baruch Plan." http://www.history.com/this-day-in-history/the-united-states-presents-the-baruch-plan.

Holley, Joe. "Richard J. Barnet Dies; Founder of Institute for Policy Studies." *Washington Post*, December 24, 2004, B6.

Holmes, Michael, ed. and trans. *The Apostolic Fathers: Greek Texts and English Translations*. 3rd. ed. Grand Rapids: Baker Academic, 2007.

Hong, Christine. "Learn to Love the Bomb: Trump's Strangelovian Nuclear Presidency." November 2017. http://www.rosalux-nyc.org/learn-to-love-the-bomb/.
Hoover, J. Edgar. "Communism: The Bitter Enemy of Religion." *Christianity Today*, June 22, 1959, 3–5.
———. "Storming the Skies: Christianity Encounters Communism." *Christianity Today*, December 21, 1962, 3–5.
Hornborg, Alf. *The Power of the Machine: Global Inequities of Economy, Technology, and Environment*. Walnut Creek, CA: AltaMira, 2001.
Hossein-zadeh, Ismael. *The Political Economy of U.S. Militarism*. New York: Palgrave Macmillan, 2006.
Hudson, Michael. "Dollar Hegemony and the Rise of China." July 12, 2010. https://michael-hudson.com/2010/07/dollar-hegemony-and-the-rise-of-china/.
———. "US Military Spending and the Upcoming G-20 Meeting." March 29, 2009. https://michael-hudson.com/2009/03/u-s-military-spending-and-the-upcoming-g-20-meeting/.
Iasiello, Louis V. "*Jus Post Bellum*: The Moral Responsibilities of Victors in War." *Naval War College Review* 57 (2004) 33–37.
Illich, Ivan D. *The Rivers North of the Future: The Testament of Ivan Illich*. As told to David Cayley. Toronto: House of Anansi, 2005.
———. "Vernacular Values." In *Shadow Work*, 27–51. New York: Marion Boyars, 1981.
Institute for Policy Studies. "The Souls of Poor Folks: Auditing America 50 Years after the Poor People's Campaign Challenged Racism, Poverty, the War Economy/Militarism, and Our National Morality." April 2018. https://ips-dc.org/souls-of-poor-folks/.
Institute for Security and Development Policy. "THAAD on the Korean Peninsula." October 2017. http://isdp.eu/publication/korea-thaad/.
International Consortium of Investigative Journalists. "Outsourcing War." September 26, 2012. https://www.icij.org/investigations/us-aid-latin-america/outsourcing-war/.
Isenberg, David. *Shadow Force: Private Security Contractors in Iraq*. Westport, CT: Praeger Security International, 2009.
Janzen, Waldemar. *Old Testament Ethics: A Paradigmatic Approach*. Louisville: Westminster John Knox, 1994.
Jarecki, Eugene. *The American Way of War: Guided Missiles, Misguided Men, and a Republic in Peril*. New York: Free Press, 2008.
Jenkins, Philip. *The Next Christendom: The Coming of Global Christianity*. 3rd ed. Oxford: Oxford University Press, 2011.
Jensen, Wollom A., and James M. Childs Jr. *Moral Warriors, Moral Wounds: The Ministry of the Christian Ethic*. Eugene, OR: Cascade, 2016.
John Chrysostom, Saint. *On Wealth and Poverty*. Translated by Catharine P. Roth. Crestwood, NY: St. Vladimir's Seminary Press, 1984.
John of Naples. "Should a Christian King Use Unbelievers to Defend His Kingdom?" In *The Cambridge Translations of Medieval Philosophical Texts: Volume Two, Ethics and Political Philosophy*, edited by Arthur Stephen McGrade, John Kilcullen, and Matthew Kempshall, 326–48. New York: Cambridge University Press, 2001.
John Paul II, Pope. *Evangelium Vitae*. http://w2.vatican.va/content/john-paul-ii/en/encyclicals/documents/hf_jp-ii_enc_25031995_evangelium-vitae.html.

———. *Veritatis Splendor*. http://w2.vatican.va/content/john-paul-ii/en/encyclicals/documents/hf_jp-ii_enc_06081993_veritatis-splendor.html.

Johnson, Kelly S. *The Fear of Beggars: Stewardship and Poverty in Christian Ethics*. Grand Rapids: Eerdmans, 2007.

Johnson, Torrey, and Robert Cook. *Reaching Youth for Christ*. Chicago: Moody, 1944.

Johnson, Walter. "The Pedestal and the Veil: Rethinking the Capitalism/Slavery Question." *Journal of the Early Republic* 24 (2004) 299–308.

Johnston, David, and John M. Broder. "F.B.I. Says Guards Killed 14 Iraqis without Cause." *New York Times*, November 14, 2007. https://www.nytimes.com/2007/11/14/world/middleeast/14blackwater.html.

Jones, Robert P. *The End of White Christian America*. New York: Simon & Schuster, 2017.

Jonsen, Albert R., and Stephen Toulmin. *The Abuse of Casuistry: A History of Moral Resasoning*. Berkeley: University of California Press, 1988.

Jost, Lynn. "Psalm 33, America, and Empire." *Direction* 35 (2006) 70–81.

Judd, Walter H. "World Issues and the Christian." *Christianity Today*, June 23, 1958, 6.

Kang, Seonjou, and James Meernik. "Civil War Destruction and the Prospects for Economic Growth." *Journal of Politics* 67 (2005) 88–109.

Kaye, Anthony E. "The Second Slavery: Modernity in the Nineteenth-Century South and the Atlantic World." *Journal of Southern History* 75 (2009) 627–50.

KDKA. "11 Dead, Several Others Shot at Pittsburgh Synagogue." October 27, 2018. https://pittsburgh.cbslocal.com/2018/10/27/heavy-police-presence-near-synagogue-in-squirrel-hill/.

Keeley, Louise Carroll. "The Parables of Problem III in Kierkegaard's *Fear and Trembling*." In *International Kierkegaard Commentary: "Fear and Trembling" and "Repetition"*, edited by Robert L. Perkins, 127–54. Macon, GA: Mercer University Press, 1993.

Kelsay, John. "How to Refine and Improve Just War Criteria." In *Religious Perspectives on War: Christian, Muslim, and Jewish Attitudes toward Force*, edited by David R. Smock, 27–32. Rev. ed. Washington, DC: United States Institute of Peace Press, 2002.

Kierkegaard, Søren. *Fear and Trembling; Repetition*. Translated by Howard V. Hong and Edna H. Hong. Princeton: Princeton University Press, 1983.

Kiernan, Ben, and David Simon. "Donald Trump Just Threatened to Commit Genocide." *Washington Post*, September 26, 2017. https://www.washingtonpost.com/news/posteverything/wp/2017/09/26/donald-trump-just-threatened-to-commit-genocide/.

Kim, Christine, and Heekyong Yang. "Experts Warn North Korea Missile Crisis Could Trigger Arms Race." *Time*, August 11, 2017. http://time.com/4896754/north-korea-missile-south-korea-crisis/.

Kim, Nami, and Wonhee Anne Joh, eds. *Critical Theology against US Militarism in Asia: Decolonization and Deimperialization*. New Approaches to Religion and Power. New York: Palgrave Macmillan, 2016.

King County Zero Youth Detention. "Peacemaking Circle Pilot Shows New Path for Juvenile Justice." November 2, 2016. https://zeroyouthdetention.com/2016/11/02/peacemaking-circle-pilot-shows-new-path-for-juvenile-justice/.

———. "The Sharing of Peace." June 22, 2018. https://zeroyouthdetention.com/2018/06/22/the-sharing-of-peace/.

King, Martin Luther, Jr. *A Testament of Hope: The Essential Writings and Speeches of Martin Luther King, Jr.* Edited by James Melvin Washington. San Francisco: HarperSanFrancisco, 1991.
Kinzer, Stephen. *The Brothers: John Foster Dulles, Allen Dulles, and Their Secret World War.* New York: Times Books/Henry Holt, 2013.
———. *Overthrow: America's Century of Regime Change from Hawaii to Iraq.* New York: Times Books, 2006.
Klare, Michael. "Militarizing America's Energy Policy." February 11, 2018. http://www.tomdispatch.com/blog/176384/.
Klingner, Bruce. "The Importance of THAAD Missile Defense." *Journal of East Asian Affairs* 29 (2015) 21–41.
Koop, Karl, ed. *Confessions of Faith in the Anabaptist Tradition, 1527–1660.* Translated by Cornelius J. Dyck et al. Kitchener, ON: Pandora, 2006.
Kornbluh, Peter. *The Pinochet File: A Declassified Dossier on Atrocity and Accountability*, Updated ed. New York: New Press, 2013.
Korten, David. "Sustainability and the Global Economy." In *Visions of a New Earth: Religious Perspectives on Population, Consumption, and Ecology*, edited by Harold Coward and Daniel C. Maguire, 29–42. Albany: State University of New York Press, 2000.
Kruse, Kevin. *One Nation under God: How Corporate America Invented Christian America.* New York: Basic Books, 2015.
Kwak, Tae-Hwan, et al., eds. *US-Korean Relations, 1882–1982.* Seoul: Kyungnam University Press, 1982.
Langan, John. "An Imperfectly Just War." *Commonweal* 118 (June 1, 1991) 361–65.
Lederach, John Paul. *The Moral Imagination: The Art and Soul of Building Peace.* New York: Oxford University Press, 2005.
Lee, Brianni. "THAAD Deployment in South Korea: Militarism Leading to Political Regression." *Harvard International Review* 38 (2017) 34–37.
Lee, Lewis Jeffery. *Moral Injury Reconciliation: A Practitioner's Guide for Treating Moral Injury, PTSD, Grief, and Military Sexual Trauma through Spiritual Formation Strategies.* London: Jessica Kingsley, 2018.
Lee, Manwoo, Ronald D. McLaurin, and Chung-in Moon, eds. *Alliance Under Tension: The Evolution of South Korean-US Relations.* Boulder, CO: Westview, 1988.
Leffler, Melvyn P. *Safeguarding Democratic Capitalism: US Foreign Policy and National Security, 1920–2015.* Princeton: Princeton University Press, 2017.
Leggett, Paul. "Panama Canal: Three Myths." *Sojourners* 5 (October 1976).
Leo XIII, Pope. *Rerum Novarum*. http://w2.vatican.va/content/leo-xiii/en/encyclicals/documents/hf_l-xiii_enc_15051891_rerum-novarum.html.
LeoGrande, William M. *Our Own Backyard: The United States in Central America, 1977–1992.* Chapel Hill: University of North Carolina Press, 2000.
"Letter from Central America." *Sojourners* 6 (November 1977) 9.
Levine, Aaron, ed. *The Oxford Handbook of Judaism and Economics.* Oxford: Oxford University Press, 2010.
Levy, Harold O., and Jonathan A. Plucker. "Brains, Not Brawn: America's Lack of STEM Students Is Bad for National Security." June 5, 2015. http://www.usnews.com/news/the-report/articles/2015/06/05/lack-of-stem-students-is-bad-for-national-security.

Lindo-Fuentes, Héctor, and Erik Ching. *Modernizing Minds in El Salvador: Education Reform and the Cold War, 1960–1980.* Albuquerque: University of New Mexico Press, 2012.

Liska, Adam J., and Richard K. Perrin. "Securing Foreign Oil: A Case for Including Military Operations in the Climate Change Impact of Fuels." *Environment: Science and Policy for Sustainable Development* 52 (2010) 9–22.

Little, Lester K. *Religious Poverty and the Profit Economy in Medieval Europe.* Ithaca: Cornell University Press, 1978.

Liu, Henry C. K. "Dollar Hegemony." https://henryckliu.com/page2.html.

Long, Michael G., ed. *I Must Resist: Bayard Rustin's Life in Letters.* San Francisco: City Lights, 2012.

Longman, Tremper, and Daniel G. Reid. *God Is a Warrior.* Grand Rapids: Zondervan, 1995.

Luther, Martin. *The Freedom of a Christian.* In *Martin Luther: Selections from His Writings,* edited by John Dillenberger, 42–85. Garden City, NY: Doubleday, 1962.

———. *Trade and Usury.* In *The Christian in Society II,* edited by Walther Brandt. Volume 45 of *Luther's Works.* Philadelphia: Muhlenberg, 1962.

Lynch, Ernesto Guevara. *Aquí va un soldado de América.* Barcelona: Plaza y Janés, 2000.

Magnuson, Stew. "Talent Strategies and the Competitiveness of the US Aerospace and Defense Industry." A research report of the Economist Intelligence Unit; sponsored by Oracle. April 2011.

Mahmood, Mona, et al. "From El Salvador to Iraq: Washington's Man behind Brutal Police Squads." *The Guardian,* March 6, 2013. https://www.theguardian.com/world/2013/mar/06/el-salvador-iraq-police-squads-washington.

Malina, Bruce J. *The New Testament World: Insights from Cultural Anthropology.* 3rd ed. Louisville: Westminster John Knox, 2001.

Marsden, Lee. "Faith-Based Diplomacy: Conservative Evangelicals and the United States Military." *Politics and Religion* 7 (2014) 475–98.

Marshall, Ellen Ott. *Though the Fig Tree Does Not Blossom: Toward a Responsible Theology of Christian Hope.* Nashville: Abingdon, 2006.

Marx, Karl. *Capital, Volume One.* In *The Marx-Engels Reader,* edited by Robert C. Tucker. 2nd ed. New York: Norton, 1978.

Marx, Karl, and Friedrich Engels. *The Communist Manifesto.* New York: Penguin, 2004.

Masco, Joseph. "Nuclear Technoaesthetics: Sensory Politics from Trinity to the Virtual Bomb in Los Alamos." *American Ethnologist* 31 (2004) 349–73.

Maslin, Sarah Esther. "El Salvador Strikes Down Amnesty for Crimes during Its Civil War." *Washington Post,* July 14, 2016.

Mathewes, Charles. *A Theology of Public Life.* New York: Cambridge University Press, 2007.

May, Rachel A. "'La verdad' y comisiones de la verdad en América Latina." *Investigación & Desarrollo* 21 (2013) 494–512.

McBride, James, and Andrew Chatzky. "The National Debt Dilemma." Council on Foreign Relations. https://www.cfr.org/backgrounder/national-debt-dilemma.

McClendon, James William, Jr. *Systematic Theology.* Vol. 1, *Ethics.* Nashville: Abingdon, 1986.

McConville, J. G. *God and Earthly Power: An Old Testament Political Theology, Genesis-Kings.* Library of Hebrew Bible/Old Testament Studies 454. Edinburgh: T&T Clark, 2006.

McCoy, Alfred W. *In the Shadows of the American Century: The Rise and Decline of US Global Power*. Chicago: Haymarket, 2017.

Meagher, Robert Emmet, and Douglas A. Pryer, eds. *War and Moral Injury: A Reader*. Eugene, OR: Cascade, 2018.

Merle, Renae, and Ellen McCarthy. "6 Employees from CACI International, Titan Referred for Prosecution." *Washington Post*, August 26, 2004. http://www.washingtonpost.com/wp-dyn/articles/A33834-2004Aug25.html?noredirect=on.

Michel, Virgil. *The Christian in the World*. Collegeville, MN: Liturgical, 1939.

Mies, Maria. *Patriarchy and Accumulation on a World Scale: Women in the International Division of Labour*. New York: Zed, 1986.

Mies, Maria, and Veronika Bennholdt-Thomsen. *The Subsistence Perspective: Beyond the Globalised Economy*. Translated by Patrick Camiller et al. New York: Zed, 1999.

Mignolo, Walter D. *The Idea of Latin America*. Malden, MA: Blackwell, 2005.

Milbank, John. *Theology and Social Theory: Beyond Secular Reason*. 2nd ed. Malden, MA: Blackwell, 2006.

Miles, Stephen. "Congress Went Bigly on the Budget." February 9, 2018. inkstickmedia.com/congress-went-bigly-budget/.

Minow, Martha. "Outsourcing Power: How Privatizing Military Efforts Challenges Accountability, Professionalism, and Democracy." *Boston College Law Review* 46 (2005) 989–1026.

Mohrmann, Margaret. "History of Christian Ethics." Unpublished manuscript.

Monahan, David, ed. *The Shepherd Cannot Run: Letters of Stanley Rother, Missionary and Martyr*. Oklahoma City: Archdiocese of Oklahoma City, 1984.

Moore, Don. "Life in Community with Dan." In *Apostle of Peace: Essays in Honor of Daniel Berrigan*, edited by John Dear. Maryknoll, NY: Orbis, 1996.

Moore, James R. "Mission as Subversion." *Post-American* 2 (December 1973) 6.

Moore, Jason W. "Name the System! Anthropocenes and the Capitalocene Alternative." https://jasonwmoore.wordpress.com/tag/anthropocene/.

———. "Nature/Society and the Violence of Real Abstraction." https://jasonwmoore.wordpress.com/2016/10/04/naturesociety-the-violence-of-real-abstraction/.

———. "The Rise and Fall of Cheap Nature." https://jasonwmoore.wordpress.com/2016/11/22/jason-w-moore-in-toronto-dec-13-the-rise-fall-of-cheap-nature/.

Morell, Michael J. *The Great War of Our Time: The CIA's Fight against Terrorism—from Al Qa'ida to ISIS*. New York: Twelve, 2015.

Moreton, Bethany. *To Serve God and Wal-Mart: The Making of Christian Free Enterprise*. Cambridge: Harvard University Press, 2009.

Moss, Candida R. *The Other Christs: Imitating Jesus in Ancient Christian Ideologies of Martyrdom*. New York: Oxford University Press, 2010.

The Movement for Black Lives. "End the War on Black People." https://policy.m4bl.org/end-war-on-black-people/.

———. "Platform" https://policy.m4bl.org/.

Murdoch, James C., and Todd Sandler. "Economic Growth, Civil Wars, and Spatial Spillovers." *Journal of Conflict Resolution* 46 (2002) 91–110.

Murphy, Jarrett. "Cheney's Halliburton Ties Remain." *CBS News*, September 26, 2003. https://www.cbsnews.com/news/cheneys-halliburton-ties-remain/.

Nairn, Allan. "Behind the Death Squads." *The Progressive*, May 1984, 20–29.

National Academy of Engineering and National Research Council. *Assuring the US Department of Defense a Strong Science, Technology, Engineering, and Mathematics (STEM) Workforce.* Washington, DC: The National Academies, 2012. https://doi.org/10.17226/13467.

Newsweek. "Rotary President Taylor: 50 Years to the Good." February 28, 1955, 25-32.

Niebuhr, Reinhold. *The Children of Light and the Children of Darkness: A Vindication of Democracy and a Critique of Its Traditional Defense.* New York: Scribner's, 1960.

———. *Christianity and Power Politics.* New York: Scribner's, 1946.

Noll, Mark. *The Scandal of the Evangelical Mind.* Grand Rapids: Eerdmans, 1994.

Norris, Kristopher. "'Never Again War': Recent Shifts in the Roman Catholic Just War Tradition and the Question of 'Functional Pacifism.'" *Journal of Religious Ethics* 42 (2014) 108-36.

Novak, Michael. *The Spirit of Democratic Capitalism.* Lanham, MD: Madison, 1991.

Novak, Michael, and John W. Cooper, eds. *The Corporation: A Theological Inquiry.* Washington, DC: AEI, 1981.

Ockenga, Harold John. "Christ for America." *United Evangelical Action,* May 4, 1943, 3-4, 6.

O'Connell, Maureen. "Jus Ante Bellum: Faith-Based Diplomacy and Catholic Traditions on War and Peace." *Journal for Peace and Justice Studies* 21 (2011) 3-30.

O'Donovan, Oliver, and Joan Lockwood O'Donovan, eds. *From Irenaeus to Grotius: A Sourcebook in Christian Political Thought, 100-1625.* Grand Rapids: Eerdmans, 1999.

Office of the Assistant Secretary of Defense for Logistics & Material Readiness. "Contractor Support of US Operations in the USCENTCOM Area of Responsibility to Include Iraq and Afghanistan." Corrected ed., November 8, 2012. https://www.acq.osd.mil/log/PS/.CENTCOM_reports.html/5A_Oct2012_CORRECTED_EDITION.doc.

Office of the Historian, US Department of State. "NSC-68, 1950." https://history.state.gov/milestones/1945-1952/NSC68.

Office of the United Nations High Commissioner for Human Rights. *Rule-of-Law Tools for Post-Conflict States: Truth Commissions.* New York: United Nations, 2006. https://www.ohchr.org/Documents/Publications/RuleoflawTruthCommissionsen.pdf.

Olsen, Tricia D., Leigh A. Payne, and Andrew G. Reiter. "At What Cost? The Political Economy of Transitional Justice." *Taiwan Journal of Democracy* 6 (2010) 165-84.

Omang, Joanne. "D'Aubuisson Honored by Conservatives at Capitol Hill Dinner." *Washington Post,* December 5, 1984.

"An Open Letter to North American Christians." *Vanguard,* January-February 1977, 4-5.

Orend, Brian. "Jus Post Bellum." *Journal of Social Philosophy* 31 (2000) 117-37.

———. "Jus Post Bellum: A Just War Theory Perspective." In *Jus Post Bellum: Towards a Law of Transition from Conflict to Peace,* edited by Carsten Stahn and Jann K. Kleffner, 31-52. Cambridge: Cambridge University Press, 2008.

Otto, Rudolph. *The Idea of the Holy.* New York: Oxford University Press, 1923.

Padilla, René. "Evangelism and the World." In *Let the Earth Hear His Voice,* edited by J. D. Douglas, 116-46. Minneapolis: World Wide Publications, 1975.

Padilla, René, and Lindy Scott. *Terrorism and the War in Iraq: A Christian Word from Latin America.* Barcelona: Ediciones Kairos, 2004.

Palmer-Fernández, Gabriel. "Just War Moralities." *Journal of Religious Ethics* 45 (2017) 580–605.
Pannell, William. "Evangelicals and the Social Crisis." *Post-American* 3 (October 1974) 11.
Pattison, James. "The Legitimacy of the Military, Private Military and Security Companies, and Just War Theory." *European Journal of Political Theory* 11 (2011) 131–54.
Paul VI, Pope. *Humanae Vitae*. http://w2.vatican.va/content/paul-vi/en/encyclicals/documents/hf_p-vi_enc_25071968_humanae-vitae.html.
Peace Corps. "Peace Corps Congressional Budget Justification, Fiscal Year 2016." http://files.peacecorps.gov/multimedia/pdf/policies/peacecorps_cbj_2016.pdf.
Pear, Robert. "Falwell Denounces Tutu as a 'Phony.'" *New York Times*, August 21, 1985.
Peralta, Eyder. "Reports: Sikh Temple Shooter Acted Alone, Had No Drugs In System." November 21, 2012. https://www.npr.org/tags/158190895/sikh-temple-shooting.
Percy, Sarah. *Mercenaries: The History of a Norm in International Relations*. New York: Oxford University Press, 2007.
Peters, Heidi M., and Sofia Plagakis. "Department of Defense Contractor and Troop Levels in Iraq and Afghanistan: 2007–2017." https://fas.org/sgp/crs/natsec/R44116.pdf.
Pierard, Richard V. "*Pax Americana* and the Evangelical Missionary Advance." In *Earthen Vessels: American Evangelicals and Foreign Missions, 1880–1980*, edited by Joel A. Carpenter and Wilbert R. Shenk, 155–79. Grand Rapids: Eerdmans, 1990.
Polanyi, Karl. *Great Transformation: The Political and Economic Origins of Our Time*. Boston: Beacon, 2001.
Polner, Murray, and Jim O'Grady. *Disarmed and Dangerous: The Radical Life and Times of Daniel and Philip Berrigan, Brothers in Religious Faith and Civil Disobedience*. Boulder, CO: Westview, 1998.
Pontifical Council for Justice and Peace. *Compendium of the Social Doctrine of the Church*. http://www.vatican.va/roman_curia/pontifical_councils/justpeace/documents/rc_pc_justpeace_doc_20060526_compendio-dott-soc_en.html.
———. *Vocation of the Business Leader: A Reflection*. http://www.justiceandpeace.va/content/dam/giustiziaepace/VBL/Vocation_ENGLISH_4th%20edition.pdf.
Ponting, Clive. *A New Green History of the World: The Environment and the Collapse of Great Civilizations*. New York: Penguin, 1991.
Pranis, Kay. *The Little Book of Peacemaking Circles: A New/Old Approach to Peacemaking*. Intercourse, PA: Good Books, 2005.
Pranis, Kay, Barry Stuart, and Mark Wedge. *Peacemaking Circles: From Crime to Community*. St. Paul, MN: Living Justice, 2003.
Presbyterian Church (USA). *A Reformed Understanding of Usury for the Twenty-First Century*. https://www.pcusa.org/site_media/media/uploads/_resolutions/usury.pdf.
Pyper, Hugh S. "World." In *The Oxford Companion to Christian Thought*, edited by Adrian Hastings, Alistair Mason, and Hugh Pyper, 761–62. Oxford: Oxford University Press, 2000.
Rabe, Stephen G. *Eisenhower and Latin America: The Foreign Policy of Anticommunism*. New ed. Chapel Hill: University of North Carolina Press, 1988.
———. *The Killing Zone: The United States Wages Cold War in Latin America*. New York: Oxford University Press, 2016.

Ramsey, Paul. *War and the Christian Conscience: How Shall Modern War Be Conducted Justly?* Durham: Duke University Press, 1961.
Ratner, Steven R., and Jason S. Abrams. *Accountability for Human Rights Atrocities in International Law: Beyond the Nuremberg Legacy*. 2nd ed. New York: Oxford University Press, 2001.
ReadyNation. "Building the Defense Industry's Workforce of the Future through High-Quality Early Learning." http://readynation.s3.amazonaws.com/wp-content/uploads/Industry-Brief-Defense.pdf.
The Reconciliation and Reunification Commission of the National Council of Churches in Korea. "Sadgago Pyonghwaora" [Go Away THHAD, Come Peace]. http://www.kncc.or.kr/admin/bbs/down.php?code=board_02_8&idx=18301&no=2.
Reese, Boyd. "Structure of Power." *Post-American* 3 (January 1974) 8–9.
Reuters in San Salvador. "El Salvador Will Cooperate in the Arrest of 17 Former Soldiers Accused of Killing Priests." *The Guardian*, January 6, 2016. https://www.theguardian.com/world/2016/jan/06/el-salvador-arrest-former-soldiers-killing-priests-civil-war.
Ricks, Thomas E. "South Korea Agrees to Hasten Upgrade of Military, Acquire US-Made Gear." *Wall Street Journal*, April 21, 1994, A10.
Right On. "The Revolutionary Catechism." October 27, 1970, 2.
Roberts, Alexander, and James Donaldson, eds. *The Ante-Nicene Fathers: Translations of the Writings Down to A.D. 325*. 10 vols. 1885–87. Reprint, Buffalo: Christian Literature Publishing Co., 1885–96.
Robinson, Cedric J. *Black Marxism: The Making of the Black Radical Tradition*. Chapel Hill: University of North Carolina Press, 2000.
Rockman, Seth. "Review: What Makes the History of Capitalism Newsworthy?" *Journal of the Early Republic* 34 (2014) 439–66.
Rockwood, Kate. "How a Handful of Countries Control the Earth's Most Precious Materials." *Fast Company*, November 1, 2010. https://www.fastcompany.com/1694164/how-handful-countries-control-earths-most-precious-materials.
Romero, Óscar Arnulfo. "The Church's Mission amid the National Crisis: Fourth Pastoral Letter." August 6, 1979. http://www.romerotrust.org.uk/sites/default/files/fourth%20pastoral%20letter.pdf.
———. *Homilías*. Edited by Miguel Cavada Diez. 7 vols. San Salvador: UCA Editores, 2005–17.
———. *La voz de los sin voz: La palabra viva de Monseñor Óscar Arnulfo Romero*. Edited by Rodolfo Cardenal et al. San Salvador: UCA Editores, 1986.
Rom-Shiloni, Dalit. "Psalm 44: The Powers of Protest." *Catholic Biblical Quarterly* 70 (2008) 683–98.
Roosevelt, Franklin Delano. "The Great Arsenal of Democracy." December 29, 1940. http://www.americanrhetoric.com/speeches/fdrarsenalofdemocracy.html.
Rostow, W. W. *The Stages of Economic Growth: A Non-Communist Manifesto*. 3rd ed. Cambridge: Cambridge University Press, 1991.
Russell, Frederick H. *The Just War in the Middle Ages*. New York: Cambridge University Press, 1975.
Rustin, Bayard. *Time on Two Crosses: The Collected Writings of Bayard Rustin*. Edited by Devon W. Carbado and Donald Weise. San Francisco: Cleis, 2003.
Ruth, John L. *Forgiveness: A Legacy of the West Nickel Mines Amish School*. Harrisonburg, VA: Herald, 2011.

Sachs, Jeffrey D. "The Fatal Expense of American Imperialism." *Boston Globe*, October 30, 2016. https://www.bostonglobe.com/opinion/2016/10/30/the-fatal-expense-american-imperialism/teXS2xwA1UJbYd1oWJBHHM/story.html.

Sanders, Barry. *The Green Zone: The Environmental Costs of Militarism*. Oakland: AK, 2009.

Sankaran, Jaganath, and Bryan L. Fearey. "Missile Defense and Strategic Stability: Terminal High Altitude Area Defense (THAAD) in South Korea." *Contemporary Security Policy* 38 (2017) 321–44.

Scheffran, Jürgen, et al. "The Climate-Nuclear Nexus: Exploring the Linkages between Climate Change and Nuclear Threats." World Future Council, November 2015.

Schlabach, Gerald, ed. *Just Policing, Not War: An Alternative Response to World Violence*. Collegeville, MN: Liturgical, 2007.

Schlesinger, Stephen, and Stephen Kinzer. *Bitter Fruit: The Story of the American Coup in Guatemala*. Expanded ed. Cambridge: Harvard University Press, 1999.

Schoultz, Lars. *Beneath the United States: A History of US Policy toward Latin America*. Cambridge: Harvard University Press, 1998.

Schroeder, Paul W. "Work with Emerging Cooperative Forces in the International System." In *Just Peacemaking: The New Paradigm for the Ethics of Peace and War*, edited by Glen Stassen, 154–65. New ed. Cleveland: Pilgrim, 2008.

Schuck, Michael. "When the Shooting Stops: Missing Elements in Just War Theory." *Christian Century* 111 (October 26, 1994) 982–84.

Schulman, Jeremy. "Defense Contractor: Climate Change Could Create 'Business Opportunities.'" *Mother Jones*, August 14, 2013. https://www.motherjones.com/environment/2013/08/raytheon-climate-change-security/.

Schwartz, Moshe, and Jennifer Church. "Department of Defense's Use of Contractors to Support Military Operations: Background, Analysis, and Issues for Congress." May 17, 2013. https://fas.org/sgp/crs/natsec/R43074.pdf.

Second Vatican Council. *Gaudium et spes*. http://www.vatican.va/archive/hist_councils/ii_vatican_council/documents/vat-ii_const_19651207_gaudium-et-spes_en.html.

Seibert, Eric A. *The Violence of Scripture: Overcoming the Old Testament's Troubling Legacy*. Minneapolis: Fortress, 2012.

Shay, Jonathan. *Achilles in Vietnam: Combat Trauma and the Undoing of Character*. New York: Scribner, 1995.

———. "Moral Injury." *Psychoanalytic Psychology* 31 (2014) 182–91.

Sherman, Nancy. *Afterwar: Healing the Moral Wounds of Our Soldiers*. New York: Oxford University Press, 2015.

Shin, Gi-Wook. *One Alliance, Two Lenses: US-Korea Relations in a New Era*. Stanford: Stanford University Press, 2010.

Sider, Ronald J. *Rich Christians in an Age of Hunger: A Biblical Study*. Downers Grove: InterVarsity, 1977.

Simpson, Bradley Robert. *Economists with Guns: Authoritarian Development and US-Indonesian Relations, 1960–1968*. Stanford: Stanford University Press, 2008.

Sinclair, Andrew. *Che Guevara*. New York: Viking, 1970.

Singer, P. W. *Corporate Warriors: The Rise of the Privatized Military Industry*. Ithaca: Cornell University Press, 2003.

———. "Outsourcing War." *Foreign Affairs*, March/April 2005, 119–32.

Sjursen, Danny. "Trump's National Defense Strategy: Something for Everyone (in the Military-Industrial Complex)." February 20, 2018. http://www.tomdispatch.com/blog/176388/.

Slade, Kara N. "Unmanned: Autonomous Drones as a Problem of Theological Anthropology." *Journal of Moral Theology* 4 (2015) 111–30.

Smith, Michael Joseph. "Strengthen the United Nations and International Efforts for Cooperation and Human Rights." In *Just Peacemaking: The New Paradigm for the Ethics of Peace and War*, edited by Glen Stassen, 166–76. New ed. Cleveland: Pilgrim, 2008.

Smith, Peter H. *Talons of the Eagle: Latin America, the United States, and the World.* New York: Oxford University Press, 1996.

Snead, A. C. "The Foreign Missionary in a Changing World." *United Evangelical Action* 7 (May 1, 1948) 3–4.

Sparks, Jack. "The American Condition." Box 2, CWLF Collection, Graduate Theological Union Archives, Berkeley, California.

———. "The End of Affluence." *Right On* 6 (April, 1975) 7.

Spillius, Alex. "Dick Cheney Iraq 'Quagmire' Video Hits the Web." *The Telegraph*, August 21, 2007. https://www.telegraph.co.uk/news/worldnews/1560915/Dick-Cheney-Iraq-quagmire-video-hits-the-web.html.

Stachowitsch, Saskia. "Military Privatization as a Gendered Process: A Case for Integrating Feminist International Relations and Feminist State Theories." In *Gender and Private Security in Global Politics*, edited by Maya Eichler, 19–36. Oxford: Oxford University Press, 2015.

Stackhouse, Max L. "Business, Economics and Christian Ethics." In *The Cambridge Companion to Christian Ethics*, edited by Robin Gill, 228–42. Cambridge: Cambridge University Press, 2001.

Stackhouse, Max L., et al., eds. *On Moral Business: Classical and Contemporary Resources for Ethics in Economic Life.* Grand Rapids: Eerdmans, 1995.

Stafford, Tim. "Ron Sider's Unsettling Crusade." *Christianity Today* 36 (March 17, 1992) 18–22.

Stanger, Allison. *One Nation under Contract: The Outsourcing of American Power and the Future of Foreign Policy.* New Haven: Yale University Press, 2009.

Stanger, Allison, and Mark Eric Williams. "Private Military Corporations: Benefits and Costs of Outsourcing Security." *Yale Journal of International Affairs* 2 (2006) 4–19. http://yalejournal.org/wp-content/uploads/2011/01/062101stanger-williams.pdf.

Stanley, William. *The Protection Racket State: Elite Politics, Military Extortion, and Civil War in El Salvador.* Philadelphia: Temple University Press, 1996.

Stassen, Glen, ed. *Just Peacemaking: The New Paradigm for the Ethics of Peace and War.* New ed. Cleveland: Pilgrim, 2008.

Stockholm International Peace Research Institute (SIPRI). "Increase in Arms Transfers Driven by Demand in the Middle East and Asia, Says SIPRI." February 20, 2017. https://www.sipri.org/media/press-release/2017/increase-arms-transfers-driven-demand-middle-east-and-asia-says-sipri.

Stohl, Rachel, and Suzette Grillot. *The International Arms Trade.* Cambridge: Polity, 2009.

Stringfellow, William, and Anthony Towne. *Suspect Tenderness: The Ethics of the Berrigan Witness.* New York: Holt, Rinehart & Winston, 1971.

Suh, Jae-Jung. "Allied to Race? The US-Korea Alliance and Arms Race." *Asian Perspective* 33 (2009) 101–27.

———. *Power, Interest, and Identity in Military Alliances*. New York: Palgrave Macmillan, 2007.

Supple, James O. "Patriotic Note Marks Service at Soldier Field." *Chicago Sun*, May 31, 1945. Photo Album I, Collection 285.

Swartz, David R. *Moral Minority: The Evangelical Left in an Age of Conservatism*. Philadelphia: University of Pennsylvania Press, 2012.

Tamez, Elsa. *Bible of the Oppressed*. Maryknoll, NY: Orbis, 1982.

Tanner, Norman P., and Giuseppe Alberigo, eds. *Decrees of the Ecumenical Councils*. Vol. 1, *Nicaea I to Lateran V*. Washington, DC: Georgetown University Press, 1990.

Taylor, Herbert. *God Has a Plan for You*. Old Tappan, NJ: Revell, 1968.

Thorpe, Helen. *Soldier Girls: The Battles of Three Women at Home and at War*. New York: Scribner, 2014.

Tian, Nan, et al. "Trends in World Military Expenditure, 2017." Stockholm International Peace Research Institute, May 2018. https://www.sipri.org/publications/2018/sipri-fact-sheets/trends-world-military-expenditure-2017.

Tomich, Dale W. *Through the Prism of Slavery: Labor, Capital, and World Economy*. Lanham, MD: Rowman & Littlefield, 2004.

Tomich, Dale, and Michael Zeuske. "Introduction, the Second Slavery: Mass Slavery, World-Economy, and Comparative Microhistories." *Review (Fernand Braudel Center)* 31 (2008) 91–100.

Topik, Steven C., and Allen Wells, eds. *The Second Conquest of Latin America: Coffee, Henequen, and Oil during the Export Boom, 1850–1930*. Austin: University of Texas Press, 1998.

Tracy, David. *The Analogical Imagination: Christian Theology and the Culture of Pluralism*. New York: Crossroad, 1998.

Troeltsch, Ernst. *The Social Teaching of the Christian Churches*. Louisville: Westminster John Knox, 1931.

Union of Concerned Scientists. "The US Military and Oil." June 1, 2014. https://www.ucsusa.org/clean_vehicles/smart-transportation-solutions/us-military-oil-use.html.

United Evangelical Action. "Churches Gain Freedom, but Communists Still Anti-Religious." December 1, 1944, 6.

———. "NAE Commences Shipments of Relief Goods to War-Torn Europe." March 19, 1945, 1.

United Nations. "Charter of the United Nations." http://www.un.org/en/charter-united-nations/index.html.

United Nations Office for Disarmament Affairs. "Arms Trade Treaty." https://unoda-web.s3-accelerate.amazonaws.com/wp-content/uploads/2013/06/English7.pdf.

United States Conference of Catholic Bishops (USCCB). *The Challenge of Peace: God's Promise and Our Response*. May 3, 1983. http://www.usccb.org/upload/challenge-peace-gods-promise-our-response-1983.pdf.

United States Department of Defense. "DOD Releases Fiscal Year 2019 Budget Proposal." February 12, 2018. https://www.defense.gov/News/News-Releases/News-Release-View/Article/1438798/dod-releases-fiscal-year-2019-budget-proposal/.

———. "Sustaining U.S. Global Leadership: Priorities for 21st Century Defense." January 2012. http://archive.defense.gov/news/Defense_Strategic_Guidance.pdf.
United States Department of State. "The Post-War Economy: 1945–1960." https://www.thoughtco.com/the-post-war-us-economy-1945-to-1960-1148153.
United States Department of State Policy Planning Staff. "Review of Current Trends: US Foreign Policy." https://history.state.gov/historicaldocuments/frus1948v01p2/d4.
United States Forces Korea. "ROK and US Joint Statement: ROK-US Alliance Agrees to Deploy THAAD." July 7, 2016. https://www.usfk.mil/Media/News/Article/831175/rok-us-joint-statement-rok-us-alliance-agrees-to-deploy-thaad/.
Van Biema, David, and Jeff Chu. "Does God Want You To Be Rich?" *Time*, September 10, 2006. http://content.time.com/time/magazine/article/0,9171,1533448,00.html.
Verkuil, Paul R. *Outsourcing Sovereignty: Why Privatization of Government Functions Threatens Democracy and What We Can Do About It*. New York: Cambridge University Press, 2007.
Vine, David. *Base Nation: How US Military Bases Abroad Harm America and the World*. New York: Metropolitan, 2015.
Walkom, Thomas. "North Korea's Unending War Rages On." *The Star*, November 25, 2010. https://www.thestar.com/news/world/2010/11/25/walkom_north_koreas_unending_war_rages_on.html.
Wallis, Jim. "Invisible Empire." *Post-American* 2 (November-December 1973) 1.
———. "The Issue of 1972." *Post-American* 1 (Fall 1972) 2–3.
Walzer, Michael. *Arguing About War*. New Haven: Yale University Press, 2004.
———. *Spheres of Justice: A Defense of Pluralism and Equality*. New York: Basic Books, 1983.
Watkin, Julia. "Boom! The Earth Is Round!—On the Impossibility of an Existential System." In *International Kierkegaard Commentary: Concluding Unscientific Postscript to "Philosophical Fragments"*, edited by Robert L. Perkins, 95–113. Macon, GA: Mercer University Press, 1997.
Weber, Max. *The Protestant Ethic and the Spirit of Capitalism*. New York: Routledge, 1992.
Werrell, Caitlin, and Francisco Femia. "US Intelligence Community: Impacts of Climate Change Raise the Risk of Conflict in 2018." February 14, 2018. https://climateandsecurity.org/2018/02/14/u-s-intelligence-community-impacts-of-climate-change-raise-the-risk-of-conflict-in-2018/.
Wertheimer, Roger, ed. *Empowering Our Military Conscience: Transforming Just War Theory and Military Moral Education*. Burlington, VT: Ashgate, 2010.
———. "*Jus Ante Bellum*: Principles of Prewar Conduct." In *Routledge Handbook of Military Ethics*, edited by George Lucas, 54–68. New York: Routledge, 2015.
Whelan, Matthew Philipp. *Blood in the Fields: Óscar Romero, Agriculture, and the Politics of Common Use*. Washington, DC: Catholic University of America Press, forthcoming.
Wilkinson, Daniel. *Silence on the Mountain: Stories of Terror, Betrayal, and Forgetting in Guatemala*. Durham: Duke University Press, 2004.
Williams, Eric. *Capitalism and Slavery*. Chapel Hill: University of North Carolina Press, 1944.
Williams, Murat. "Still More Arms Won't Aid El Salvador." *New York Times*, April 17, 1980.

Williams, William Appleman. *The Tragedy of American Diplomacy*. Cleveland: World, 1959.
Winright, Tobias. "Hawks and Doves: Rival Versions of Just War Theory." *Christian Century* 123 (December 12, 2006) 32–35.
———. "Militarized Policing: The History of the Warrior Cop." *Christian Century* 131 (September 17, 2014) 10–12.
———. "The Morality of Cluster Bombing." *Studies in Christian Ethics* 22 (2009) 357–81.
———. "Predictably Horrific: The Afterlife of Cluster Bombs." *Commonweal* 138 (March 25, 2011) 11–12.
———. "Two Rival Versions of Just War Theory and the Presumption against Harm in Policing." In *The Annual of the Society of Christian Ethics* 18, edited by John Kelsay and Summer B. Twiss, 221–39. Washington, DC: Georgetown University Press, 1998.
Winright, Tobias, and E. Ann Jeschke. "Combat and Confession: Just War and Moral Injury." In *Can War Be Just in the 21st Century? Ethicists Engage the Tradition*, edited by Tobias Winright and E. Ann Jeschke, 169–87. Maryknoll, NY: Orbis, 2015.
Wittenburg Door. "Door Interview." August-September 1976, 17.
Wittman, Hannah, and Laura Saldivar-Tanaka. "The Agrarian Question in Guatemala." In *Promised Land: Competing Visions of Agrarian Reform*, edited by Peter Rosset, Raj Patel, and Michael Courville, 23–39. Oakland: Food First, 2006.
Wolf, Kenneth Baxter. *The Poverty of Riches: St. Francis of Assisi Reconsidered*. Oxford: Oxford University Press, 2003.
Wong, Kenman L., and Scott B. Rae. *Business for the Common Good: A Christian Vision for the Marketplace*. Downers Grove: InterVarsity, 2011.
Woodward, Bob. *The Agenda: Inside the Clinton White House*. New York: Simon & Schuster, 1995.
Worthen, Molly. *Apostles of Reason: The Crisis of Authority in American Evangelicalism*. Oxford: Oxford University Press, 2014.
Wright, J. Elwin. "Park Street Church in Boston Leads Way in Foreign Relief." *United Evangelical Action* 5 (October 15, 1944) 1.
Wright, Jacob L. *David, King of Israel, and Caleb in Biblical Memory*. New York: Cambridge University Press, 2014.
Yeo, Andrew. "US Military Base Realignment in South Korea." *Peace Review* 22 (2010) 113–20.
Yoder, John Howard. "The Biblical Mandate for Evangelical Social Action." In *For the Nations: Essays Evangelical and Public*, 180–98. 1997. Reprint, Eugene, OR: Wipf & Stock, 2002.
———. *Body Politics: Five Practices of the Christian Community Before the Watching World*. Scottdale, PA: Herald, 2001.
———. *The Christian Witness to the State*. Scottdale, PA: Herald, 2002.
———. "Just War Tradition: Is It Credible?" *Christian Century* 108 (March 13, 1991) 295–98.
———. *Nevertheless: The Varieties and Shortcomings of Religious Pacifism*. Rev. and expanded ed. Scottdale, PA: Herald, 1992.
———. *The Priestly Kingdom: Social Ethics as Gospel*. Notre Dame: University of Notre Dame Press, 1984.

———. *When War Is Unjust: Being Honest in Just-War Thinking.* 2nd ed. Maryknoll, NY: Orbis, 1996.

Zakim, Michael, and Gary J. Kornblith, eds. *Capitalism Takes Command: The Social Transformation of Nineteenth-Century America.* Chicago: University of Chicago Press, 2012.

Contributors

Justin Bronson Barringer is a PhD candidate in Religious Ethics at Southern Methodist University. He is coeditor of *A Faith Not Worth Fighting For: Addressing Commonly Asked Questions about Christian Nonviolence* (Cascade, 2012) and coeditor of *Practicing the Kingdom: Essays on Hospitality, Community, and Friendship in Honor of Christine Pohl* (forthcoming from Cascade).

Pamela K. Brubaker is Professor of Religion Emerita, California Lutheran University (CLU). Her books include *Globalization at What Price? Economic Change and Daily Life* (Pilgrim, 2007); *Justice Not Greed*, coedited with Rogate Mshana (WCC, 2010); and *Justice in a Global Economy: Strategies for Home, Community, and World*, coedited with Rebecca Todd Peters and Laura Stivers (Westminster John Knox, 2006). She has also published numerous chapters and articles.

Bradley B. Burroughs is Visiting Assistant Professor of Philosophy and Religious Studies at Allegheny College in Meadville, Pennsylvania. He is also the author of *Christianity, Politics, and the Predicament of Evil: A Constructive Theological Ethic of Soulcraft and Statecraft* (Lexington, 2019) and articles in the *Journal of the Society of Christian Ethics*, *The Journal of Lutheran Ethics*, and *The Christian Century*.

Stan Goff is the author of *Borderline: Reflections on War, Sex, and Church* (Cascade, 2015) and *Mammon's Ecology: Metaphysic of the Empty Sign* (Cascade, 2018). He has also written numerous articles on socioeconomic issues since 1995. He is a former career soldier, and current peace activist.

Nathaniel Hibner is Director of Ethics for the Catholic Health Association. His doctoral studies in healthcare ethics and moral theology focused on the discernment of theological scandal in organizational decision-making.

James McCarty is the Director of the Center for Equity and Inclusion at the University of Washington-Tacoma. He has published articles on Christian ethics, racial justice, restorative justice, and peacebuilding in books and journals such as *the Journal of the Society of Christian Ethics, Journal of Law and Religion*, and *Theology and Sexuality*.

Christina G. McRorie is Assistant Professor of Theology at Creighton University. She is a research fellow at the Institute for Advanced Studies in Culture at the University of Virginia, an affiliated fellow with the F. A. Hayek Program for Advanced Study in Philosophy, Politics, and Economics at George Mason University, and serves on the editorial board of the *Journal of Catholic Social Thought*.

Wonchul Shin is Visiting Assistant Professor of Christian Ethics and Theology and Louisville Institute Postdoctoral Fellow at Columbia Theological Seminary in Decatur, Georgia. He has published articles and reviews in *the Journal of the Society of Christian Ethics* and *The Journal of Asian American Theological Forum*.

Kara N. Slade is Associate Rector of Trinity Church in Princeton, New Jersey, as well as Associate Chaplain at the Episcopal chaplaincy to Princeton University and Princeton Theological Seminary. A former research engineer in the aerospace and defense sector, she holds a PhD in mechanical engineering and materials science as well as a PhD in theology, both from Duke University. She is Canon Theologian of the Episcopal Diocese of New Jersey.

David R. Swartz is an associate professor of history at Asbury University. He is author of *Moral Minority: The Evangelical Left in an Age of Conservatism* (University of Pennsylvania Press, 2012) and writes at the The Anxious Bench blog.

Matthew Tapie is Assistant Professor of Theology and Director of the Center for Catholic-Jewish Studies at St. Leo University. He is the author of *Aquinas on Israel and the Church: The Question of Supersessionism in the Theology of Thomas Aquinas*.

Jonathan Tran is Associate and Graduate Professor of Theology and Ethics at Baylor University where he holds the George W. Baines Chair of Religion. His next books are *Yellow Christianity: An Intervention on Antiracist Thinking* (forthcoming 2020) and, with Stanley Hauerwas, *Christianity and the Promise of Politics* (forthcoming 2021).

Myles Werntz is Associate Professor of Christian Ethics and Practical Theology at Logsdon Seminary, Hardin-Simmons University, where he holds the T. B. Maston Chair in Christian Ethics. He is the author and editor of five books in theology and ethics.

Matthew Philipp Whelan is a St. Andrews Postdoctoral Fellow in Theology & Science, hosted by Baylor University. His book *Blood in the Fields: Óscar Romero, Catholic Social Teaching, and Land Reform* is forthcoming from Catholic University of America Press. His articles have appeared in *Modern Theology, Journal of the Society of Christian Ethics* (forthcoming), *Journal of Moral Theology, Nova et Vetera, Crosscurrents, Biodiversity and Conservation*, and *Agriculture, Forestry, and Fisheries*.

Tobias Winright is an Associate Professor of Theological Studies and an Associate Professor of Health Care Ethics at Saint Louis University. His PhD in Christian ethics/moral theology is from the University of Notre Dame, and his MDiv is from Duke Divinity School. A former law enforcement officer in both corrections and policing, he has taught and written extensively on violence- and peace-related issues.

www.ingramcontent.com/pod-product-compliance
Lightning Source LLC
Chambersburg PA
CBHW030614230426
43661CB00053B/1978